FRANKLIN *and his* French Contemporaries

FRANKLIN
and his
French Contemporaries

Alfred Owen Aldridge

NEW YORK UNIVERSITY PRESS

Washington Square · 1957

ACKNOWLEDGMENTS

*My research in French Archives was in large measure
made possible by a Fulbright grant in 1952-1953 and a
sabbatical leave from the University of Maryland in
1954-1955. I had in addition a grant from the American Philosophical Society.*

*The friendly atmosphere of the Institut de Littéra-
ture Comparée of the Sorbonne encouraged me in the
writing of this book, and I received a number of help-
ful suggestions from Professors Charles Dédéyan, M.
Le Breton, and Henri Roddier.*

*I respectfully dedicate my work to my former col-
leagues at the Université de Toulouse and the Université de Clermont-Ferrand, the institutions where I
served as Fulbright lecturer.*

CONTENTS

1. INTRODUCTION

As Voltaire in the eighteenth century stood as a symbol of the Philosophic Enlightenment and is now considered an intellectual precursor of the French Revolution, so his American contemporary Benjamin Franklin represented the Anglo-Saxon manifestation of the same spirit and ideals. Condorcet, who knew both men, regarded each as "the apostle of philosophy and tolerance" in his own hemisphere.[1] Franklin, like Voltaire, "had often used the weapon of humour, which corrects human folly, and teaches us to regard perversity as the most pernicious folly. . . . He had honored philosophy by the genius of science, as Voltaire by that of poetry. Franklin succeeded in delivering the vast areas of America from the bondage of Europe, and Voltaire in delivering Europe from the ancient theocracies of Asia." Although few, if any, Frenchmen considered Franklin as a match for Voltaire as satirist, wit, or literary craftsman, most French contemporaries of the two *philosophes* admired Franklin as the more versatile genius. Franklin was heralded not only as a man of letters, but also as a scientist, as a practical moralist and master of economic theory, and as a diplomat respected by the entire court.

For this reason two dramatic meetings of Franklin and Voltaire became enshrined as popular anecdotes, resembling legendary tales of the gods and heroes of antiquity. Once Franklin visited Voltaire on his sickbed and asked for the blessing of the French sage upon his grandson; once at a public meeting of the Academy of Science the two men were called upon by a spontaneous demonstration of the assemblage to embrace *à la française*. Several versions of each incident exist, contributing to the fabulous nature of the encounters.

In February of 1778, Franklin, accompanied by his grandson William Temple Franklin, then eighteen years old, asked Voltaire to give the youth his benediction. In the presence of twenty witnesses profusely shedding tears of sensibility, Voltaire, according

Notes to this chapter begin on page 239.

to his own statement, pronounced only the words, "Dieu et la liberté." [2] Another report has it that he said, "Mon enfant! Dieu et la liberté," [3] and it is possible that he added, as Condorcet asserted, "this is the only appropriate benediction for the grandson of M. Franklin." [4] La Harpe, drawing on the *Journal de Paris*, reported the benediction as, "Mon enfant, Dieu et la liberté; souvenez-vous de ces deux mots." [5] According to Condorcet, since the two sages had been speaking English, Voltaire pronounced the English words "God and Liberty." [6] It had been Voltaire, according to the *Journal de Paris*, who had chosen English as the mode of communication. His niece, feeling that the other spectators might wish to profit by the exchange of greetings, begged him to speak in French. "I ask your pardon," replied Voltaire; "I gave way a moment to the vanity of speaking the same language as Monsieur Franklin." [7] *Les Mémoires secrets*, a periodical collection of scandal and personalities, true to its sensational character, gave a caustic account of the episode, one of the few uncomplimentary pictures of Franklin in French letters. Franklin "by a base, indecent and puerile adulation, and, according to certain fanatics, by a derisive impiety, asked Voltaire to give his benediction to the child. The philosopher, playing out the scene no less thoroughly than the doctor, got up, placed his hands on the head of the little innocent, and pronounced with emphasis these three words, 'God, Liberty, and Tolerance!' " [8] Surely a touching scene played with a "little innocent" of eighteen years, an illegitimate son and illegitimate grandson, who seven years later was to become in his own right the father of an illegitimate son.

The histrionic overtones of the scene were emphasized in another contemporary account, spuriously attributed to the Marquise de Créquy. In her memoirs, Franklin's grandson is said to be four years old, and Franklin's request is interpreted as a species of ridiculous adulation. "The patriarch of Ferney, no less theatrical than the American philosopher, rose up with a hierophantic air; he placed his two hands on the head of the little man, and began to cry out at the top of his voice in tones of the devil with a cold, Liberté, Tolérance et Probité." [9]

As a result of the wide publicity given to this encounter, an admirer of Franklin wrote to him from Naples, suggesting that

Franklin had introduced his grandson to Voltaire so that the young man might be able to say of Voltaire as Ovid had said of Virgil, "Virgilium vidi." [10]

The two sages met again April 29 of the same year at a public meeting of the Academy of Sciences. Although the name of neither is entered in the register of the Academy as being present that night, at least three eyewitness accounts leave little doubt that the encounter took place. A young student from the provinces in a letter to his father described the physical appearance of the two principals.[11] Franklin's simplicity stood out. He wore a plain suit of dull yellow cloth, a white hat, blending with his grey hair, and no adornments of any kind. He was quite corpulent in striking contrast to Voltaire, whose meagre bones were barely covered by a ghostlike skin, withered by eighty-four years of arduous living. Condorcet, in viewing the two patriarchs side by side, was struck by resemblances rather than contrasts.[12] Born in different worlds, each was respected for his age, his glory, and the employment of his talents, and each reflected with pleasure on the influence he had exercised on the century. As they embraced amid "noisy acclamation, one would have said that it was Solon who embraced Sophocles. But the French Sophocles had destroyed error and advanced the reign of reason; and the Solon of Philadelphia, supporting the constitution of his country on the immovable foundation of the rights of man, had no need to fear that he would see its uncertain laws during his own lifetime prepare chains for his country and open the door to tyranny." The analogy to Solon and Sophocles must have been commonplace, for it was used also by John Adams, future president of the United States, who, as joint commissioner with Franklin in Paris, was on the scene. He wrote in his diary:

> There was a general cry that M. Voltaire and M. Franklin should be introduced to each other. This was no satisfaction; there must be something more. Neither of our philosophers seemed to divine what was wished or expected; they however took each other by the hand. But this was not enough. The clamour continued until the explanation came out: *Il faut s'embrasser à la française.* The two aged actors upon this great theatre of philosophy and frivolity then embraced each other by hugging one another in their arms and kissing each other's cheeks, and then the tumult subsided. And the cry imme-

diately spread throughout the kingdom, and I suppose all over Europe: Qu'il est charmant de voir embrasser Solon et Sophocle." [13]

The comparison was not inappropriate; apart from his incontestable reputation as a master of the classic theater, Voltaire himself maintained that his intellectual masters were Sophocles and Socrates.[14]

Voltaire's great reputation rested in some measure upon respect bordering upon fear. He had fought his way to popular esteem, not, to be sure, with the bludgeon force of his personality like Dr. Johnson in England, but with the rapier-like thrusts of his wit. Franklin's reputation rested upon love and affection. He had ingratiated himself into the hearts of the populace as well as the court; he was loved for his personal modesty and simplicity and for the simple ideas and appeal to common understanding in his literary works. This phase of his public personality was well expressed by Mme. Tussaud, creator of the famous London waxworks, who claimed to have known all of the most talented men in France before the Revolution. "Statesmen, authors, men of learning and science, metaphysicians, political enthusiasts, and even the populace," she wrote, "crowded to obtain a sight of the republican delegate; and the richest embroidered suit was an object of insipidity and passed unnoticed, whilst the simple garb of Franklin was the theme of admiration. 'He unites,' said the people, 'the deportment of Phocion to the wisdom of Socrates.' " [15] Both the disciples of Voltaire's philosophical iconoclasm and moral rationalism and the exponents of Rousseau's primitivism and social and psychological sentimentalism found in the work and personality of Franklin an expression of their cherished special beliefs.

The manifold accounts of the two interviews of Franklin and Voltaire and the impressionistic terms in which they are described illustrate a major difficulty in tracing Franklin's career. As the deists said about conventional religions, when there are so many conflicting accounts and portrayals of the attributes of god, how can we be sure that any one is true? Since nearly all modern versions of the meetings of Voltaire and Franklin derive from the accounts of John Adams and Condorcet, an air of authenticity surrounds these episodes; yet all that can be assumed

about them is that they represent fictitious elaborations containing varying degrees of truth and embellishment. Other anecdotes
of Franklin may be purely apocryphal. It is almost impossible to
reach conclusions concerning the relation to historical fact of
incidents which Franklin does not allude to in his own writings.
In estimating Franklin's reputation, however, truth is of no more
consequence than fiction. We are as much interested in learning
what his contemporaries thought he said, did, or represented, as
we are in knowing the true facts of his career.

Franklin's glory survived in France long after his death. As
late as 1864, a French critic gave vivid testimony to the tremendous extent and duration of his reputation.[16]

> A strange thing, that such an enthusiasm, which in France ordi-
> narily has the duration and the éclat of a fuse, should be pro-
> longed from year to year, should be maintained and solidified, so
> to speak, to such a point that even today Franklin exists as a demi-
> god. He represents for everyone more or less the type and the
> model of all human virtues—antique simplicity, good faith and sin-
> cerity. What is there in such a conglomeration of truth or of ex-
> aggeration, of sincerity or of artificiality?

The answer to this question is to be found in the works of
Franklin's contemporaries. The hundreds of references to the
century's most famous American reveal that two, or possibly
three, Franklins existed in French letters: first, the legendary
Franklin, whose traits of character were based on his *Way to
Wealth* and on a calculated pose that Franklin consciously
adopted in Paris to create the impression that he was a rural
philosopher or primitive patriarch. This pose he adopted in part
because it suited the role he wished to play at court and in part
because the French public expected him to conform to the character of Father Abraham in *The Way to Wealth*. From this pose
developed, secondly, the purely imaginary Franklin, the character
adopted by authors of fiction and drama from the legend which
Franklin had helped to create. Finally, the actual Franklin is revealed by means of the recollections, memoirs, and eulogies of
his close friends and associates. Parallel to these in their effect
upon Franklin's French reputation are the products of Franklin's
own pen in France, particularly a group of light essays—some of
which were composed in the French language—written for the

amusement of his Parisian friends. Equally important is his autobiography, a large part of which was written at Passy and the
major part of which was published in French translation before
an English version appeared in print.

From another perspective we may speak of Franklin portrayed
by the scores of journalists, critics, essayists, and dramatists who
knew him only slightly or not at all and Franklin portrayed by
the much smaller number of intimate friends who were able to
describe his opinions, personality, and character from firsthand
observation. Nearly all the writers of any consequence who discussed Franklin, those including Turgot, d'Alembert, abbé Morellet, Condorcet, du Pont de Nemours, La Rochefoucauld, and
Cabanis, belong to the category of friends and close associates.
Apart from the abbé Raynal, Cerutti, and Marmontel, who may
be considered authors of some distinction, the group who wrote
about Franklin without an intimate acquaintance were by and
large literary hacks and propagandists or well-meaning poets and
dramatists of minor talents.

Those who presented purely fictitious accounts of Franklin
were obviously writers who lacked personal contact, and con-
versely those who portrayed the real Franklin were associates who
knew him intimately. But both groups to some extent perpetuated
the legend of Franklin—his pose of a primitive moralist. Barbeu
Dubourg and du Pont de Nemours, to cite two examples of philosophic friends who corresponded extensively with Franklin and
lived on intimate terms with him in Paris, both stress the patriarchal (to them almost avuncular) phase of Franklin's personality and consider *The Way to Wealth* as the serious expression
of moral and economic ideals.

The mass of facts, records, impressions, and feelings that combined to form Franklin's total reputation derives from both his
legendary and his actual character. No previous attempts have
been made to separate these two threads. Indeed the only works
which have hitherto touched on the subject of Franklin's reputation in France are histories of his diplomatic negotiations and
full-scale biographies, works in which Franklin's reputation has
been merely an incidental concern. It is a commonplace that
Franklin had great influence upon his French contemporaries,
but the extent of this influence in thought and literature has

never been traced. One or two anecdotes and newspaper fragments have been continually quoted and the obvious literary
products, such as elegies, have been known as titles, but no attempt has been made to show the extent to which Franklin's
name appeared in contemporary French letters or to suggest the
spirit in which French authors approached their subject.

It is possible to extract from biographical and historical materials a completely new picture of Franklin's Gallic reception.
We see that some of the opinions he expressed concerning his
host country were widely disseminated and that constitutional
theories attributed to him had a fundamental influence upon the
French Revolution. His reputation passed through several clearly-
defined stages. At first he was considered exclusively as a scientist, later as an economist, moralist and primitive philosopher,
and finally as a shrewd diplomat and distinguished statesman.
Although he eventually came to be regarded as a composite of
these characters, the progress in individual steps may be clearly
traced. His reputation as a scientist preceded his actual appearance in France, and during the course of his first visits in 1767
and 1769 he became known as a moralist and economist. The
physiocrats, his original friends and sponsors, helped to crystallize this conception by the publicity they gave to his portrayal
of Indians and to kindred moral pieces. Franklin's early journalistic work, which created for him the role of primitive philosopher, became in French translation the basis of the pose he
semiconsciously adopted throughout his later extended sojourn
in France during the American Revolution. During this latter
period, French journalists and historians gave full testimony to
the respect they felt for his diplomatic abilities and political principles. Propaganda pieces that he himself inspired served further
to spread his fame as statesman and journalist. Both complete
strangers and literary friends and acquaintances contributed to
the portrayal of this phase of his personality in French letters.
Depictions of Franklin in his public character comprise a combination of the real and the assumed, his concrete activities blended
with his subconscious pose and legendary attributes.

The portrayals of Franklin in belles lettres derive exclusively
from his legendary character; even his Polly Baker sketch contributed to the French conception of Franklin as an exemplum

of primitive rationalism. In France the double discovery was made that the sketch was a hoax and that Franklin had perpetrated it. Had French authors not taken it up, it would probably have been lost to the literary world; certainly Franklin would otherwise never have had occasion to admit his authorship. The French authors who wrote about Polly without knowing that she was Franklin's creation fostered notions concerning the primitive reason and simple morality of the American milieu out of which the Franklin legend was constructed.

Of the host of writers who celebrated Franklin in fiction, poetry, drama and allied forms, only Turgot knew him well. Turgot's tribute, a Latin epigram, is in itself graphic proof of the force of the Franklin legend. Five words elevate Franklin to epic stature. Although his achievements are compared to exploits of classical deities, his unassuming, human personality still predominates. He is a man invading the realms of supernal power and autocratic privilege for the benefit of his fellow men.

Eripuit coelo fulmen, sceptrumque tyrannis.

(He seized the lightning from the sky, and the sceptre from tyrants.)

Turgot found the legend of Franklin already formed; his epigram gave it unalterable and eternal character. Literally scores of poets imitated Turgot's line in French verse, and others turned their hand to original pieces.

Authors of fiction presented Franklin almost exclusively either in caricature or in allegory. Propagandists against the American Revolution played up the ludicrous aspects of his diplomatic negotiation; court satirists ridiculed the superficial aspects of the legend surrounding him—his alleged rural background, simplicity of manners, and humble demeanor. Allegorists and dedicators, on the other hand, eulogized him as the symbol of the political liberty of the new American nation. On the stage during the French Revolution, Franklin appeared as a stereotyped symbol of liberty and reason.

We have said that the real Franklin is to be seen in his bagatelles, his memoirs, and in the recollections of his friends. These works present as close an approximation to the real Franklin as literary works may conceivably attain, but still they represent approximations. We cannot be sure that any one of Franklin's friends—no matter how intimate or how observant—captured the essence of Franklin's personality. Nor can we be sure even that Franklin in his own work revealed his fundamental nature—his motives, impulses, desires, or opinions. Even if he were himself aware of all aspects of his nature—a doubtful assumption to make about anyone—he obviously made a careful choice of the elements to present to the public. His entertaining anecdotes concerning actual events in his early life, for example, may not have been consistently presented in their proper perspective. Certainly in his reminiscences elements of the Franklin pose are imperceptibly interwoven with historical fact. This explains the apparent paradox that most of his bagatelles seem to be the work of a facetious, somewhat cynical wit; the autobiography, the work of a serious, somewhat parsimonious moralist. The recollections of Franklin's friends illustrate a similar paradox. All exhibit his private rather than his public or official behavior, but some reveal his frailties, his facetiousness; others his intellectual curiosity, his moral earnestness. The personalities of the authors themselves as much as the manifold aspects of Franklin's character explain these variations.

The eulogies appearing after Franklin's death exhibit similar variety. La Rochefoucauld presented a crisp, unemotional record of the major events in Franklin's life; the abbé Fauchet limited himself to Franklin's moral and religious opinions and his legislative career; Condorcet stressed Franklin's ideology; Vicq d'Azyr covered all phases of Franklin's career including his scientific achievements. But all eulogists agreed with Mirabeau, who had made a dramatic oration in the National Assembly announcing Franklin's death, that Franklin was the symbol of the new order in France and America which he had in large measure helped to create—the new order of political organization in which eminence is based not upon the accident of birth, but upon service and merit.

Part
One

FRANKLIN
AS A PUBLIC FIGURE

Journalist and Statesman

2. FRANKLIN'S DEBUT IN FRANCE

The period of Franklin's glory in France was that of the American Revolution, during which he represented his government at the court of Louis XVI. Here he was admired as moral philosopher, diplomat, and scientist. His literary reputation had preceded him, however, by many years. While making his debut in France, he had been hailed first as a scientist and secondly as an economist; his reputation as moralist and diplomat came later. The spark that ignited the flare of Franklin's reputation in France was the appearance of a series of letters on electricity from Franklin to his friend Peter Collinson of the Royal Society. These had been published in London by Edward Cave in 1751 with the modest title *Experiments and Observations on Electricity, made at Philadelphia in America.* Buffon, who saw an imperfect French manuscript paraphrase of this edition, persuaded his friend Jean François Dalibard to undertake a more accurate version,[1] and in 1752 the latter published a literal translation with "Approbation & Privilège du Roy." The King not only sanctioned the publication of this work but asked that the experiments recorded therein be repeated for his special benefit; accordingly they were carried out in the King's presence by Delor at the Chateau de St. Germain. Louis XV was so delighted with this performance that he strictly commanded "the *Abbé Mazéas* to write a Letter in the politest Terms to the Royal Society, to return the King's Thanks and Compliments in an express manner to *Mr. Franklin* of *Pennsylvania,* (Pensilvania) for the useful Discoveries in Electricity, and Application of the pointed Rods to prevent the terrible Effects of Thunder-storms." So wrote Collinson in reporting the honor to his friend.[2]

During the same year in which the translation of Dalibard appeared, Franklin's experiments were described by the abbé Mangin in his *Histoire générale et particulière de l'électricité,* 1752. Here Franklin receives a just measure of attention, but he is by

Notes to this chapter begin on page 239.

no means considered the most brilliant or the most advanced of contemporary electricians. The abbé was particularly impressed by the experiment in the course of which Franklin killed a turkey that was on the other side of the Skuylkill river by means of an electric current. With the aid of his Leyden bottle he subsequently lit the fire destined to roast the bird, and he drank the health of the electricians of the world in electrified glasses. "I think," wrote the abbé, "that if Monsieur Franklin ever made a trip to Paris, he would not delay crowning his magnificent repast with a good coffee, well electrified." [3] The following year, 1753, Diderot in his *Pensées sur l'interprétation de la nature* particularly mentioned the work of Franklin as an example of sound experimental science.

Dalibard brought out a second, greatly enlarged French edition of *Expériences et Observations* in 1756, and in 1773 Barbeu Dubourg made a completely new translation as part of his *Œuvres de M. Franklin,* also with the "Approbation & Permission du Roi." On March 31, 1754, Dalibard wrote to Franklin that his name was justly reverenced by all French electrical experimenters, except a small minority like the abbé Nollet who were jealous of his discoveries,[4] and included a list of French scientists, among them Barbeu Dubourg, who wished to send their compliments. In the next year Franklin began to receive letters from other French admirers of his experiments.[5]

The story of the opposition to Franklin's theories by the abbé Nollet, parallel to the opposition of Wilson in London, represents an interesting chapter in the history of science. Nollet, who heretofore had been considered the French authority on electrical matters, felt personally aggrieved by Franklin's new theories, particularly since his name had not even been mentioned in Franklin's book. As Franklin wrote in his autobiography, Nollet "could not at first believe that such a work came from America, and said it must have been fabricated by his enemies at Paris, to decry his system." [6] Nollet immediately set to work to disparage the new system, using methods not to be recommended for their honesty. He rigged apparatus at a public demonstration of Franklin's experiments and persuaded a set of henchmen to vouch that the experiments could not be verified.[7] Unfortunately for the abbé, a nobleman who had witnessed the earlier successful demonstration before Louis XV detected the imposture and exposed the abbé's dishonesty to the world. Nollet attacked Franklin also in his *Lettres sur l'électricité* (Paris, 1753), a collection of nine letters of which five were addressed to Franklin, and in papers presented at meetings of the Académie Royale des Sciences; but Jean Baptiste Le Roy defended him at the Académie and eventually Nollet's pretensions were completely silenced.

Not until over a decade after the publication of Nollet's letters did evidence of Franklin's occupation with economic and moral problems cross the channel, shortly before his first visit to France in person. Apart from his scientific acquaintances, Franklin's sponsors in France were a group of physiocrats and philanthropists associated in publishing a monthly journal, *Ephémérides du citoyen, ou bibliothèque raisonnée des sciences morales et politiques* (1765-1772). Franklin's most intimate friends in this circle were Dr. Jacques Barbeu Dubourg, physician and translator of the first French edition of Franklin's works, who died while Franklin was still in France, and Samuel Pierre du Pont de Nemours, economist and editor, who, living through the era of the French Revolution and the Napoleonic wars, perpetuated Franklin's name and achievements in a number of periodical publications. The *Ephémérides,* described by its originators as "a critical and moral periodical work by and large in the taste of the English Spectator," became the semiofficial organ of the physiocrats.

The most precise statement concerning Franklin's intellectual relations with this group of thinkers appears in the Journal of John Baynes, an English visitor of Franklin in Passy in 1783. When asked about French publications on political affairs, Franklin replied that a series of excellent tracts on finance had given rise to a set of persons or a sect called economists. The members of this group, Franklin explained,

held that if the people were well informed on matters of finance, it would be unnecessary to use force to compel the raising of money; that the taxes might be too great—so great as in fact to diminish the revenue—for that a farmer should have at the end of a year not only wherewith to pay his rent and to subsist his family, but also enough to defray the expence of the sowing, &c. &c. of next year's crop; otherwise, if the taxes are so high as to prevent this, part of his land must remain unsown, and consequently the crop which is the subject of taxation be diminished, and the taxes of course must

suffer the same fate. Some of their principles, he observed, were
perhaps not tenable. However, the subject was discussed thoroughly.
The Marquis de Mirabeau was said to be the author of the system.
Dr. Franklin waited on him, but he assured him that he was not
the author originally—that the founder was a Dr. Chenelle, or
Quenelle [Quesnay]. The Marquis introduced Dr. Franklin to him,
but he could not make much out of him, having rather an obscure
mode of expressing himself.[8]

It was highly appropriate that the physiocrats should have sponsored Franklin's debut in France since many of his dearest friends
belonged to the group: Dubourg, du Pont de Nemours, Turgot,
who later wrote the world-famous epigram on Franklin, and Mirabeau, author of an influential work of economics and philanthropy, *L'Ami des Hommes, ou Traité de la population.* The editors of the *Ephémérides* liked to believe that Franklin subscribed
to physiocratic doctrines, and they not only reprinted those of his
works which exhibited common doctrines, but they made specific
statements of Franklin's adherence to their views. The French,
they affirmed, were the first to merge moral and political principles into an exact science, but great economic truths were found
also in the works of some eminent foreigners. "And who does not
know," they wrote, "that the English have today their Benjamin
Franklin, who has adopted the principles and the doctrine of our
French economists, a doctrine that he is so worthy of promulgating and defending." [9] Turgot, however, sharply rebuked du
Pont de Nemours for making this claim. "To announce to the
public the opinions of a man like Franklin, one must either be
commissioned by him to do so or be quite sure of his opinions.
You are not yet cured of a sectarian spirit. I find, moreover, that
you have not sufficiently taken advantage of the occasion to develop the question of colonies in extolling the opinions of Franklin, which are not at all in harmony with the true principles." [10]
Franklin himself never returned the compliment of du Pont with
a rapturous endorsement of the physiocrats, but he did praise the
Ephémérides lavishly. In a letter to du Pont de Nemours in 1772,
he wrote concerning the journal, "You are doing a great deal of
Good to Mankind, for which I am afraid you are not duly re-
warded, except in the Satisfaction that results from it to your
benevolent Mind." [11]

The first work by Franklin to appear in the *Ephémérides* was anonymous, and it is possible that the editors never knew who the author was. This is his letter "On the Price of Corn, and Management of the Poor," signed Arator, that had appeared originally in the *London Chronicle,* November 27-29, 1766. It was sent to the *Ephémérides* in 1767 by l'abbé M. "très connu dans la République des Lettres." [12] Two years later it was noticed by an English reader of the *Ephémérides* (probably Benjamin Vaughan), who remarked on its prior publication in the *London Chronicle* and sent it to the English equivalent of the *Ephémérides,* a now rarer periodical, *De Re Rustica,* or *The Repository for Select Papers on Agriculture.* Here it appeared in 1769 with a brief letter of introduction signed COLUMELLA, the version that is now reprinted in Franklin's works. The more extensive introductory remarks in the *Ephémérides,* however, present a more comprehensive view of the scope and background of the essay. Assuming that their readers were aware of the clamors and seditions in England consequent to the high price of grain, the editors analyzed the economic strife between the landholders and farmers on one hand and the manufacturers, artisans, and negotiators on the other. They interpreted the pleasantries of the English writer as a disguised serious attempt to reveal the true political means of preventing murmurs, seditions, and terrors of popular demonstrations. Probably the French editors contrived to present the English situation as more ominous than it actually was. Franklin's pleasantries conceal nothing more serious than a defense of free trade, and he seems to be less concerned with general political principles than with particular propaganda to promote the export of grain. The extension of his principles of free trade to attack all forms of social welfare, however, represents a rather heartless attitude toward suffering humanity. Fortunately for the reputation of Franklin, this work appeared anonymously in France, and shortly before his death appeared another economic work attributed to him with a social philosophy quite the contrary. We shall speak of this work in our fourth chapter.

The remaining works by Franklin in the *Ephémérides* were contributed by his friend and disciple, Dr. Jacques Barbeu Dubourg. The two began a philosophical and personal correspondence in 1768 in the course of which they frequently exchanged literary works. In 1768 Franklin sent Dubourg some of his periodical pieces as well as an account of his famous examination before the House of Commons on the subject of the stamp acts. This account had appeared in the *London Chronicle*, July 4 and 7, 1767, and Dubourg translated it for the *Ephémérides,* in which it was given the title "Des Troubles qui divisent l'Angleterre et ses colonies." [13] As a result of the opposition in America to the imposition of stamps on legal documents and printed matter, Franklin had been called before the House of Commons to give evidence during a period of four hours. His testimony does not support the principles of the physiocrats in great measure beyond its protests against restraints on trade and against benefiting one section of the nation at the expense of another, but it was printed in the *Ephémérides* probably out of respect to his character and abilities. The readers were promised detailed light on one of the most interesting events in recent times.

> . . . they will see what constitutes the superiority of intelligence, the presence of mind and the nobility of character of this illustrious philosopher, appearing before an assembly of legislators. Accustomed from childhood to fathom the truth in all the studies to which he has devoted himself, this wise American was struck, as soon as he was spoken to on the subject, by the chain of truth which during the last several years has reduced what is called the art of governing nations to an exact science. He has rapidly become one of the most skillful adepts of this sublime science, which in the country of its birth has been subject to opposition which has failed to retard its progress and to which its defenders are reconciled by the pleasure of making converts of the weight and merit of M. Franklin.

Judged by the footnotes in the *Ephémérides,* the most significant economic principle which Franklin brought out in his examination is that taxes on commerce are always passed on to the consumer. Franklin's interrogators raised the question whether taxes in Pennsylvania were imposed on industry and commerce in order to place a restraint on English commerce. Franklin replied that these taxes were no more burdensome than those on real estate and that they were levied for revenue alone. The editors of the *Ephémérides,* however, suggested that this answer was evasive since the merchants' habit of passing taxes on to the consumer makes it impossible to tax profits. They maintained in opposition to Franklin that the taxes on commerce are more onerous than those levied directly upon the producer; the merchant will not only add the amount of the tax to his product, they argued, but will also demand a profit on the money he had advanced in taxes and on expenses of administration. Franklin may have been disguising his principles as the editors suggest, but it is more likely that the editors were trying to reconcile his words with their economic doctrines. Franklin seemed to justify taxes on commerce, whereas the physiocrats opposed them completely. This account of Franklin's appearance before the House of Commons is the only one of Franklin's pre-Revolutionary political works that enjoyed a wide circulation in France. After this initial publication, it was reprinted in Dubourg's edition of Franklin's *Œuvres,* 1773, and in a number of later collections of Franklin's miscellaneous works, particularly those highlighting his *Way to Wealth* (*Bonhomme Richard*) and his *Memoirs.*

The next work from Franklin's pen to appear in the *Ephémé-rides* was his twelve "Positions to Be Examined," another work that had appeared first in the *London Chronicle* (June 29, 1769).[14] Franklin's twelve points have frequently been said to derive from the physiocrats, and certainly there are many similarities. Quesnay's fundamental maxim that all wealth comes from agriculture, not industry, is matched by Franklin's fourth and fifth points, that riches are the product of cultivating the land, and by his twelfth, that agriculture is the only honorable means to acquire wealth. Quesnay's explanation of "gain véritable" as the exchanging of value for equal value is repeated in Franklin's definition of fair commerce in his eighth point. The editors of the *Ephémérides* disagreed with Franklin on only one point, the tenth. In discussing fair prices, Franklin points out that one who is transporting one hundred bushels of wheat could make a larger profit by converting it first into flour than by carrying it as grain, for he could use easy and expeditious methods of manufacture not generally known. If strangers then buy his flour, they will not know how much time and effort were actually spent in the milling, and the merchant may then impose on the buyer by placing a false valuation on the finished product and demanding more than a fair price. The physiocrats, who seemed to be further on the road toward modern capitalism than Franklin, felt that he was a little severe on the entrepreneur. "We believe that the one who has equally well executed something with more industry and intelligence and less labor and expense can in honor claim the same reward as the one who has expended more labor and less industry." Mental endowments like physical ones, they argued, are gifts of providence, and it is in the order of justice for those who have received superior gifts to have the right to enjoy them in bettering their condition and seeking their enjoyment, with the qualification, of course, that they do not usurp the rights of others. The stalwart porter who can carry 150 pounds has the right to charge double the man who can carry only 75. Maximum production is always to the advantage of society, and those who foster it are entitled to rewards. This justification of maximum profit is not really contradictory, they add, to Franklin's general thesis that "la valeur des marchandises ouvrées, n'offre que le remboursement des frais qu'elles occasionnent." Several years later Franklin's twelve points were circulated by Grimm in his *Correspondance littéraire,* giving the impression that this was an entirely new document presented under his auspices to French readers for the first time.[15]

In the *Ephémérides* during the same year, 1769, Franklin was cited by a French admirer, probably Dubourg, as an authority on rural life. In the first of two letters, March 12, 1769, the author supported the observation of a former contributor that it would be both useful and pleasant to live in an agricultural land with homes close enough for mutual aid, but separated sufficiently to avoid mutual annoyance and corruption.[16] After citing "New York" as a very prosperous country where there are no cities, he drew directly from Franklin to describe it as one of the flourishing American colonies in which the population doubles every twenty years.

> The inhabitants, although of European origin, scorn the closed-in life of city dwellers, heaped one upon another in attached houses. . . . They love to enjoy the life-giving air and the spectacle of natural beauty which leads to the idea of its author and to the sweet and pure feeling of gratitude and respect for providence and of concern and love for our fellow-creatures which it has given us and who share with us its blessings.

The author adds that the English have several times tried to force the inhabitants into cities, but the wise and simple citizens have refused to give up country life. Although the English have built forts and trading posts at Albany and elsewhere, these are inhabited only by professional soldiers and traders. "In no other country of the world does one find more beautiful women, even at an advanced age, more well made and robust men, more elevated geniuses, more mellow characters, or more courageous hearts." This idyllic picture, purely literary and imaginary, undoubtedly came from primitivistic books and not from direct contact with native Americans.

Franklin soon pointed out the enthusiastic excesses of this picture, however, for in a later issue of the same year the author contributed a second letter to the *Ephémérides* correcting his statement that New York had no cities and giving a full description of the rural way of life in America.[17] The details of this letter were taken directly from "one of the greatest and the most enlightened and the noblest men the new world has seen born and the old world has ever admired, the celebrated Doctor Benjamin Franklin." In this letter, undoubtedly one of the first realistic descriptions of the American way of life to appear in France, the author says in substance that he was mistaken about New York since it has in reality two cities, New York and Albany, that "the beautiful country which has no cities is Virginia," whose principal community, Williamsburg, has only 200 houses, a college, and the colonial assembly. When the assembly is in session there is moderate activity, but afterwards the delegates return to their homes, and only administrative personnel and students and teachers of the college remain. The other communities in Virginia are scarcely hamlets, with never more than thirty houses. In these rural surroundings where nature permits ameliorations without number, where the advantage of one man is never at the expense of another, where all new labor assures an increase in the total production, and in social happiness, all human beings regard each other with a secret gratitude and satisfaction. These noble sentiments determine the morals and culture of America. When a new family arrives in Virginia, all their future neighbors assemble to greet them, and over a three-day period they help them clear the land of trees and together construct a rough and simple dwelling. After the first year this edifice becomes a barn, for in the meantime the proprietor has used the arts of carpentry to construct a second more comfortable dwelling. After ten years, the newcomer has a third house of stone and wood, completely European in design and commodiousness.

In speaking of the future glory and prosperity of America, the author's vision is colored by physiocratic principles. Only a century and a half is needed, he asserts, to establish in America an empire more powerful than all of Europe today—provided that when cities are finally established, the inhabitants resist the selfish spirit of the middlemen who inhabit them, that they never be seduced by the view that human interests are opposed, that they constantly seek the greatest liberty for all, that they raise no social or racial barrier, and finally, that there be no economic restrictions, no protective tariffs or embargoes, no indirect taxes, with all taxes to be levied directly on the net product of the soil in such a way as to favor the prosperity of all those who work on the land.

There can be little doubt that the original letter containing this documentation came from Franklin, since three years previously he had communicated its principal facts in a conversation that took place on a visit to Germany. Gottfried Achenwall, who had spoken at length with Franklin on this occasion, published the same details concerning American life in his *Observations on North America*, 1767.[18]

The general impression created by the *Ephémérides,* however, of America as a paradise of prosperity without arduous individual labor Franklin undoubtedly regarded as unfortunate, and his famous *Information to Those Who Would Remove to America*, 1782, was written in part to counteract such rapturous impressions as this one. Not all of the physiocrats, moreover, were enthusiastic about the Virginia article. Turgot in a letter to du Pont de Nemours (November 7, 1769) demanded ". . . what signifies all this beautiful eulogy of Virginia? Do you not know that this Virginia is a colony of negroes?" [19]

The editors of the *Ephémérides* printed only two other works by Franklin—works having very little in common—and in their comments on these works reveal themselves in a curiously ambivalent light. In considering Franklin's "Plan for Benefiting Distant Unprovided Countries," the editors appear as realistic men of the world viewing Franklin's scheme as a form of visionary idealism; in considering a literary hoax of Franklin's, "An Account of the Captivity of William Henry," in which he portrays American Indians as practical deists, the editors reveal themselves as credulous and sentimental romanticists.

Franklin's "Plan for Benefiting Distant Countries" grew out of the discovery of New Zealand and the realization that the new land had no grain, fowls, or quadrupeds except dogs.[20] A group of humanitarian Englishmen felt that providence had charged them to communicate the advantages of their own country to the newly-discovered land. Among them, Franklin announced that "he would with all his heart *subscribe* to a voyage intended to communicate *in general* those benefits which we enjoy, to countries destitute of them in the remote parts of the globe," and Dalrymple offered to take charge of the expedition. He accordingly drew up a formal declaration of the aims of the expedition, showed it to Franklin, and the latter added an introduction. In commenting on this worthy design, the French editors agreed that it is not only more noble but more useful to conquer the hearts than to exhaust the strength and riches of a newly-acquired colony, but they felt that the project was suitable only for England, a land in which the people were really at ease and in which agriculture flourished. For other nations the project would be premature, since it would be absurd to carry products to the ends of the earth which are needed for home consumption. France, in particular, would be better advised to wait until wealth and prosperity flourished at home before engaging in philanthropic projects elsewhere. The printing of Franklin's project had far-reaching results. A Dutch nobleman, having read it in the *Ephémérides,* wrote to Franklin (November 12, 1772) that although impecunious and burdened with four children, he coveted the honor of contributing four Holland ducats to the noble purpose.[21]

Franklin's hoax concerning Indians, a work in the literary tradition of the imaginary voyage, the editors of the *Ephémérides* accepted with great seriousness.[22] It is fortunate that they did so, for had they not reprinted it from the *London Chronicle,* where it appeared anonymously, it is possible that the work would never have been attributed to Franklin.[23] The focal point of Franklin's literary hoax is one of his richest and most original humorous narratives, a burlesque Indian cosmogony, which informs us that tobacco first appeared on the earth when and where the daughter of the Great Spirit first allowed her noble posterior to touch the ground.

> Nine *Oneida* Warriors passing near a certain hill, not far from the head of Sasquehanah, saw a most beautiful young Woman descend naked from the clouds, and seat herself on the ground upon that hill. Then they said, this is the great Manitta's Daughter, let us go to her, welcome her into our country, and present her some of our venison. They gave her a fawn's tongue broiled, which she eat, and thanking them, said, come to this place again after twelve moons, and you will find, where I now sit, some thing that you have never yet seen, and that will do you good. So saying she put her hands on the ground, arose, went up into the clouds, and left them. They came accordingly after twelve moons, and found growing where she had pressed the ground with her right hand, corn, where with her left hand, beans; and where her back parts had pressed it, there grew tobacco.

When the "Captivity of William Henry" appeared in the *London Chronicle,* Franklin attempted to foster the illusion that it was an extract from a complete book of 160 pages. Assuming the style of a reviewer, therefore, he introduced his remarks with a supposed condensation of the unessential narrative details of the book.

> This Writer, who is an Englishman, gives a plain short account of his education in human learning at an academy in Northampton; his settlement in America as a trader with the *Ohio* Indians; his being surpriz'd and made prisoner at the breaking out of the late war; his spiritual change or conversion during his sickness and other afflictions; and then among a multitude of other particulars, relating to the Indians, says.

Immediately after this introduction appear the pretended direct quotations from the imaginary William Henry. After three years of captivity, Henry had succeeded in learning the Indian language and in so doing had gained the respect of his captors. He frequently engaged in conversation with "Old Canusatego," a "Warrior, Counsellor, and the chief man" of the village. In real life this Canusatego had been an actual Indian chief whom Franklin had known on the Pennsylvania frontier in 1744.[24] He had been widely known for his skill in oratory, and Franklin in the "Captivity" amuses himself with the picturesque declamations of his fictional counterpart. In other passages Franklin rather severely ridicules his principles of formal rhetoric.

When not orating, Old Canusatego occupies a role similar to that of the King of the Brobdingnagians in *Gulliver's Travels*. The Indian chieftain would often enquire of his captive concerning "our wars, history, customs, arts, &c. and sometimes about our religious opinions." As Gulliver wished for the tongue of Demosthenes or Cicero that he might justly celebrate the praise of his own dear native country, William Henry regretted his incapacity to reply to the chief's questions because in his youth he "had so unhappily refused the advantage . . . of acquiring store of divine knowledge under the pious instructions of Dr. Doddridge."

One day while William Henry contemplates the Gulliverian task of making the Indians perceive the wisdom and goodness of European "regulation of commerce, by which one nation proposes to make advantage to itself in distressing the trade of others," a young warrior begins a discourse on creation, the one which is printed above concerning the beautiful young woman descending from the clouds. This cosmogony is not allowed to go unchallenged, for all the young Indians laugh heartily at the origin of tobacco described therein, and Old Canusatego rebukes the narrator for telling this foolish Oneida tale to their white captive. "If you tell him such tales, what can you expect but to make him laugh at our Indian stories as much as you sometimes do at his." To atone for the foolishness of the young warrior, Old Canusatego tells the true story of the beginnings of the country, prefacing it with a correction of William Henry's notion that there is but one "great good Manitta," usually called the "Great Manitou" in other Indian literature.

> If there were but one, how unhappy must he be without friends, without companions, and without that equality in conversation, by which pleasure is mutually given and received! I tell you there are more than a hundred of them. [Franklin's note: They commonly use a hundred to express any great unknown or indeterminate number.] They live in the sun and in the moon; they love one another as brethren; they visit and converse with each other; and they sometimes visit, though they do not often converse with us. Every country has its great good Manitta, who first peopled that country.

After establishing a "good Manitta" to people every land, Old Canusatego continues with an account of the peopling of Akanishionegy, the land of the five Indian nations, an account which combines primitive animism with a crude form of scientific evolution. Having dedicated the land to red men, who are the best of men, the good Manitta strewed the fertile fields of Onondaga with five handfuls of red seeds, like the eggs of flies.

> Little worms came out of the seeds, and penetrated the earth, where the spirits who had never yet seen the light entred (sic) into and united with them. Manitta watered the earth with his rain, the sun warmed it, the worms with the spirits in them grew, putting forth little arms and legs, and moved the light earth that covered them. After nine moons they came forth perfect boys and girls. Manitta covered them with his mantle of warm purple cloud, and nourished them with milk from his finger ends. Nine summers did he nurse, and nine summers more did he instruct them how to live.

One does not have to be a Freudian to wonder how much of this imagery Franklin intended as sexual and embryological. On the surface, however, it remains simply a myth of cosmogony—the Five Nations springing from the five different handfuls of seeds. In a loose paraphrase of the second chapter of Genesis, Old Canusatego pictures the great good Manitta assembling his five children, naming them (Mohocks, Oneidas, Sennekers, Cayugas, and Onondagoes), and providing each with a characteristic foodstuff. Manitta crowns his act of creation with a forecast of things to be.

> The bodies I have given you will in time grow old and wear out, so that you will be weary of them; or from various accidents they may become unfit for your habitation, and you will leave them. . . . I have enabled you therefore, among yourselves, to produce new bodies, to supply the place of old ones, that every one of you when he parts with his old habitation may in due time find a new one, and never wander longer than he chuses under the earth, deprived of the light of the sun.

We may well pause at this point to inquire how much of this system of metempsychosis and pre-existence Franklin intended seriously and how much as straight burlesque. His cosmogony of the naked woman from the clouds is not a serious substitute for the first and second chapters of Genesis; neither is it a masterpiece of primitive wisdom, as it was interpreted by the editors of the *Ephémérides*. Franklin is having as much fun with the deists as with the orthodox in this work that is supremely eclectic in its humor. But although Franklin has rejected orthodoxy, he is still speculating on the plurality of worlds, and realizing the ethereal nature of his speculation, he finds amusement in his own attempts to solve the problem of life and individual identity. Metempsychosis and pre-existence are no more seriously intended than is the character of Old Canusatego himself. The latter is so wise and so philosophically erudite and he expresses himself with such vigor and grace that he could almost serve as an Indian Franklin. Yet just as Franklin ascribed some realistic traits and practical comments to the ancient chief, he probably thought seriously about some of the esoteric metaphysical concepts he introduces. He may, on the other hand, have been merely lightly mocking himself for retaining such esoteric notions, the persistence of which may have both annoyed and amused him.

In the remainder of the work, Franklin discards metaphysics and tackles the economic system. Here his distress at moral deficiencies is genuine and earnest. He introduces an apologue concerning the discord caused by economic competition and greed, a narrative that in its sombre invective resembles the style of Swift. In this section Franklin repeats the same principles of free trade he had expressed in the earliest of his works to appear in the *Ephémérides,* "On the Price of Corn"; however, in suggesting that free trade could have prevented the commercial wars between the English and the French, Franklin uses much stronger language than he had used in the mild and good-humored letter "On the Price of Corn."

The concluding paragraph of the "Captivity" returns to the satirical method of *Gulliver's Travels.* With obvious irony, William Henry disclaims sympathy with the Indians and categorically asserts the superiority of western orthodox beliefs.

Now it is well known that some who have before me been among these Indians, have reported highly of their stories, as if there were something superexcellent in them. I have therefore given this story of theirs at full length translated as well as I am able; and I can faithfully assure my readers it is one of their very best, by which may be seen the miserable darkness these poor creatures labour under, and how far inferior their best instructions do appear when compared with the unerring oracles that we possess, and the histories contained in them.

The editors of the *Ephémérides* presented William Henry's adventures under the title, "Mithologie et Morale Iroquoises," remarking that they had first taken this "petit morceau de Philosophie" for a fairy story, but since it had been sent to them by Franklin they finished their reading and so discovered that it was a sample of Iroquois morality, "qui ne paraît pas mal absurde, quoiqu'elle ne le soit peut-être pas plus au fonds, que celles des Egiptiens, des Phéniciens, des Grecs & des Romains, qui renfermoient des principes très sages & très vrais, sous une apparence de folie extrême."

The bibliographical history of this deft burlesque of the philosophical Indian in literature touches France at several points. Two years before the "Captivity of William Henry" appeared in the *London Chronicle,* Franklin had narrated his Indian cosmogony to friends in Germany, and it appeared in Achenwall's *Observations on North America,* 1767.[25] He told it again in one of his most famous tracts, *Remarks concerning the Savages of North America,*[26] first published at Franklin's press at Passy in separate French and English versions. The title of the French version, *Remarques sur la politesse des sauvages de l'Amérique septentrionale,* emphasizes the characteristics of primitive nobility which had delighted the editors of the *Ephémérides.* The *Remarks* was later printed in several editions in the same volume with *Information to Those Who Would Remove to America.* Presumably Franklin did not intend either piece for general publication. After learning of their appearance in London in 1784, he wrote to Benjamin Vaughan to inquire concerning the circumstances of their being printed. The latter wrote to Franklin, November 21, 1784, "I know not *who* published your pieces on the Indians & on Imigrations, nor have I yet seen them. The latter piece the Abbé Morellet sent Lord Shelburne, from whom I had it; The Bishop of St. Asaph's family afterwards had my whole packet of your pieces for many weeks." [27]

One of the passages from the *Remarks* (but not in "William Henry") Franklin based on an actual event which had occurred at an Indian Treaty, a record of which Franklin published at his Philadelphia press in 1744. Nine years later he paraphrased the incident in a letter to Peter Collinson, May 9, 1753. In his *Remarks* Franklin incorporated this material, emphasizing the droll aspects of the scene to illustrate Indian politeness. The commissioners at the close of the treaty had informed the Indians that there existed an academy at Williamsburg with funds for the education of Indians. They invited the Indians to send six of their young men to learn the language and customs of the white people. The day following, the Indians gave their reply.

> We are convinc'd . . . that you mean to do us Good by your Proposal; and we thank you heartily. But you, who are wise, must know that different Nations have different Conceptions of things; and you will therefore not take it amiss, if our Ideas of this kind of Education happen not to be the same with yours. We have had some Experience of it; Several of our young People were formerly brought up at the Colleges of the Northern Provinces; they were instructed in all your Sciences; but, when they came back to us, they were bad Runners, ignorant of every means of living in the Woods, unable to bear either Cold or Hunger, knew neither how to build a Cabin, take a Deer, or kill an Enemy, spoke our Language imperfectly, were therefore neither fit for Hunters, Warriors, nor Counsellors; they were totally good for nothing. We are however not the less oblig'd by your kind Offer, tho' we decline accepting it; and, to show our grateful Sense of it, if the Gentlemen of Virginia will send us a Dozen of their Sons, we will take great Care of their Education, instruct them in all we know, and make Men of them.[28]

While Brissot de Warville was employed in London as a rising young journalist he saw this passage in a London newspaper in 1785. Translating it as "Anecdote sur les Sauvages de l'Amérique septentrionale," he sent it to the *Journal de Paris,* where it appeared as an anonymous work, April 7, 1785.

It is apparent that the sections of both the "Captivity" and the *Remarks* that appealed most to French readers were those exhibiting the naive wisdom of the Indians. The cosmogony of the beautiful woman descending from the skies is common to both works but serves two quite distinct purposes. In the "Captivity" it is derided, called a foolish Oneida tale, and contrasted with the rhapsodical discourse on metempsychosis and the origin of the Five Nations, whereas in the *Remarks* it stands by itself with no comment of any kind. Perhaps in the interim between the publication of the two works, Franklin realized that regardless of its absurdity or disharmony with his own religious beliefs, the tale had great narrative and character interest. Thus, in the

Remarks it is told entirely for its own sake as an amusing anecdote parallel to the preliminary narrative of the Indians refusing
the academic advantages of the college at Williamsburg. The
"Captivity" is a satire on universal human frailties exemplified
by the religious myths of braves and missionaries and the economic policies of the British Empire, while the *Remarks,* on the
other hand, is an amusing local color sketch of Indian character
and customs. The "Captivity" bristles in the satirical vein of
Jonathan Swift deriding the Lilliputians; the *Remarks* glows in
the tolerant spirit of Joseph Addison discoursing indulgently on
fans and patches.

The editors of the *Ephémérides* found in the "Captivity" only
what they wished to find—"Mithologie et Morale Iroquoises."
No doubt this is what Franklin's friend, the duc de La Rochefoucauld, later found admirable in the *Remarks* and led him in
1784 to translate the work for Franklin's private press at Passy.

3. POOR RICHARD

With the publication of the fragment, "Mithologie et Morale
Iroquoises," the Franklin legend had begun to develop, but it did
not take permanent form until the arrival of Franklin in France
as American commissioner and the concomitant publication of
Quétant's translation of his *Way to Wealth* under the title of
La Science du Bonhomme Richard. The Way to Wealth is a
compilation of proverbs from an almanac that Franklin had
edited and published in Pennsylvania from 1733 until 1758. To
make his almanac more entertaining than those of his competitors, Franklin had invented a harassed husband, Richard Saunders,
and his determined spouse, Bridget. In the preface to the almanac
for nearly every year in which it appeared, Saunders or his wife
wrote about each other or their competitors in the vein of
Isaac Bickerstaff, the imaginary astrologer of Jonathan Swift and

Notes to this chapter begin on page 241.

Richard Steele. In addition to prefatory essays, poetry, and domestic hints, the pages of the almanac were filled with a variety
of proverbs. The annual production bore the title *Poor Richard's
Almanac,* but in French, because of the paradox inherent in a
literal translation, the name of Franklin's rural philosopher was
usually converted to Bonhomme Richard.

In the summer of 1757 while on a packet en route to England,
Franklin looked over his almanacs for the preceding two decades,
extracted the best proverbs concerning thrift and industry, and
combined them in an ingenious narrative. This narrative he published as the Preface to the Almanac for 1758 and gave it the title
The Way to Wealth. The scene is a country fair in Pennsylvania,
where Poor Richard, passing by on horseback, pauses to hear a
hoary patriarch, named Father Abraham, haranguing the crowd
on taxes and hard times. The best weapons to combat both, maintains the old man, are labor and economy; his immediate counsel
to his auditors is to abandon the folly of the fair. Nearly each one
of his sentences contains a proverb or two—most of them drawn
from previous almanacs and introduced with some variant of the
phrase, "As Poor Richard says." The old gentleman concludes
his discourse, the people solemnly approve, and immediately
proceed to act upon the contrary doctrine. The only one to be
visibly influenced is Richard Saunders himself, whose vanity has
been touched by hearing his name mentioned throughout, and
who goes away without buying the coat he had attended the fair
to acquire.

During his middle age Franklin was fond of amusing himself
by constructing magic squares and circles—numbers arranged in
various patterns to produce identical sums when added in various
directions. His *Way to Wealth* is essentially a *tour de force* of the
same nature—the construction into a continued narrative of a
series of proverbs on a single theme taken from a larger collection
of heterogeneous sayings.

The first French translation of *The Way to Wealth* appeared
in 1773 as part of Dubourg's edition of the *Œuvres de M. Franklin,* 1773.[1] It created almost no comment. A second translation
by Antoine François Quétant in 1777 immediately gained thou-
sands of readers.[2] Some preliminary facts concerning the relations
between Franklin's own visits to France and the translations of

his works will help to explain why the early translation of *The Way to Wealth* was given almost no attention, whereas another version only three years later became the most widely read American work in France.

Although some authorities attribute the two volumes of Franklin's *Œuvres* to Jean Baptiste Lesqui (or LeCuy), a member of the religious order of the Prémontres, the correspondence between Franklin and Dubourg proves without a doubt that they are entirely the work of the latter. Both Lesqui and Jean Baptiste Le Roy had begun translating some of Franklin's scientific works in 1772, perhaps at Dubourg's instigation, but both gave up the task almost at its commencement, leaving it entirely in Dubourg's hands.[3] Dubourg's translation is based on the fourth edition of Franklin's *Experiments and Observations in Electricity made at Philadelphia in America* (London, 1769), but Dubourg included a mass of materials not found in this edition. His work, therefore, represented the most complete collection of Franklin writings printed to that time. The first volume contains documents concerning Franklin's electrical experiments; the second volume, material on economic, political and miscellaneous subjects. Of the miscellaneous pieces, *The Way to Wealth* and an essay on demography, *Observations concerning the Increase of Mankind,* were the most influential.

The latter essay was the only one to receive critical attention in the French press and the only one which stimulated Dubourg to extensive editorial comment. To his translation Dubourg added a number of explanatory notes and a supplementary essay of his own, hoping by them to persuade Franklin to write further on the subject. Dubourg felt that Franklin's comments on Pennsylvania should be extended to generalizations on the population of the entire world; he accordingly presented ten demographic principles of his own, which portray a broader international and humanitarian vision than that of Franklin. Dissenting from Franklin's observation that a nation is strengthened doubly by "increasing its own people, and diminishing its neighbours," Dubourg asserts that the advantages drawn from the misfortune of one's neighbors are often more imaginary than real, that the principles of justice and the sources of felicity are the same both for nations and for individuals. Although presuming to expand the scope of Franklin's observations, Dubourg agreed with their general principles. Mirabeau, however, who saw Franklin's essay before its appearance in print, wrote on a manuscript translation in his possession in 1771, "Observations on population by Mr. Franklin given by him to me before he had any notion of economics, and it is here apparent." [4]

Dubourg added no original comments to his translation of *The Way to Wealth,* but it is apparent from his later imitation of its proverbial wisdom that he considered the work to be even more significant than the *Observations* on population. Dubourg's title is literal and comprehensive: "Le Moyen de s'enricher, Enseigné clairement dans la Préface d'un vieil Almanach de Pensylvanie, intitulé: Le Pauvre Henri à Son Aise." This pioneer translation seems to have been virtually ignored by the French public although extracts appeared in the *Journal Encyclopédique* (June 1773) as part of an appraisal of the *Œuvres.*[5] It enjoyed no separate editions, inspired no commentaries or eulogies—except Dubourg's own imitation of Franklin's almanac, *Calendrier de Philadelphie, ou Constitutions de Sancho-Pança et du Bon-Homme Richard, en Pensylvanie,* 1777. In this same year, 1777, appeared the new translation of *The Way to Wealth* by Quétant, *La Science du Bonhomme Richard, ou Moyen Facile de payer les impôts,* a translation that went through four editions in two years and at least five others before the end of the century. It was widely quoted in periodicals and extravagantly praised. In this dress, *La Science du Bonhomme Richard* came to be almost universally considered a work of sublime morality, and its sententious maxims were compared to those of Bacon and La Fontaine.

Let us review the chronological record. *The Way to Wealth* appeared originally in Philadelphia in 1758, was widely reprinted in America and England, but remained unheard of in France until 1773 when it appeared as part of Franklin's complete works. The editor, Dubourg, and one or two journalists recognized that it had literary merits beyond Franklin's other pieces, but it nevertheless fell into virtual neglect. Then a brief four years later a new translation brought the work widespread attention and effusive praise. The conclusions are inevitable. Either the two translations brought about this state of affairs—the deficiencies of one and the excellencies of the other—or other completely unrelated circumstances were responsible.

A comparison will show almost at a glance that the two translations vary hardly at all in literary merit. Dubourg's is more literal and slightly more expansive than that of Quétant and in general preserves the constructions of the original, preferring to give an exact rendering of the English idiom than to convert to the French equivalent. Quétant, however, maintains a colloquial French style, selecting the language which Franklin would have used had he been a rural philosopher speaking to the average Frenchman of his time. These characteristics may be seen in the rendering of the English proverb, "God helps those who help themselves," which Franklin probably took from James Howell's *Lexicon Tetraglotton*, 1660. Dubourg gives the completely literal translation "Dieu aide ceux qui s'aident eux-mêmes"; whereas Quétant gives the French idiomatic equivalent, "Aide-toi, je t'aiderai," almost as it appears in La Fontaine's "Le Chartier Embourbé" ("Aide-toi, le Ciel t'aidera").

An anecdote concerning this proverb has been recorded by Sainte-Beuve and associated with Franklin. Two prominent Jansenists imprisoned in the Bastille were visited by the governor, who was in a very good humor. Finding them in a tranquil frame of mind, he remarked upon it, "Doesn't God say in his Gospel, 'God helps those who help themselves'?" The two prisoners looked at each other and smiled at the citation of the new gospel. But we may well smile in turn at their astonishment, Sainte-Beuve added, so much has our Christianity been humanized since and translated *à la Franklin*.[6]

The event which brought *The Way to Wealth* to instant popularity in France was Franklin's arrival, December 21, 1776. Franklin's appearance and personality created an immediate sensation, not only among the scientists and philosophers who had known and admired him previously, but among the diplomats on one side and the common people on the other. *Les Mémoires secrets* reported (February 4, 1777) that he had been much wined, dined, and applauded by the savants. The details of his appearances at court and in public we may read in newspapers, personal letters, and private memoirs; all agreed on Franklin's paternal and benevolent demeanor. The *Mémoires secrets* noted his "handsome physiognomy, partial baldness, and a fur cap which he wore constantly on his head." So popular did Franklin become that his likeness appeared on every hand. His portrait was offered for sale in medallions of various sizes, "some to be set in the lids of snuffboxes and some so small as to be worn in rings; and," he wrote to his daughter, "the numbers sold are incredible. These, with the pictures, busts, and prints (of which copies upon copies are spread everywhere), have made your father's face as well known as that of the moon, so that he durst not do anything that would oblige him to run away, as his phiz would discover him wherever he should venture to show it." [7] Louis XVI, not exactly pleased with the homage paid to this hero of democracy but not prepared openly to discountenance it, paid his respects to the mode by presenting to the Comtesse Diane de Polignac a handsome chamber pot with Franklin's physiognomy on the inner side of its base.[8]

The consequent success of *La Science du Bonhomme Richard* came about not only because Franklin was in the public eye, but also because his own personality came to be associated with that of Bonhomme Richard. No better evidence of this can be given than the following description of Franklin by Hilliard d'Auberteuil, a fellow member with Franklin of the Masonic lodge of the Nine Sisters.

> Everything in him announced the simplicity and the innocence of primitive morals. . . . Franklin had lain aside the wig which formerly in England hid the nudity of his forehead and the useless adornment which would have left him at the level of the other English. He showed to the astonished multitude a head worthy of the brush of Guide [a painter of old men] on an erect and vigorous body clad in the simplest of garments. His eyes were shadowed by large glasses and in his hand he carried a white cane. He spoke little. He knew how to be impolite without being rude, and his pride seemed to be that of nature. Such a person was made to excite the curiosity of Paris. The people clustered around as he passed and asked, "Who is this old peasant who has such a noble air?" [9]

In appearance Franklin seemed to be a village philosopher; those who knew him, therefore, considered his Bonhomme Richard as village philosophy.

Franklin himself, however, never had such a view of his work.

To him it was a collection of proverbial wisdom, some of which he believed and had practiced, some of which he considered to be of limited application. There is little doubt that he included much of it to sell almanacs and that he gave little or no thought to either its practical value or moral tone. We have already pointed out that *The Way to Wealth* was drawn from the pages of *Poor Richard's Almanac* of previous years, that it was a careful selection of those passages inculcating thrift and industry. The complete *Poor Richard* does more than advocate worldly prudence; indeed, much of its philosophy is contradictory. In general, the sayings are bawdy and practical in the early years; paradoxically, moral and cynical in the later. Several of them were derived ultimately from La Rochefoucauld.

The French journalists who praised Bonhomme Richard for his sublime morality would have been surprised to learn that he had formerly advised his Philadelphia townsmen:

> Love your Neighbour; yet don't pull down your Hedge. 1754
>
> There's none deceived but he that trusts. 1736
>
> Onions can make ev'n heirs and widows weep. 1734

Franklin did not exactly view life as a dog-fight, but he portrayed many unconventional aspects of life that were completely ignored in *The Way to Wealth*. His attitude toward sex, for example, is more cynical than sublime.

> You cannot pluck roses without fear of thorns
> Nor enjoy a fair wife without danger of horns. 1734
>
> Neither a fortress nor a maidenhead will hold out long after they begin to parley. 1734

Indeed the prudential worldliness of *The Way to Wealth* is in general controverted by the following maxim from *Poor Richard*.

> Avarice and happiness never saw each other, how then should they become acquainted. 1734

Not to speak of the French couplet which Franklin used in 1742,

> Fiente de chien & marc d'argent,
> Seront tout un au jour du jugement.
>
> (Dog's dung and silver marks
> Are all one at the day of judgment.)

Even in *The Way to Wealth* itself Franklin gently satirizes his prudential advice and his method of inculcating it: "I own that to encourage the practice of remembering and repeating those wise sentences, I have sometimes quoted myself with great gravity." Franklin's French contemporaries, however, completely missed this suggestion of irony and were completely unaware that many of the proverbs in the complete *Poor Richard's Almanac* epitomized worldly or bawdy views of life.

Despite the many editions and periodical reprints of Quétant's version, other translations followed. In Lausanne, *The Way to Wealth* appeared under the title *Manuel de Philosophie Pratique, Pour servir de suite à la Science du Bonhomme Richard* (1795) as the nucleus of a collection of little-known English moral fragments.[10] Notably this is the only translation in which Poor Richard is literally translated in the text as "pauvre Richard," although the title of the piece reads, "Le secret du bon homme Richard pour faire une bonne maison." The translated narrative is brisk and colloquial, but somewhat condensed, the anonymous translator going even further than Quétant in converting Franklin's proverbs to idiomatic French equivalents.

A fourth translation by J. Castéra appeared in his edition of Franklin's autobiography in 1798.[11] Referring to Quétant's prior version, he remarked that the work was so interesting that he felt obliged to give a fresh translation. He provided also a new title, "Le Chemin de la Fortune, ou La Science du bonhomme Richard." A fifth separate translation appeared in Paris in 1817 with the title *Extrait de la Science du Bonhomme Richard*,[12] a highly compressed version that omits the entire narrative framework and all reference to Father Abraham, but is otherwise literal. This translator is unknown.

Most French critics admired *Bonhomme Richard* for its simplicity, its appeal to the common man, and its sublime morality. Brissot, who had previously met Franklin in Pennsylvania and had praised him extensively in an account of his voyages, devoted an article in his periodical *Le Patriote François* to *Poor Richard*, portraying it as an indirect cause of the French Revolution.[13] Repeating the commonplace that the Revolution was not the fruit of an insurrection but the work of fifty years of enlightenment, he observed that as the enlightenment had first established

liberty it was the subsequent function of enlightenment to maintain it; that the true friends, the true defenders of the Revolution
are those who spread instruction among the people. As Franklin
had established liberty in America, Penn had established the
republic. Franklin in particular influenced his age through his
simple, naive, and familiar style, which was as useful to the common people as it was agreeable to those of literary culture. *The
Way to Wealth,* which Brissot describes as proverbial exhortation,
he concludes is a masterpiece of popular literature. In a later
address at the Jacobin's Club, Brissot repeated his political interpretation: "The patriot *par excellence* is a philosopher. Behold
how Poor Richard and Franklin were always friends of the
people." [14]

An even more enthusiastic appraisal was given by the abbé
Fauchet in his *Eloge Civique* of Franklin. Apparently referring
to Dubourg's translation, he stated that "Les Proverbes du
Vieux Henri, la Science du Bonhomme Richard are in the hands
of the learned and the ignorant: it is the most sublime practical
morality presented for the common man; it is for all humanity
the catechism of happiness." [15]

Even the ladies, who shared in many of Franklin's activities
in Paris, joined in acclaiming Bonhomme Richard. While Franklin was still in residence, a young married lady distributed copies
of the work to a number of her friends; one of these, a romantic
admirer, wrote some verses on the subject that were published
in the *Journal de Paris* (March 14, 1781). On the one hand, he
regretted that a young and pretty maiden should show in her
demeanor nothing but good sense, for at the age of polite accomplishments too much reason leads to misanthropy. On the
other hand, he applauded her resolution since she gave endless
pleasure by preaching in Poor Richard's style; even those whom
she condemned by her principles involuntarily admired her moral
sobriety.

Grimm in his *Correspondance littéraire* was almost the only
critic to say anything adverse about *Bonhomme Richard* (although
his general opinion is favorable). Impressed chiefly by the economic features of the work, he pointed out its grand principle
that personal extravagance may be more onerous than public
taxes. "This moral is developed in a series of apophthegms full

of reason, energy, and clarity," Grimm admitted, but at the same time he objected to "the eternal repetition of the phrase *as Poor Richard says,* which makes reading a little tiresome." He concluded, nevertheless, that he knew of no other book more worthy of universal circulation than this one of Dr. Franklin.[16]

Other critics praised the economic features of the work. Jean Baptiste Say, famous economist during the period of the Directory and authority on public education, specifically asserted in reference to Franklin that practical economics and high morality are mutually dependent. In a work of utopian fiction, *Olbie, ou essai sur les moyens d'améliorer les moeurs d'une nation,* 1791, he describes the erecting of temples celebrating the principal virtues,[17] with wall inscriptions of moral precepts chosen from among the most useful and practical that literature has to offer, including maxims of political economy, since they are conducive to morality. By this means, farmers, traders, and manufacturers who travel to other communities may read these maxims and may be apprised of their own true interests. Among examples of proverbs notable for their simple forcefulness and ease of retention, Say gives one each from La Fontaine and Bacon and six from Franklin.

Say collaborated with du Pont de Nemours in 1794 in publishing a volume of Franklin material, including the Quétant translation of *The Way to Wealth.*[18] The highly-significant review of this volume in *La Décade Philosophique,* the organ of du Pont de Nemours and fellow minds, summarizes the importance of *Bonhomme Richard* to Franklin's vogue in France: [19] "It is in this work that are found these numerous adages, these moral axioms that have made a part of the reputation of Franklin. *La Science du Bonhomme Richard* is a masterpiece of good sense, of concision, of simplicity—one could almost add, of finesse, if a word so decried could be applied to the most sublime, the most useful notions of political and private economy." After a cursory summary of Franklin's work, the reviewer adds, "Nothing which concerned the interests of humanity was below him. One senses how he had been obliged to make this light framework interesting by the manner in which he has carried it out. At every moment one perceives his profound knowledge of the qualities and eccentricities of men. He had seen much; he had experienced much; and he knew how to observe. There are few works which comprise so many things in such a small volume. At every instant one encounters one of these maxims which astonish by their justness, their concision, their profundity." Finally, the reviewer praises the literary skill that enabled Franklin to appeal to all classes of readers. "At the same time that he develops the truths that he gives you with such skill, he brings them within the comprehension of every reader. That which an unpracticed mind does not grasp under one form, it grasps under another. One may say of Franklin as has been said of La Fontaine from another point of view: his writings are those of all ages, of all minds, of all conditions."

Shortly after the publication of this volume containing *Bonhomme Richard*, Say wrote to the Executive Commission of Public Instruction offering to provide copies of the volume at a negligible price to be used as an elementary textbook in the public schools. Reporting on the offer, the Commission remarked, "To have named this work is to have eulogized it." [20] Because of the merit of the book, its nominal price, and the dearth of elementary books in all sections of the republic, the Commission recommended that copies be obtained and distributed in the various departments.

Du Pont de Nemours, perhaps with this transaction still in his mind, prescribed *The Way to Wealth* as a textbook for the American educational system. In a discussion of national education in the United States, written while du Pont was in New York, he advocated *The Way to Wealth* as the only literary work in existence suited to the elementary grades; [21] an adequate ABC, he felt, was the most difficult type of textbook to prepare.

> I know only a single book which has the grace, the lightness, the deep sense, the art of dissimulating art, which this genre of work requires. It is by Franklin. It is *la Science du Bonhomme Richard*. It has been imitated in France by the honest *Mathon de la Cour* in *le Testament de Fortuné Ricard;* but what a great difference in talent and how little application it has to childhood. The *Testament* has as its aim merely to demonstrate the value of thrift in spending and the accumulating of interest from capital—and then to show the useful projects a government with several millionaires may undertake.

Franklin himself knew *le Testament de Fortuné Ricard* and wrote to Mathon de la Cour (July 9, 1785) that he had read it with pleasure and conceived a high opinion of its author; indeed, it had such a strong influence upon him that he later attributed to it the impulse which led him to provide in his will for a trust fund of £2000 sterling for the cities of Boston and Philadelphia to be used in aiding "young beginners in business." [22] When *le Testament de Fortuné Ricard* first appeared in France, it was taken to be the work of Franklin.[23]

Mathon de la Cour was the first of a series of French economists and sociologists, including Jean Baptiste Say and Frédéric Bastiat, who were strongly influenced by *Poor Richard*. Bastiat wrote to one of his friends at the age of 26, exulting over the discovery of a volume of Franklin's moral and political miscellanies, "I am so enthused over it that I intend to follow the same method to become as good and as happy as he." [24] Bastiat's biographer, describing him as "le Bonhomme Richard de la science économique française," felt sure that he adopted from Franklin his familiar and simple tone and his attitude of popular good nature when he wished to instruct the masses.[25]

The pedagogical value of *Bonhomme Richard* was similarly stressed by the translator of the Lausanne, 1795, edition, who remarked that literature offers for children a large number of works presenting the most noble sentiments, the greatest simplicity, and the best manner of instruction, but that few works are available that are designed for the period of early youth, that highly critical age when the young man begins to sense his importance, to pride himself on the title of man, and to scorn everything that recalls the child. At this period in life, the young man needs reading material devoted exclusively to his needs, to satisfy his zest for noble thoughts and philosophic systems. The editor, in reference to the pieces that he had selected with *Bonhomme Richard* as their nucleus, concluded that "morality is above all sophisms and essentially related to the maintenance of public felicity because of its direct influence on the happiness of individuals."

Condorcet, finding *Bonhomme Richard* suitable for informed as well as burgeoning minds, admired Franklin for concealing his intellectual superiority in seeming to descend to the common level.[26] Franklin at the outset of his career "did not want any class of citizen to remain without instruction," Condorcet observed in his famous eulogy; he did not wish to see

> any one condemned to receive only false ideas by books designed to flatter his credulousness or nourish his prejudices. A common printer [Franklin] did for America what the wisest governments have had the arrogance to neglect or the weakness to fear. He later gathered all of these lessons in the work so famous under the title of Bonhomme Richard, a unique work in which one cannot help recognizing the superior man without it being possible to cite a single passage where he allows his superiority to be perceived. Nothing in the thoughts nor in the style is above the least developed intelligence, but the philosophic mind easily discovers noble aims and profound intentions. The expression is always natural, often indeed commonplace, and all the wit is in the choice of ideas. In order that his lessons might be most useful he did not reveal to his readers that a philosopher of the town had condescended to instruct them and he hid himself under the name of Poor Richard, pretending to be ignorant and humble like them.

In the following year, Joseph Antoine Cerutti, famous Revolutionary figure, himself an exponent of adult education, published in his *La Feuille Villageoise* a similar interpretation of Franklin's career.[27] The human race owes less to Franklin's politics and his lightning rods, he remarked, than his compatriots owe to his pamphlets. "Twenty years before he established the liberty of the American people, he cultivated their reason." Cerutti's periodical was designed especially to enlighten the provinces concerning the progress of the Revolution. Although apparently without any specific knowledge concerning Franklin's extended editorial supervision of his newspaper *The Pennsylvania Gazette,* Cerutti felt that his own enterprise was similar to Franklin's. "He was a printer; he wanted to be a journalist; no doubt he produced *Feuilles villageoises* (Village Newspapers)." In a subsequent article on *Poor Richard,* Cerutti explained that Franklin

> having observed how the people he wished to liberate still lacked enlightenment, conceived the plan of publishing a weekly paper where morality was presented in varied and intriguing forms, and where political principles were taught in a clear and simple language. It was by this essentially simple proceeding that he succeeded in rectifying the common ideas and in creating in some measure for

the multitude a new spirit capable equally of braving perils and of avoiding excesses. His paper had an enormous success; it fell into the hands of the ignorant and the intelligentsia; some of the articles it contained, worthy of Voltaire and of Montesquieu, have circulated throughout the entire world. Among them is *La Science du Bonhomme Richard,* a science made for our villagers.[28]

This account contains much rapture, little accuracy. Cerutti makes no distinction between Franklin's newspaper, *The Pennsylvania Gazette,* and *Poor Richard's Almanac. Poor Richard* had absolutely no connection with the *Gazette,* and the famous political tracts and moral pieces that contributed to Franklin's vogue in Paris were all written subsequently to his period as newspaper editor. While Cerutti gives a fair statement of Franklin's purposes in the *Gazette,* he is completely mistaken about his achievements, for although Franklin wrote a number of pieces of genuine literary merit for the *Gazette,* they were not at the time widely read.

Cerutti by nature cared more for embellishment than for accuracy. This characteristic influenced even the extracts from *Poor Richard* he selected from the Quétant translation as printed in the Buisson edition of Franklin's *Memoirs;* he touched up the style, enlivened the narrative to suit his own fancy, but paid no attention to literal meaning. Thus, his is not a new translation, but an embellishment of Quétant's. The nature of Cerutti's treatment is well revealed in the conclusion of the piece, to which Cerutti gave a novel twist completely contrary to Franklin's ending. According to Cerutti,

As the old preacher finished his harangue, the people listened with mouths agape and smiling. They clapped their hands when he finished speaking. Indeed they did even better; taking advantage of his advice, some ran to pay their debts, others went to take up their work, and still others remained for the sale, but bought only necessary articles; and all paid their taxes through the savings of virtue and the reform of vice. American national prosperity profited through the science and the proverbs of Bonhomme Richard. Since this famous discourse, no one in America pronounces a moral sentence, a political maxim, an aphorism of jurisprudence, a historical apophthegm, a popular proverb, a popular adage, or any kind of saying, without adding "as Poor Richard says."

In this embellishment, Cerutti is right about little except the colloquial style of *Poor Richard.* In America, it was the style rather than the sense of Franklin's proverbs that made *Poor Richard* a best-seller; intellectually Franklin's proverbs were so diverse and contradictory that they could not possibly have had a consistent effect. In France, Bonhomme Richard became so closely associated with brisk, colloquial style that a periodical came out in 1790 with the title *Le Bonhomme Richard aux Bonnes-Gens.* Anti-revolutionary propaganda, it ran to only two issues, but in imitating the homespun style of *Poor Richard,* it attempted to reconcile workers, servants, and the unemployed with the status quo and to forfend further disturbances. During Year III of the revolutionary epoch appeared another periodical under the title of *Journal du Bonhomme Richard,* a political daily, presenting opinions corresponding to those of Bonneville and Fauchet. The author, Antoine F. Lemaire, introduced Bonhomme Richard as a man with normal human characteristics and from time to time allowed him to present his moral thoughts.[29]

Other evidence shows that Bonhomme Richard and his proverbs actually entered into common parlance. In a periodical dedicated entirely to the theater, for example, an author began a letter in the year after the Quétant translation with the phrase, "Bonhomme Richard is indeed right in saying," and ended the same letter with another proverb and the words, "as Bonhomme Richard also says." [30]

Amid all the notice created by *Bonhomme Richard,* however, the most extraordinary manifestation of interest was that of a society of deists, who included it in a compilation of works of religious and moral contemplation. Franklin, who wrote at least one ritual for his own private devotions and collaborated in the preparing of another for public use, would probably have been amazed to see his utilitarian proverbs regarded as a religious and moral system. Yet a précis of *The Way to Wealth* appeared under the title of "Pensées Morales de Franklin" in the *Année Religieuse des Théophilantropes, ou Adorateurs de Dieu et Amis des Hommes,*[31] published by the Théophilantropes, a moral and philanthropic society that held public services celebrating its three major doctrines, the existence of God, the existence of the soul, and the hope of a future life. In the *Année Religieuse, Bonhomme Richard* appeared as a parallel to the moral thoughts of Penn, La Bruyère, Fénelon, Young, Voltaire, and Rousseau. The text, based on Quétant but eliminating all narrative elements, presents Franklin's didactic utilitarianism in unrelieved simplicity. The editors apparently received inspiration or moral strength from the stark homily, spaced in the fashion of prayer books or meditations.

> . . . Par exemple, notre *paresse* nous prend deux fois autant que le gouvernement;
> Notre *orgueil*, trois fois;
> Et notre *imprudence*, quatre fois autant encore.

It may be worth noting that the section which the Theophilanthropists changed most radically from the Quétant version is the only one in which Franklin departs from the theme of prudential economy to suggest the higher theme of social benevolence. Franklin had stated that the good things of prosperity were of little value without the blessings of heaven, and he exhorted his readers to petition these for themselves and to care for their neighbors who lacked material and spiritual comfort, giving as an example the transition of Job from poverty to happiness.

> N'allez pas cependant vous confier uniquement à votre industrie, à votre vigilance & à votre économie. Ce sont d'excellentes choses à la vérité, mais elles vous seront tout-à-fait inutiles, si vous n'avez, avant tout, les bénédictions du Ciel. Demandez donc humblement ces bénédictions; ne soyez point insensibles aux besoins de ceux à qui elles sont refusées; mais donnez-leur des consolations & des secours. Souvenez-vous que Job fut pauvre, & qu'ensuite il redevint heureux.

The Theophilanthropists, perhaps because of their deistical notions, deleted the references to prayer and to Job.

> N'allez pas cependant vous confier uniquement à votre industrie, à votre vigilance et à votre économie. Ce sont d'excellentes choses, à la vérité; mais il faut encore à votre bonheur les bénédictions du Ciel. Rendez-vous en dignes, par la pratique de toutes les vertus; ne soyez pas insensibles aux besoins de vos frères, mais donnez-leur des consolations et des secours.

If taken seriously, *The Way to Wealth* must be condemned as a handbook of bourgeois respectability. (That Franklin himself did not take it seriously, the narrative elements with which he adorned it are ample proof.) [32] The Theophilanthropists and other French contemporaries who read concepts of sublime morality into the work must have been touched by the personality of Franklin and so attributed to his work the virtues they perceived in his character. They seem to have considered the work a companion piece to Franklin's *Liturgy on the Universal Principles of Religion and Morality,* 1776, written in collaboration with David Williams, which the Theophilanthropists adopted almost in its entirety in 1797.

This respect for Franklin bordering upon adulation may be perceived also in the previously-mentioned imitation of *Poor Richard's Almanac* entitled *Calendrier de Philadelphie, ou Constitutions de Sancho Pança et du Bon-Homme Richard, en Pensylvanie,* 1777. This work is a calendar in the sense that the book is divided into twelve major sections, one for each month, and the subsections correspond to the days of the month. The contents, however, comprising a maxim or subject of meditation for each day, are not primarily proverbs and wise sayings, like Franklin's, but moral and philosophical *pensées,* in structure more like Pascal's, though in the liberal and deistical principles they set forth, almost antithetical to Pascal's. This work has been attributed to Dr. Barbeu Dubourg, and there is good reason for believing that it is his in part; many of the maxims are taken from the *Petit code de la raison humaine,* a deistical work definitely known to be Dubourg's. I am convinced, however, that Dubourg had absolutely nothing to do with a long introductory narrative of twenty-five pages in which Sancho Pança and Bonhomme Richard converse with each other and with two original characters, Sir Thomas and Mistress Rachel. My reason for this conclusion is that the introductory narrative incorporates the Quétant translation of *The Way to Wealth* almost verbatim, whereas the quotations from Franklin in the almanac section are based on the Dubourg translation. It is hard to imagine that Dubourg would use his own translation as the source of quotations in the text of the work and at the same time use a rival translation in its entirety in an introduction. The probable explanation is that Dubourg himself compiled the almanac section and that the editor or printer added the introduction in order to swell the contents of the work and make it more readily salable.[33] But whatever the reason for the combination, the book is a rarity in literature. I know of no other original production based upon and includ-

ing quotations from two entirely different translations of a work
that it imitates.

The evidence that the introduction and the body of the *Calendrier* are by different hands explains an obvious esthetic and intellectual incompatibility between the two sections. The printer
may have considered the introduction a scintillating and original
jeu d'esprit, but the situation is clumsy and artificial and the
humor forced. It can be justified merely on the grounds that
through it Sancho is enabled to harangue a multitude with a
translation of *The Way to Wealth,* but even the introducing of
Franklin's proverbs is of doubtful value. Franklin's melange of
practical morality does not blend very well with Dubourg's
broader and more philosophical maxims in the body of the work.

The introduction explains how it comes to pass that Sancho
Pança figures as a lawmaker in Pennsylvania. Everyone, the author asserts, is acquainted with his brilliant career as governor
of the island of Barataria, and with his celebrated judicial skill
worthy to be ranked with Solomon's. Like Solomon, he possessed
a mind stored with proverbs, particularly those illustrating and
glorifying prudence. After the death of his master Don Quixote,
Sancho, having had too much taste for knight errantry to remain
content with the mediocrity of life in his simple village with its
curate and barber, revisited the cavern of Montesinos to renew
his acquaintance with the enchanter Parasaragaramus. In a
proverb-crammed speech, Sancho complains of his ennui and
implores the enchanter for surcease. The latter replies that all
will be well; Sancho has followed destiny in coming to the magic
cavern. He is to remain there during the passage of the centuries
until awakened to become the legislator for a populous nation,
where his eminent good sense and his storehouse of proverbs will
then make his regime as successful as the one he had enjoyed on
the island of Barataria. His new subjects are to be primitive
Christians, who will never swear, lie, nor make war. The time
will come when they must be defended against a race of mis-
creants, who, under the pretext that these primitive moralists
have descended from their kinsmen, will seek to ravish their
liberties and seize half of their property. These Christians are
saints, but saints not canonized by virtue of services rendered to
the popes. Like Socrates, Titus, Trajan, Epictetus, Aristides, and

Marcus Aurelius, they have much greater virtues than all the saints of the Golden Legend.

After his forecasted sleep of centuries, Sancho reawakens in Philadelphia in the company of Poor Richard, the almanac-maker. As the two stroll through the city, the latter explains the measures by which the English are seeking to confiscate more than half of the Philadelphia income—by taxing tea and requiring that stamps be affixed to all documents. When he asks Sancho to use his legislative skill and knowledge of proverbs in behalf of his townsmen, Sancho recommends first of all that everything that serves only for ornamentation must be suppressed, or at least be permitted only to thieves and courtesans. Happening upon an auction at which nothing but ornaments is offered for sale, Sancho finds confirmation of his fear that love of luxury is the source of the nation's evils. He harangues the throng, therefore, on the folly of luxury, repeating the entire Quétant translation of *The Way to Wealth*. At the conclusion of this melange of proverbs, everyone in the audience applauds, praises the good sense and reason of the speech, and congratulates the speaker. Just as Poor Richard begins to weep with joy at the thought of his dear townsmen renouncing their vanities and occupying themselves henceforth with useful pursuits, the auctioneer announces the beginning of the sale, and all the beholders rush madly to buy. Sancho and Richard retreat in sorrow to Richard's house, where they console themselves with food and drink and speculate on the means of converting their errant fellow citizens to reason. Richard invites two of his friends, Mistress Rachel and Sir Thomas, to join the consultation, in which, discarding sumptuary laws as ineffectual, the four decide that they should circulate "un petit Cours abrégé de morale simple & insinuante, divisé en léçons courtes & faciles à retenir, qu'on put regarder comme un livret de tous les jours & de toutes les heures." They will publish their defense of reason in the form of an almanac, but an almanac of universal, not provincial, utility, one without holidays and phases of the moon and serviceable in any year.

This episode of Sancho and Richard is not only clumsy, but inconsistent. The tergiversation of Sancho's audience at the conclusion of the tale may have seemed an amusing touch, but it obviously nullifies everything the enchanter Parasaragaramus had previously said concerning the primitive morality of the Quakers. The trouble comes from mixing two themes. Franklin had suggested a boycott of all British goods as a means of defeating the Stamp Acts, and the beginning of the tale seems to be designed to prepare the reader to interpret Sancho's harangue as an attack on importations only. *The Way to Wealth* was written long before the Stamp Acts, however, and it denounces domestic luxury as well as imported; hence, it does not really serve as a rejoinder to the Stamp Acts. Also, as a reviewer in the *Courrier de l'Europe* points out, it is out of keeping with the sober moral tone of the work to introduce Sancho Pança, who inevitably suggests ideas of pleasantry and ridicule.[34]

The almanac itself, however, not the introduction, is the real work of art. Although it is Dubourg's most original and imaginative work, he is forced by the rigid censorship to keep up the fiction that it is a translation. In the preface he expresses fear that his translation may not be exact or agreeable, and that the sentiments of a pretended religious reformer may not be relished in a monarchical and Catholic state. He asserts in defense that wise and judicious readers of the work have assured him that it contains no sophisms or sarcasms against essential doctrines of religion and that it demonstrates, moreover, that a simple monarchy is the only form of government which may render a great nation happy and flourishing.

True enough, the almanac does not praise democracy at the expense of monarchy, for Dubourg sincerely believed that monarchy was the best form of government for France. Despite his pretended concern for Catholicism, however, the work can be called nothing less than anti-Catholic. Dubourg devotes more space to religion than to any other three subjects, and of this space, about half is devoted to deistical theories and the other half to attacks on Catholic doctrines and institutions. Monasticism in particular aroused his ire, reflected in his charges that monastic life encourages nothing but laziness, that it is expensive and unproductive, that it defies nature in requiring celibacy, and that it thrives on the wealth of others. Despite the disclaimers in his preface, Dubourg even attacks doctrine.

Il n'est fait mention dans le nouveau Testament, ni de la conception de la sainte Vierge, ni de sa nativité, ni de sa présentation, ni

de son assomption. Toutes ces fêtes ont été instituées par les papes
pour réchauffer la dévotion des fidèles, depuis que la sainteté de
leurs moeurs a commencé à s'altérer.

Les Romains croient que les prières des vivants peuvent être utiles
aux morts; les Américains comptent que Dieu traitera chaque
homme suivant ses mérites, ou ses démérites.

Dubourg has many other comments on the luxury of the church,
on its lust for money, and on its fanaticism. He also gives his own
deistical view of what true religion should be.

Aimer Dieu souverainement, & nous conformer en tout à l'ordre
qu'il a établi; aimer notre prochain comme nous-mêmes, & embrasser tout le genre humain dans la sphère de notre bienveillance;
voilà en deux mots le sommaire de notre religion; & de qui l'avons
nous reçue? De Dieu même.

As a contrast to the Catholic system, Dubourg makes several
comments about his favorites, the Quakers, praising their sobriety,
their pacifism, their refusing to swear, their simple faith, and their
high morality. His system of deism is sketched in nearly complete
form in the *Calendrier,* many of the entries being identical with
passages in his *Petit code.*

Among the famous writers whom Dubourg quotes are Franklin,
Catherine the Great, Montesquieu, La Rochefoucauld, and Solomon. Franklin is cited more than any of the others; *The Way
to Wealth* is seen to be the inspiration of the French *Calendrier*
both in spirit and in form.

Other editions of the *Calendrier* appeared, the last in 1823
under the title *Almanach de Philadelphie,* in which the introduction is cut just at the point where Sancho is about to quote
The Way to Wealth. Both the Quétant and the Dubourg translations appear in the *Almanach,* however, in an even more curious combination than in the original *Calendrier;* that is, passages
from both appear in the almanac section, the text of which in
the 1823 version is not the same as in the original edition. Although some passages are repeated from the 1777 edition, some
are completely different. Of the passages from *The Way to
Wealth,* those that had appeared in 1777 are still from the Dubourg translation; the added ones are from the Quétant version.

This edition also has a new preface—obviously not written by
Dubourg—with the following tribute to Franklin.

B. Franklin, under the name of Poor Richard and under the commonplace form of an almanac yearly introduced into households, circulated the precepts of a salutary morality to citizens and heads of families. The alliance of all public and private duties was the basis of these annual lessons. For he wished to make his fellow-citizens enemies of despotism, submissive to law, jealous of their independence as well as industrious, upright, and temperate. He had recognized the intimate relation between the private virtues and the civic virtues, of liberty with morals, of particular interest with general interest; and to establish the happiness of his country upon the indissoluble union of these diverse elements was the effort of all his life.

This paragraph epitomizes the impression that *Poor Richard* made upon French thought. Fifty years after Dubourg's translation, the fallacy was still current that Franklin had considered his almanac a means of inculcating moral precepts and that it had political significance. Both concepts are completely false but will probably continue to be ineradicably associated with the Franklin legend.

In both England and America, *The Way to Wealth* accounted for a large measure of Franklin's contemporary literary reputation, but nowhere except in France was it taken seriously as a work of sublime morality. Indeed, largely as a result of this work, at least one Englishman considered Franklin as "a philosophical Quaker full of mean and thrifty maxims." [35] Another called his *Poor Richard's Almanac* "a heap . . . of Scoundrel maxims." [36] In both England and America there have been a number of disparaging opinions, but there is not to be found a single unfavorable reference in eighteenth-century France.

4. FRANKLIN'S DIPLOMATIC MISSION

Neither Father Abraham nor Franklin himself was actually a "philosophical Quaker," but Franklin pretended to this character during the period of his diplomatic negotiations in France.

Notes to this chapter begin on page 242.

He adopted this guise no doubt because of the high reputation accorded to the Quakers in France deriving from Voltaire's *Lettres sur les Anglais* and other works. Franklin assumed Quaker garb, adopted an extreme simplicity of manner, and affected a grave demeanor, quite out of keeping with his natural fun-loving disposition. In a sense, Franklin's public character as diplomat and statesman represented Father Abraham in action.

The story of Franklin's diplomatic career in France belongs to the history of the American Revolution and cannot be completely told as long as hundreds of official documents in various archives remain unpublished. The influence of Franklin's political activities upon French-American literary relations and upon his own reputation, however, has little to do with these manuscript sources. For this subject we must turn to contemporary printed works. Of particular interest are reports concerning his negotiations at Versailles, tributes to his political talents and principles, and propaganda pieces that he himself inspired.

The broad outlines are clear and consistent in all contemporary reports: Silas Deane, the original commissioner, created little interest and enjoyed scant success; Franklin, who succeeded him, won from the moment of his arrival a fantastic renown and the adulation of the people. At first when the British seemed to possess military supremacy, he remained in seclusion and could not be openly received at official functions. After Burgoyne's defeat and the treaty of alliance, however, he was celebrated everywhere, including the court, and became a popular idol.

The most widely read—or at least the most widely quoted—contemporary account of Franklin's reception in France was the *Mémoires secrets,* which periodically presented colorful episodes concerning one phase or another of Franklin's personality. The most ambitious attempt to incorporate the record of Franklin's negotiations into a literary framework, however, was a collection of political comment, gossip, and literary criticism entitled *L'espion anglois,* a blend of fanciful situations with actual documents and eyewitness accounts. Inspired by *L'espion turc* of Marana and something on the order of Montesquieu's *Lettres persanes,* or Goldsmith's *Citizen of the World,* the collection has less satire and moralizing, more gossip and politics.

In it, the uneventful sojourn of Deane is contrasted with the

stir caused by Franklin's arrival, the reputed English spy reporting that as soon as Franklin landed the adulation began; a spectator at Nantes writes that the voyage had tired him a little
and that he seemed a little too old for worldly happiness; when
curious folk speculated on the reasons for his coming to France,
"the gullible were told that he was seeking rest, that he had
brought his children to be given a Parisian education, and that
he and his compatriots wished to Frenchify (*franciser*) their
race."[1] This relatively authentic portrayal of Franklin's arrival
may be compared with a contemporary manuscript journal in
which Franklin is called a rich American more than eighty years
old who has come to France in his character of orator and President of Congress.[2]

The English spy prints at length a letter by the abbé Flamarens
(January 15, 1777) describing Franklin's early days in Paris. Parts
of this letter were printed also in the *Mémoires secrets* under different dates (January 17, February 4), from which latter source
they have been widely quoted and paraphrased ever since. The
first two paragraphs in particular are among the most famous
ever written about Franklin in France.

> Dr. Franklin, who arrived a short time ago from the English
> colonies, is much sought after and entertained, not only by his
> learned colleagues, but by everyone who can gain access to him,
> for he shows himself rarely and lives in a seclusion which is said
> to be prescribed by the government. This Quaker wears the full
> dress of his sect. He has a handsome physiognomy, glasses always
> on his eyes, very little hair, a fur cap, which he always wears on
> his head, no powder, but a neat appearance. Extremely white linen
> and a brown habit are his sole ornaments. He carries as his only
> defense a cane in his hand.
>
> He is very circumspect in public concerning the news from his
> country, which he praises constantly. He says that heaven, jealous
> of its beauty, sent the scourge of war. Our free thinkers have
> adroitly sounded him on his religion, and they maintain that they
> have discovered that he was of their own, that is, that he had none
> at all.
>
> There has been no lack of prints of Franklin, whose portrait has
> become the fashionable New Year's gift for this year. People keep
> it on the mantle as they formerly kept a statuette, and the simple
> and singular costume of this grave personage leads our fops and
> women to turn his likeness into ridicule almost in the manner of

those futile knick-knacks which served as playthings thirty years ago.

This new representative of the Insurgents, moreover, has not yet appeared at Versailles. It is believed that this has been agreed upon in order not to upset the British Ambassador, who has made vigorous protests on the subject and who would have wished that Franklin had not been admitted to the capital or even that he had been sent out of France as soon as he arrived. If he sees our ministers, it is at Paris, it is at night, it is in the greatest secrecy. But he has frequent conferences with Messrs. Beaumarchais and le Ray de Chaumont. The first is the bow-wow of Monsieur and Madame de Maurepas and most likely the go-between. The second is an ardent, industrious and greedy man, who would grasp, if he could, the commerce of the thirteen united colonies, for himself alone.

There follows after this genuine letter an imaginary dialogue between Franklin and the pretended English spy, who had purportedly known Franklin in England, and who petitions him for an interview, which is granted at Franklin's residence. The Englishman assures his host that he is filled with admiration for the determination of the colonists to resist British tyranny, but wonders whether they did not go too far in publishing their Declaration of Independence, which removed all possibility of reconciliation and left no possibility of reunion with England except through conquest and slavery. Franklin replies that there were wise men among them who had similar thoughts—some who still retain them—but independence was forced by necessity. Without it, they could never have hoped for military aid from France. And without it, France would have continued to enrich its commerce and would have been pleased to see both sides exhaust their men and resources. America needed France, Franklin further explains, but France did not need America. Vergennes had given him to understand that France could not offend England and thus instigate a war without the certainty that war would bring about a diminution of British power by the absolute and irrevocable separation of the colonies. There was a further political reason: if France declared war first, it would appear that the American revolt came as a result of French action, whereas by joining a conflict already in progress France would seem to be merely taking advantage of the right to increase its commerce. The purported spy then expresses his opinion that the

Declaration of Independence should have been followed by heroic military actions that, he observes, seem to be lacking; indeed, the British seem to have had the upper hand in the last campaign, particularly in Long Island. Franklin answers that one of the reasons for his mission is to explain to the French that the American retreat was a necessary and strategic one; had they been able to defeat Howe, they would not have needed French aid at all. They lack equipment, arms, uniforms, and trained soldiers but possess the courage and determination to fight a delaying action until France provides the necessary material aid. The Englishman then mentions rumors that the Americans have been deceived and disappointed by the indirect aid that France has hitherto furnished. Franklin declares that nothing could be more true.

> Not only do they sell their merchandise extremely dear, but they give us only their rejects. In regard to arms especially, they have given us only discarded muskets, which have become in our hands more deadly to those who carry them than to our enemies; as for personnel, America has been the sewer of France. In place of the experienced officers which we need, good artillerymen, skilled engineers, we have received only blackguards, swindlers, men ruined in reputation or head over heels in debt, or conceited fops, insulting our sincerity, our good nature, seeking to debauch our wives and our daughters, fitted to infect us with their own corruption, carrying vices until then unknown among us.

To the Englishman's remarks that they have had bad luck with their agents—there could be little in common between the frivolous Beaumarchais and the austere republican Deane—Franklin acknowledges the fact that the commissioners had not chosen Beaumarchais; the liaisons were begun with him and they were forced to continue with him. As the Englishman continues to cast more and more gloom over the chances of victory, suggesting that if the Americans lose because of the indifference or neglect of France, England may accord them advantageous terms provided that they promise to turn their efforts against France, Franklin indignantly retorts that they would never accept any offensive alliance with England, much less against France, their benefactor. He trusts the Minister of Foreign Affairs, Vergennes, and knows that he is too much of a politician to allow the occasion of humiliating England to pass. The Englishman, in turn, asserts that he loves his own country and cannot help regretting the prospect of seeing France exalt herself on the ruins of England and America. Franklin is forced to admit that France inwardly mocks at American suffering and calamities, that France is not aiding the Americans out of conviction of the justice of their cause nor out of desire to avenge the wrongs of suffering humanity, that secretly France regards them as rebels, and that France has behaved in even more tyrannical fashion than England toward her own colonies. Relating a few circumstances partially exonerating the French, Franklin then concludes with the statement, "In politics as in medecine in crises endangering life, one seeks to remedy the greatest and the most urgent evil; we cannot foresee what is going to happen in a century or in fifty years." With these words, Franklin bursts into tears, reflecting the deep concern he feels for the welfare of his country.

Although purely fictitious, this is a shrewd contemporary analysis of the situation that actually prevailed. Later historical research can add to these details little except the knowledge that France initiated negotiations with the colonists in 1775—a year before Franklin's voyage—and that Franklin himself had at first been opposed to seeking French aid.[3]

In an entry of later date, May 15, 1777, the English spy further sketches the indecision of the French government in its policy of waiting for a colonial military victory. Franklin had been officially instructed not to show himself at public assemblies, and the celebrity-seekers who had attended the April public meeting of the Academy of Sciences had been disappointed by his absence. Even more significant, royal permission and approbation of the dedication to Franklin of a scholarly book had been revoked. This suppressed dedication is one of the most interesting and concrete records of the symbolic role that Franklin played in the diplomatic negotiations of 1777. Virtually unknown in Franklin scholarship, it appeared in *Œuvres de Bernard Palissy* published by Ruault in 1777.[4]

> In offering you the works of Bernard Palissy, it is to honor the memory of the greatest natural philosopher which France produced in a time when natural history was still in its cradle. This profound observer, nearly forgotten for two centuries, could not reappear

more worthily than under your auspices. The genius which characterized him is rediscovered in your works. Like him you announce the greatest truths with this modest tone which so well agrees with the true sage, and there is such a great analogy between Palissy's method and that which you have used for the discovery of phenomena of natural philosophy that I could not associate two names more worthy of the admiration of savants. But the French philosopher, devoted entirely to the seeking of the secrets of nature, did not penetrate at all into those of politics, a science which the sages of antiquity cultivated as one of the most important of philosophy. You have realized its great value, Monsieur. Your works have for their purpose only the happiness of a free and virtuous people. Every nation which is concerned with the wisdom of its government has doubtless owed much to its first law-maker, but what does it not owe to those whose enlightenment and courage tend only to give a form more perfect and more stable to its laws.

The people is fitted, said Montesquieu, "to choose those to whom it must confide a part of its authority; it makes its decisions only by things it is aware of and by facts which come under its observation."

This dedication is signed by the bookseller Ruault, but the English spy asserts that it is certainly not by him.

By the end of the year news of Burgoyne's defeat had given America a new prestige in France, and Franklin was now free to make public appearances. The English spy observed, December 29, 1777, that Franklin had been given a tumultuous ovation both at the public meeting of the Academy of Sciences (November 12) and at the opera.[5] The little taste that this grave and philosophical sage had for the glitter and spectacle of the occasion made the English spy conjecture that the situation had been contrived by the ministry. Franklin had been applauded by the grave and serious at the Academy and by the gallant and frivolous at the opera. But the surest indication of the success of his negotiations, the spy assumed, was his casting off the reserve that he formerly exhibited in regard to his country's affairs. "He says openly that the conquest of the siege of the Congress is a blunder of General Howe, that it was not he who had taken Philadelphia, but Philadelphia who had taken him; that surrounded by enemy positions and lacking communication by a free river, he must either evacuate in turn or be Burgoynized (*burgonisé*)."

During and after Franklin's successful negotiations, many French writers attempted to characterize his diplomatic aims and talents—or to relate his political career to his personality or to his careers as scientist, journalist, or moralist. Since these writers by and large repeated the same generalities, there is little value in attempting to summarize their accounts. One of the best, by Charles Mayo, will serve as illustration. In a comparison between the United States and the federations of Switzerland and Holland published in 1787, Mayo describes the enthusiastic reception accorded to Franklin.[6]

> . . . He was not given the title *Monsieur;* he was addressed simply Doctor Franklin, as one would have addressed Plato or Socrates. His genealogy was traced—an attempt was made to claim him for France. What is most certain is that he was like Curtius, the offspring of his virtues. He must have considered it a happiness to be born in a country where a genius for law-making could be displayed, where probity, temperance, frugality were qualities esteemed and observed. Free in his thoughts, observations, writings and speech, he had given to his character this energy which makes science useful for oneself and profitable to others. He began by observing nature; this sky which is not so elevated that it is to be considered beyond the man of genius; he had explained the causes of the aurora borealis and subsequently he demonstrated the secrets of electricity. If it is true that Prometheus was only a man, may one not believe that he was a natural philosopher like Franklin, who, like him, drew a line to the fire of heaven, but whose discovery has not been attended to. If he was not the first; if he had collaborators in the formation of the United States, . . . it is nonetheless true that Franklin made a great contribution.

A footnote referring to genealogical studies explains that an attempt had been made to trace Franklin's ancestors to a family from Pontoise. This is probably based on a report in the *Gazette of Amiens,* April, 1780, that the name Franklin had French rather than English origins, that the name Franquelin is very common in Picardy, and that the Doctor's ancestors probably went to England with the fleet of Jean de Biencourt.[7]

Franklin himself was not at all averse to the stories about him in the French press. Even in the period before Burgoyne's defeat, any kind of publicity for Franklin was good publicity for the American cause. Franklin himself also directly engaged in journalistic activities in France; his most elaborate project concerned participation in *Affaires de l'Angleterre et de l'Amérique,* a propaganda periodical published in Paris in the interests of the Amer-

ican governments.[8] Edited by Edmond-Charles Genet, the first issue appeared in May, 1776, before Franklin's arrival in Paris and
featured a series of letters written by a fictitious Dutch banker
living in Antwerp, a device with many resemblances to that of
L'espion anglois. Franklin, soon after his appearance in Paris,
began feeding propaganda items to Genet, most important, the
constitutions of the various American states, which appeared separately in *Affaires de l'Angleterre* and were later reprinted in 1783
in *Constitutions des treize Etats-Unis.*[9] Franklin himself was the
patron and sponsor of this significant edition, the first complete
translation of all the state constitutions to be published. Franklin
made arrangements with the printer and wrote to Vergennes asking him to use his influence with the Keeper of the Seals to obtain permission for its prompt appearance.[10] Official approbation
was granted June 16th.

On at least one occasion Franklin sponsored a propaganda
piece in the *Journal de Paris,* edited by his friend Cadet de Vaux.
The abbé Jean Louis Soulavie's *Historical and Political Memoirs of the Reign of Lewis XVI* is the source of all that is known
of this piece allegedly concerted by Franklin and Soulavie, but
there is no reason to doubt the truth of his narrative.[11] The correspondence of Soulavie and Franklin on scientific subjects still exists, and the document that Soulavie maintains was the product
of their collaboration was actually published in the *Journal de
Paris.*[12] In reporting a conversation with Franklin, Soulavie indicates that Franklin asked him to explain the geological changes
in sea and land that Soulavie had observed in southern France.
Theories of naturalists had variously maintained that the sea re-
tires, that it diminishes and loses its level, and that the mass of
its water rises and increases. Franklin communicated his own observation "that the rocks of Derbyshire abound with oyster-shells,
and are greatly above the level of the sea; while the rock of the
coal-mines of Whitehaven, covered with vegetation, is as much
below as the former are above the same level." Franklin actually
had this conversation with Soulavie, for on September 22, 1782,
Franklin sent him a letter concerning it, keeping a copy, which
he endorsed, "Letter to Abbé SOULAVIE, occasioned by his
sending me some Notes he had taken of what I had said to him
in conversation on the theory of the Earth. I wrote it to set him

right in some points wherein he had mistaken my meaning." [13]
This letter was read at a meeting of the American Philosophical
Society, November 21, 1788, with the title "On the Theory of
the Earth." In it Franklin remarks in terms parallel with Soulavie's version of their conversation that he had noticed oyster shells
mixed in the stone of the lowest part of the calcareous rock in
Derbyshire, "and part of the high county of Derby being probably as much above the level of the sea, as the coal mines of
Whitehaven were below it, seemed a proof that there had been
a great *bouleversement* in the surface of that Island, some part
of it having been depressed under the sea, and other parts which
had been under it being raised above it." [14] Since this much of
Soulavie's account can be verified, it is logical to assume that the
rest also is completely reliable. But even though it be fictitious,
it provides a unique portrait of Franklin as a political theorist.

According to Soulavie, Franklin in August, 1781, pointed out
to him an article in *Le Courrier de l'Europe,* dated August 3rd,
in which Soulavie's *Histoire naturelle de la France méridionale*
had been favorably mentioned. The writer had called for explanation of Soulavie's affirmation that the protestants of the
Cévennes district in southern France had been in a rebellious
state for two centuries and "had listened to the natural enemies
of France, and, assisted by them, had endeavoured to establish
a republic in the very center of the nation, defended by inac-
cessible rocks, and the loftiest mountains." Franklin in his conversation drew a parallel between the attempts of the French
protestants to create an independent state and the geological
changes that Soulavie had reported in southern France; these
revolutions in nature Franklin compared to those in the moral
or political world. "One continent becomes old, another rises
into youth and perfection. But the perfected continent will in
its turn correct the other. Monarchies, by way of restoration, become republics, republics sink into monarchies; and the author
of the *Courrier de l'Europe,* as curious as myself, and my tea
party, desires to learn from you, who is the natural enemy you
mention of the French monarchy, that wished to raise a protestant
republic in the heart of your southern mountains."

Soulavie answered that just as the French in ages past had
made secret war upon England by assisting their insurgents, so

England had encouraged the protestants of the Cévennes to revolt, with the hope of there establishing an independent protestant republic. Franklin thereupon suggested to Soulavie that he
write the history of this movement and submit it to Louis XVI
and Vergennes, who would certainly approve it. Soulavie objected that Franklin, as a protestant, even though a professed
friend of France, must inevitably "approve the desire England
has shown of dismembering France, for the benefit of liberty."
Franklin replied,

> Were I a Frenchman, a Cévegnol, a mountaineer, a protestant, sub-
> ject of Lewis XVI, and harassed by his dragoons, I should prefer
> the safety of my country to the disagreeable alternative of seeking
> in a foreign land the protection of an English or Prussian monarch;
> but we are at a period already remote from this, a relation of which
> may serve to show the justice of the present war, by way of reprisal
> on the part of France; since it is but repaying the injury which Eng-
> land has already committed against her, by interfering in her in-
> ternal concerns, and raising up a religion in the state which dis-
> sents from the head of the state. I certainly love liberty, and esteem
> a republican government; but a republican minister, though de-
> voted to his country, may know how to forget his own predilection
> in favour of a friendly monarchy. Therefore, considering this at-
> tempt of the English as equally rash and criminal, I shall thankfully
> receive your papers; and if you will give me a letter to M. de
> Vergennes, I will present it to him, and recommend the papers with
> the force which a matter of so much importance merits.

Soulavie agreed to compose a letter, but dissented from Franklin's opinion that the English scheme was rash or unpolitic. He
argued that the religious protestants present no threat to internal
security because the government leaves them alone, but protestants of another kind, "the ignorant class of the lower people,
who are burdened with imposts, and the more enlightened, who
are malcontents"—these constitute a real danger.

> The party that desires, and the party that dreads, a new order of
> things, agree in this, that France will one day suffer a greater revo-
> lution than that which America has experienced. I speak of the
> clergy, who said officially to Lewis XV, before his death, that a
> revolution was preparing in the state, similar to the English one
> of 1688; and I refer to the philosophers, who long for a revolution,
> and are preparing one against religion. I refer particularly to
> Buffon, who said to me in December 1778, that this revolution

would direct its first efforts against the French clergy, and who advised me to take care of myself.

These remarks forecasting the French Revolution were not, we must remember, written until after the event and thus may reflect the prescience of a retrospective view. According to Soulavie, Franklin not only did not foresee the Revolution, but repudiated Soulavie's forebodings:

> France is in a state strongly constituted, and, I doubt not, will long resist the spirit of innovation that overturns government. I therefore think, that neither you or I shall live to see the changes you speak of, and for this reason, that the continent is equally old in all its parts, and France the youngest and most robust of all its states. At the same time it must be owned, that the protestants are no friends to a government, at the head of which is the body who treated them so ill; but they would hardly expose their frail existence to the danger of a sedition. They possess no longer that characteristic turbulence by which they were marked prior to the reign of Lewis XIV, who polished all degrees of the French: nor do the government or the clergy carry their intolerance to the same excess to which they extended it in past ages. The time is come when history can record the faults of both parties; and, in my opinion, a narrative of the attempts made by England to raise a revolt among the French protestants under Lewis XIV, would be a point of history truly interesting.

Under the urging of Franklin, Soulavie prepared a letter setting forth the discoveries of his historical research, which Franklin passed on to Vergennes. In his letter Soulavie showed that from 1627 until the beginning of the eighteenth century, the English had continually acted in France to fix a spot noted for protestant worship as "the central point of an independent republic, to be divided into provinces, and to have cities, and a capital, at the expense of the rest of the kingdom."

In the following year when a party in France developed as a focus of opposition to the American war, Franklin urged Soulavie to publish his discoveries, hoping that they would show the need of retaliating against the English. "The *Journal de Paris*," he said, "will readily insert an article so curious; which, however, must be written in a form, that, while the truth done to history is observed in it, the protestants may take no offense at it."

Soulavie again agreed to do Franklin's bidding, but argued that the work would "neither alter the English plans, nor influence the fate of France." England, he felt, was actively engaged not only in fomenting a spirit of independence among the Cevennese protestants, but also of encouraging independence and republicanism among the philosophers; in other words, he suggested that the English government consciously promoted the French Revolution, a rather unrealistic view. He stated to Franklin, nevertheless, "I shall execute my task the more willingly, as, in opposition to the republican and political commotions aimed at by England, you agree with me as to the propriety of pointing out at the same time the moral remedies to be attempted by a wise and prudent government to the miseries of the revolution and anarchy, of which the clergy and the philosophers so eternally warn us."

Soulavie's article appeared in the *Journal de Paris,* June 26, 1782, as an appendix to an announcement concerning the manuscripts he had discovered during his research in the southern provinces of France. In his *Mémoires historiques* he added the title, "The Former Plans of England for Erecting our Southern Protestant Provinces into a Republic." In this essay he sketches very briefly the efforts of the English to separate the southern protestants, but prudently assures his readers that the dissensions have long been at an end and the spirit of fanaticism extinct. After indicating an intention of preparing a History of the Establishment and Progress of Protestantism in France and Europe, he suggests that his primary aim will be to solve the political problem.

> When a portion of a great monarchy has, for many ages, experienced intestine commotion and religious wars, and the rebellion raised in the state has opposed the monarch, what are the means, most conformable to humanity, which reason and experience dictate, for the restoration of public tranquillity?

Soulavie remarked that this article planned by himself and Franklin had appeared in the *Journal de Paris* exactly as submitted except that some additional political remedies against anarchy were rejected by the editors on the grounds that since the state of the nation had never been more tranquil or more remote from revolution, the remedies against anarchy were out of place. Since these remedies seem to show the hand of Franklin they are worth reprinting.

The most effectual way to alleviate the tumults of a state, is, to divert the attention of the parties from the subjects. This may be done by directing their minds—

To a species of learning that has no connexion with any thing seditious, nor with polemical writings and factions, which are the pests of a state.

To a system of general commerce.

To the study of the fine arts.

To great undertakings, such as national buildings.

To the ridicule of past violences and errors, political or religious (but this with the utmost caution).

To pleasure, festivals, amusements, fashions, dances, and luxury. —And lastly,

By softening the manners of the turbulent; taking every means of gaining the surviving leaders, and especially the means of negotiation.

Of these remedies, Soulavie asserted that Franklin agreed that

to divert men's minds, was the only way, after great events of allaying the seditious spirit of a people. But he did not fully approve the last means, that of softening their manners. He said, that the societies established in Europe were already too much softened. He acknowledged, however, that fanaticism, anarchy, and all the vices of an impetuous class, originate in a state of mind, which force and violence tend to increase rather than correct; and, he observed, that the very best way of softening those who laboured under them, was to treat with the factious. He was of the opinion, that attachment to kings, and the love of liberty, were two powerful and laudable springs of action, which had produced great effects; and, though in this country the republican and royal parties had entered into a struggle for superiority, he felt the utmost veneration for Lewis XVI, whom he looked upon as the founder of the liberties of the United States.

Nothing in this opinion is incompatible with views Franklin expressed in his correspondence or with the principles he followed in his own behavior. If Soulavie's portrayal of Franklin is not a literal transcript of actual conversations, which it purports to be, it is at least an accurate reflection of both his manner of expression and habits of thought.

Another political-economic work that helped establish French opinion of Franklin as a diplomat and statesman appeared originally in the *Journal d'économie publique* (10 Ventôse An V— February, 1797). The editors remarked that this essay, "Hausse-

ment des salaires en Europe, effet de la prospérité de l'Amérique,"
had been given to them by "a friend of M. Franklin, and having
been found in his papers, is very probably by this illustrious philosopher." This highly-significant essay contains a number of
clearly-stated political maxims—particularly the forthright declaration that the object of all political association is the happiness
of the greatest number. Although Franklin during his public
life wrote hundreds of political documents and propaganda pieces,
in none of them does he directly set forth in this manner the theo-
retical foundations of the particular schemes he advocates. After
its initial appearance in French, this piece attracted the attention
of J. W. von Archenholz in Hamburg, who translated it for his
Minerva, ein journal historischen und politischen, where it appeared in the following month.[15] When J. Castéra, French translator of the works of Franklin, published his edition in 1798, he
took this essay from the *Minerva,* translating it for the second
time, for he had been unable to find a copy of the *Journal d'économie publique.*[16] Finally, the American editor of Franklin, Jared
Sparks, took the essay from the edition of Castéra, retranslating
it for the third time.[17]

It is unfortunate that Castéra was unable to find a file of the
Journal d'économie, for in the subsequent issue we are told that
the essay is not by Franklin! We find a second essay with the following explanation:

> We had believed these two works to be Franklin's since they
> were given to us in 1791 by M. de la Rochefoucauld, who told us
> they came to him from the philosopher himself, who was his friend.
> Our conjecture has been proved false. The essay which has ap-
> peared, and the one which now appears, are by another friend of
> Franklin, the abbé Morellet.

It appears, however, that the edition of Castéra was much more
widely circulated and read in France than was the explanation of
the editors of the *Journal d'économie publique,* particularly when
we remember that Castéra was unable to find a copy of the latter. For the French public, therefore, the social and political principles of Franklin were those of the essay of the abbé Morellet—
imbued with benevolence and philanthropy.

5. FRANKLIN'S OPINION OF FRANCE

The essay on political theory that we have just discussed appeared several years after Franklin's death. During the period of Franklin's actual sojourn in France, no comprehensive statement of his political beliefs circulated in print. Surprising as it may seem, his reputation as a political leader was based exclusively on his personality and his reported or purported opinions. His anti-British propaganda pieces that appeared in *Affaires de l'Angleterre et de l'Amérique* tell us nothing about political theory except that the British method was manifestly improper for holding an empire together. While working tirelessly as a propagandist for the American cause, Franklin circulated in France the theories of his compatriots rather than his own ideas. An American document that he caused to become one of the most widely read in France was the state constitution of Pennsylvania, the framing of which he had been partially responsible for, and French opinion assumed that it was completely a reflection of his own political theories. His attitude toward hereditary aristocracy and a legislature of a single house, moreover, had a direct influence upon several leaders of the French Revolution—even though his writings on these subjects were carefully concealed during his residence in France. Franklin died within a year after the outbreak of the French Revolution, but prior to his death he wrote to some of his friends on the new turn of events.

Before examining the influence of his reputation on the French Revolution, let us consider his early attitude toward the people and policies of the French nation—an attitude that explains in some measure his conduct as a diplomatic representative at the court of Louis XVI. As we have already seen, Franklin first came to the attention of the French public as a scientist. He was so pleased with the praise of Louis XV, "this sweetest kind of music," that he copied out for a friend the passage from Peter Col-

Notes to this chapter begin on page 243.

linson's letter announcing his triumph.[1] Before his first visit to France, however, Franklin could not have been considered in any sense a Francophile; on the eve of his departure, he wrote to his son (August 28, 1767), "I fancy that intriguing nation would like very well to . . . blow up the coals between Britain and her colonies; but I hope we shall give them no opportunity." [2] During his first two weeks in France, he was presented at Versailles to the King and Queen. Although favorably impressed by the serenity and benignity of the Queen, the graciousness and cheerfulness of the King, he insisted that "no Frenchman shall go beyond me in thinking my own King and Queen the very best in the world, and the most amiable." [3] He noticed among all stations of Frenchmen a uniform courtesy and politeness—especially to strangers. This led him to inquire, "Why don't we practise this urbanity to Frenchmen? Why should they be allowed to outdo us in any thing?" He readily adapted himself to the French mode. "I had not been here Six Days, before my Taylor and Perruquier had transform'd me into a Frenchman. Only think what a Figure I make in a little Bag-Wig and naked Ears!" This is Franklin at the age of sixty-one. Ten years later he created a sensation by laying aside his wig and powder and wearing his hair *au naturel*.

When he returned to France as a Commissioner from Congress, he continued to remark on the cordiality, respect, and affection with which Americans were received and treated in France. He noticed the boorishness of the English, the graciousness of the French, on a national as well as an individual level. "America has been *forc'd* and *driven* into the Arms of France. She was a dutiful and virtuous Daughter. A cruel Mother-in-Law turn'd her out of Doors, defam'd her, and sought her Life. All the World knows her Innocence, and takes her part; and her Friends hope soon to see her honourably married." [4]

In the next year Franklin continued to compliment the French people on their politeness and civility.

They have certainly advanced in those Respects many degrees beyond the English. I find them here a most amiable Nation to live with. The Spaniards are by common Opinion suppos'd to be cruel, the English proud, the Scotch insolent, the Dutch Avaricious, &c., but I think the French have no national Vice ascrib'd to them.

They have some Frivolities, but they are harmless. To dress their Heads so that a Hat cannot be put on them, and then wear their Hats under their Arms, and to fill their Noses with Tobacco, may be called Follies, perhaps, but they are not Vices. They are only the effects of the tyranny of Custom. In short, there is nothing wanting in the Character of a Frenchman, that belongs to that of an agreeable and worthy Man. There are only some Trifles surplus, or which might be spared.[5]

Franklin found the French ladies, in particular, eager to please and to shower kindnesses upon him. Their complaisance he explained in detail to one of his nieces.

This is the civilest nation upon Earth. Your first Acquaintances endeavour to find out what you like, and they tell others. If 'tis understood that you like Mutton, dine where you will you will find Mutton. Somebody, it seems, gave it out that I lov'd Ladies, and then every body presented me their Ladies (or the Ladies presented themselves) to be embrac'd, that is to have their Necks kiss'd. For as to kissing of Lips or Cheeks it is not the Mode here, the first, is reckon'd rude, & the other may rub off the Paint. The French Ladies have however 1000 other ways of rendering themselves agreeable; by their various Attentions and Civilities, & their sensible Conversation. 'Tis a delightful People to live with.[6]

On his return to Philadelphia, he wrote to Mme. Lavoisier his most gracious tribute to the courtesy and charm of the French nation. Now on his native heath and enjoying everything that a reasonable mind could desire—an adequate income, a comfortable home of his own construction, an affectionate daughter, promising grandchildren, old friends, and public honors and distinction —all could not make him forget Paris and the nine years' happiness he enjoyed there, "in the sweet Society of a People, whose Conversation is instructive, whose Manners are highly pleasing, and who above all the Nations of the World, have in the greatest Perfection the Art of making themselves belov'd by Strangers.— And now, even in my Sleep I find, that the Scenes of all my pleasant Dreams are laid in that City, or in its Neighbourhood." [7] In the same year, he wrote to La Rochefoucauld that his vital interest in French current events came from his love for that country— a love for which he had a thousand reasons. Its happiness concerned him, he wrote, as would the happiness of his own mother.[8]

After the outbreak of the Revolution, Franklin wrote to Benjamin Vaughan, "The Revolution in France is truly surprising. I sincerely wish it may end in establishing a good constitution for that country. The mischiefs and troubles it suffers in the operation, however, give me great concern." [9] The importance of this passage is not the affection shown for France—it is evident in scores of other Franklin letters—but the admission that the French Revolution came as a surprise to Franklin, for at least two French authors during the revolutionary period maintain that Franklin had actually predicted the social upheaval in their country. Before I discuss these French sources I wish to present another statement by Franklin prior to 1789 in which he clearly expressed the view that France was a benevolent monarchy with its administration in no danger whatsoever of a revolt from below. He foresaw revolution in Europe but assumed that it would take place through the aid of the French king. This statement, not found in any edition of Franklin's works, appeared in a newspaper, where it was described as a letter from Franklin to a friend in London.[10] The analysis of political tensions in the letter would quite logically have developed from Franklin's experience in both Great Britain and France.

> The political world, within the last half century, has assumed a variety of aspects, and from present appearances, it is still as unsettled as ever. The states of Europe are ripe for slavery, and their respective governments are ready and prone to take every advantage of the people. It is not easy to decypher the various problematic governments of the several powers on the continent; but there is none of them which does not seem very much interested in the politics of England. Your patriots have certainly served their country. The reform which they broached is the only expedient the poor peasantry of England have yet in reserve to protect themselves from plunder and despotism. The Irish may probably make a bad cause of a very good one. The shame in that country seems too rapid and fierce to be lasting; those of property expect nothing but ruin from the idleness and dissipation of their dependants; and in this situation it requires more public spirit than they have yet discovered to refuse a bribe. The Scotch are a selfish, but cool, intrepid, and ingenious people. They will carry their object, because they adopt no measures which are not rational and plausible.—How truly respectable and great does the French king appear, in the midst of all these intrigues and impending revolutions! His memory will go down to posterity, loaded with glory; it will be said of him, that he protected the states general from imperial tyranny. It is not

impossible, but it may also be said of him, that both Ireland and Scotland were emancipated by his means from their present miserable subjection to their haughty English task-masters.

If this is a genuine letter—and there is every reason to think that it is—it is hard to imagine that Franklin in any sense predicted the French Revolution. Yet a reviewer of his *Mémoires* in the *Journal de Paris* states flatly that he did.

> One thing that is certain is that circumstances serve more and more, to keep the memory of Franklin interesting, for one is aware that in contributing so effectively toward making his country free he had greatly accelerated the progress of political ideas among us. He even predicted the future influence that they were bound to have upon the French. "You see," he said, "liberty establish itself one day in a society nearly under your eyes; soon you will wish to procure it for yourselves." [11]

An even stronger and more explicit statement was made by Cerutti in his notes to *Les Jardins de Betz,* 1792. We are familiar with Cerutti's expansive rhetoric from our previous discussion of *Bonhomme Richard.* The following discourse, however, is probably not mere rhetorical embellishment of something Franklin once said; it is more likely pure fantasy.[12]

> American independence is, so to speak, the tocsin of universal liberty. Europe sooner or later will become insurgent. France will provide the example. The fatality of circumstances, the part that she has had in the triumphs of America, the prodigious flight of modern philosophy, and the irresistible character of an impatient and variable people, everything augurs, everything promises a revolution. The immortal Franklin predicted it: "You will not delay," he announced to us, "to follow the impulse of America and you will go even farther than America. In fact, we had only to repel a distant power; you will be required to stifle three enemy nations. We had only recent and visible wounds to cure; you will have to extirpate deep and inveterate cancers. The centuries, the tyrants, the slaves in place—more dangerous than the tyrants, have accumulated, interwoven, organized your abuses in such a way that they are made to seem natural and indestructible; they compose in their monstrous disorder an apparent order that sustains itself by its general effect and imposes itself by its mass. Your philosophers have uncovered this gothic assemblage, but they have not been able to overthrow a prejudice which serves as its prop: this prejudice consists in some brilliant souvenirs of your history, in some fortunate epochs of your nation; finally, in this disastrous but daz-

zling splendor which from the height of the French throne seems to cover far and wide all the ruins of monarchy. Thus in order to repair everything you will be forced to dissolve everything. The haste of reforms, the slowness of substitutions, the most ruinous impact of blind resistance, the sudden defiance or the sudden apathy of an unthinking or irritated multitude, the ferocious cry of some eloquent tigers, the rapid influence of subterranean factions, which, without revealing themselves, give blows to the earth, all will contribute to throw you into the convulsions and the chaos of anarchy. You will come out of it bleeding and mutilated. A single night of anarchy, say the Neapolitan slaves, causes more havoc than a century of despotism. But liberty sows upon a fertile field and slavery upon a dead earth. Five hundred oriental empires are deserts despite their renown; the Janissary Turk has destroyed them, not by the sword, but by the tyranny of his depredations. The marshes of Holland, the rocks of Switzerland, the plains of our colonies have flourished anew after frightful devastations. Is it possible to escape this scourge of the moment? No. Would it be preferable to remain in the mire of abuse? No. There is no mechanical art, no important occupation which does not expose the most useful citizen to constantly reviving perils. Must one abdicate employment, desert workshops, in order to seek a haven in inertia and uselessness? . . . Frenchmen, you have a struggle facing you, and you will be victorious. Parliaments will not be the most difficult colossus to overthrow. Although they seem to be interwoven with the foundations of monarchy, they are merely concealed under old ruins, and they will collapse like a tower founded upon crumbling rocks. The nobles, proprietors of half of the realm, will oppose the weight of riches against that of number. They will wish first to bury themselves under the throne, then to bury themselves under their chateaux, finally, to bury themselves under the childish mass of their arms and decorations. The clergy can never detach itself either from Rome, which gives it its independence, or from its abbeys, which give it its splendor, or from this superb domination which they exert over the people and which they extend over philosophy. They will resist to the death. Do you remember the words of King Edward: "I succeeded in ridding England of all the wolves in the land. I wanted to banish two turbulent priests, but was unable to do so."

Like the words of King Edward, this narrative is probably purely apocryphal.

Whether he predicted it or not, Franklin had influence upon the progress of the French Revolution. The air *Ça ira,* which became the battle song of the popular forces, owed its inspiration to Franklin, according to a number of authorities, among them an English observer of the Revolution, Helen Maria Williams. "To those who asked as an idle question how the American Revolution was progressing, he customarily replied laconically, *ça ira*. This response, which he hurled indistinctly at the curious, was later adopted by the patriots, and the remark of Franklin became the refrain of the revolutionary song." [13]

At a fete in Auteuil in the summer of 1792, the mayor paid tribute to "the patriarch of free men."

> He was an expert printer, excellent farmer, great scientist, profound legislator and politician. America owes him its independence; the world owes him its lightning-rods. His genius inspired a revolution on the earth and in the sky. . . . He was the first village journalist; he invented the proverbs of Poor Richard; he even invented the refrain *ça ira*, this air dear to the patriots.

Cerutti, who reported this ceremony in *La Feuille Villageoise*, gave the conventional explanation that when news from America seemed to be bad and Franklin's friends inquired of him anxiously, he replied always with assurance, "Soyez tranquille, ça ira." [14]

While the whole populace sang *Ça ira*, the intellectuals, alone, studied Franklin's words on hereditary aristocracy and the constituency of a legislature. His sentiments on the first subject were introduced to the French public by Mirabeau, who, as Franklin knew, was engaged in translating an American work by Aedanus Burke denouncing the recently-formed Society of the Cincinnatus. At about the same time, Franklin's daughter, Sarah Bache, wrote to him to ask his opinion of the Society, and in his answer Franklin exposed the ridiculousness of the organization. After rereading his remarks, written originally as a purely personal epistle, Franklin apparently perceived that they merited publication for a wider audience. He arranged with Mirabeau, therefore, that the latter incorporate the most important passages of the letter in the notes to Mirabeau's translation of Aedanus Burke's book under the title of *Considérations sur l'ordre de Cincinnatus*, 1785.

Bernard Faÿ in considering this work has given full information on the circumstances of publication and on the relations between other writings of Franklin and the letter to Sarah Bache, but he completely ignores the participation of Chamfort,[15] who, as the letters of Mirabeau to Chamfort will show, engaged in the translation with Mirabeau. These letters provide, moreover, valuable information concerning the circumstances of publication.

In his letter to Sarah Bache, one of the most politically radical of his entire life, Franklin declares the organizing of an order of hereditary knights to be contrary to the good sense of the country. The notion of honor descending to posterity is not only groundless and absurd, he declares, "but often hurtful to that Posterity, since it is apt to make them proud, disdaining to be employ'd in useful Arts, and thence falling into Poverty." [16] He shows by mathematical calculations that the same blood does not descend in its entirety to subsequent generations (a man's son acquiring half of his blood from the wife's family). In nine generations—a period of only 300 years—the share of a distinguished ancestor's blood in a male heir would be but a 1/512th part.

Franklin first of all transmitted his remarks on hereditary distinctions to the abbé Morellet for translating. The latter turned them into French, but advised his friend not to publish them,[17] pointing out that some of Franklin's aristocratic acquaintances might be offended and suggesting that the piece be shown only to those with enough of the true philosophy to perceive the absurdity of the aristocratic system. Unfortunately, we cannot be sure whether Mirabeau and Chamfort saw the manuscript merely as two of these advanced spirits or whether Franklin expressly presented them with a copy to be used as they saw fit. All we know is that Franklin noted in his journal, July 13, 1784, that Mirabeau and Chamfort visited him to read their translation of the *Considérations*. They intended it, he wrote, "as a covered satire against *noblesse* in general. It is well done." [18] Two months after this visit, Franklin wrote to Benjamin Vaughan, asking him to help arrange the printing of the piece, which he described as "extremely well written, with great Clearness, Force and Elegance." [19] Mirabeau's adopted son declared in 1834 that Franklin had urged Mirabeau to undertake the work, but Franklin's personal journal indicates that Mirabeau and Chamfort themselves took the initiative. Mirabeau himself remarked to an admirer that he had written the *Considérations* in order to gain money for his own sustenance and that of his mistress, Mme. de Nerac,[20] for at the time he had no other means of support but his pen. It is of interest to note that this is the first work that Mirabeau published under his own name.

The first of the printed correspondence between Mirabeau and Chamfort that concerns the *Considérations* (letter unfortunately without date) indicates that Chamfort began the enterprise alone.

> . . . for a spirit as fresh and as strong as yours, such a subject is an inspiration, especially when the writer presents a theory which is almost exclusively his own and the practice of which has composed and directed his life. It is, however, a remarkable and curious thing that philosophy and liberty should arise in the heart of Paris to warn the new world of the dangers of servitude and to show to it from afar the fetters which menace its posterity. Never has eloquence defended a more noble cause. Perhaps it is only the corrupt nations which are able to give enlightenment to the burgeoning ones. Enlightened by their own evils, they can at least teach the new nations to avoid them, and even servitude may be useful in becoming the school-master of liberty.[21]

The contemporary editor who published these letters assures us that this passage concerns the work on the Cincinnatus, "of which the most brilliant passages are Chamfort's."

In the next letter on the subject, Mirabeau asserts that Franklin wanted the material to be published as quickly as possible, and it appears that Mirabeau shared his impatience. The ambiguities in the writing are obviously caused by the fear that these letters might be intercepted by the royalist authorities.

> . . . so much has it been necessary for me to engage in explanation with F . . . in order to explain the delay. Do not rely on the time that is necessary for me, for if I had the manuscript which M. Thomas has kept in order to make his notes, all would be rearranged—since the passages of transition are ready. Of course it is a new work, but this is not a reason that it should take forever, especially since it is talked about: for the waiting to complete is always a painful destiny.[22]

The first of the letters bearing a date, August 30, 1784, reveals that Mirabeau is acquainted with the intimate friends of Franklin, the abbé de la Roche and Le Veillard. In addition, he exhorts Chamfort to persuade Franklin to interest Doctor Richard Price in the publication of the work.

. . . Here is what is urgent: Doctor Price is in London; he is an intimate friend of Franklin. That Franklin recommend the work to him or at least the author. Then I should turn to account a useful book undertaken to please them—something for which I have the greatest need. Do not neglect this I implore you.[23]

In another letter, November 10, 1784, Mirabeau explains that he proposes to add a translation of Price's pamphlet *Observations on the importance of the American Revolution* to the book on the Cincinnatus, and in his next letter, December 30, he points out that a large part of the essay entitled "Réflexions sur l'ouvrage précédent," printed as an appendix to the work of Price, was written by the friend of Franklin, the advocate Target.

Finally, we learn from Mirabeau some of the circumstances of the publication of his work, from an undated letter, in which he informs Chamfort that the best means of dying of hunger in London is to be a good French author.

. . . For the rest, the Cincinnati is being printed, which will bring me very little, but at least will cost me nothing, and which a man of much talent has well translated [Sir Samuel Romilly] so that the English edition will appear almost as soon as the French. But judge by what occurs in this regard of the scant resources which the English printing trade offers. Two booksellers of Paris—useless to name them by post, but one is rich and solid—have offered to take 1500 copies at 50 sous provided that they be delivered at a certain city at the border. We had great trouble to persuade the English bookseller to set the French edition at 1500 copies, and if the work had not produced a very great effect upon some men of renown here, not a single bookseller would have printed it at his own risk.[24]

We know now that despite the hesitation of the English printers the work had a great success. Chamfort was at first inclined to allow to Mirabeau all of the credit for the work, but later during the French Revolution when accused of being a defender of the nobility, disclosed the role he had played in its composition. In the following passage he speaks of himself in the third person.

It is a man to whom this so-called mania against the nobility dictated the most vigorous passages inserted in the book on the American order of Cincinnatus, work published in 1786, which delivered the most forceful blows against the French aristocracy in public opinion.[25]

To these proofs of the collaboration of Mirabeau and Chamfort, we need add merely the comment on Mirabeau presented by the contemporary editor of Chamfort's works.

> Chamfort had a great part in many of his first works and in the one which brought him the greatest honor; in other words, in his work on the order of the Cincinnatus, the most eloquent passages are Chamfort's. . . . This fact is very well known by all who are acquainted with the literary productions of this period. Those who are not will find obvious proofs in the letters of Mirabeau which are ready to appear.[26]

It is unquestionable, moreover, that Chamfort enjoyed intimate relations with Franklin's circle of friends. It was he, for example, who furnished Castéra the letter from Franklin to Mme. Helvétius.[27]

Franklin's complete letter on the Cincinnatus was apparently not published during his lifetime, but three months after his death—one month after public homage was paid to him in the National Assembly—Morellet's translation was printed in full as a weapon in the movement to destroy the system of hereditary nobility in France.[28] An introductory essay by Phillipe Antoine Grouvelle, friend of Chamfort and later the member of the Convention who read the death sentence to Louis XVI, pointed out that it was important for the French to understand Franklin's reasons for opposing a system of deadly prejudice at its inception in America, as they were the same reasons the French had for contending against it in its decadence.

Grouvelle used the example of Franklin himself as one of the principal arguments against the system. The advocates of the noblesse, who maintain that patriotic service, virtue, and heroic actions are the origin of aristocracy, could not find a man more distinguished in virtue and accomplishment than Franklin; yet the general effect of glory and illustriousness that he personified does not in the least require the creation of a system of nobility parallel to that which has just expired. "Can you imagine that Franklin's son and his nephews will be any otherwise distinguished in Boston than by their own individual advantages? Ask them whether they do not rather dread the unfavorable comparison which their name will always suggest at the expense of their persons."

Citing Franklin's work, not only because in it he attacks the superstition of the nobility, but because he ridicules all kinds of frivolous and dangerous distinctions in society, Grouvelle regretted that Franklin did not remain in France—that he had been unable to witness the marvels of the Revolution and that he had been unable to assist the patriots with his experience. Finally, he compared Franklin to the philosophers of antiquity, who anticipated the knowledge of centuries and who were as superior to posterity as to their contemporaries.

Two years later the letter was again translated in an article, "Suppression of the Nobility of Titles, Arms, etc." [29] Here it is used as propaganda against the view that titles and other signs of hereditary nobility are harmless and should not be molested. The author, after describing the history of the Society of the Cincinnatus, suggested that as a result of Franklin's satirical attack the organization fell into disrepute, with its American members uniformly explaining their adherence as a moment of shameful weakness and only a few of its French members still wearing its insignia to nourish their foolish and puerile vanity. After these remarks, he presented the complete text of Franklin's letter with one notable divergence from the text printed by W. T. Franklin—a divergence that expands and clarifies Franklin's meaning and is significant whether it is an emendation of Franklin or of the French editor. In the English text Franklin remarks that the project to distinguish men who have participated in the American Revolution by a badge or ribbon is harmless—provided that it has no hereditary force. This badge

> will save modest Virtue the Trouble of calling for our Regard, by awkward roundabout Intimations of having been heretofore employ'd in the Continental Service.

The French version specifies that only the French volunteers are indicated by this passage.

> Cette distinction visible sauve au mérite modeste l'embarras d'attirer l'attention: et, par exemple, en France, elle dispense les gens de m'apprendre, toujours avec un peu de gaucherie, que je parle à un homme employé ci-devant comme officier au service de l'Amérique, et qui a contribué à la liberté et au bonheur de mon pays.

The editor explains in a footnote that this passage incorporates a subtle irony against a swarm of young courtiers, who toward

the end of the American Revolution wanted to follow the fashion and participate in it for at least a few months so as to receive
military promotion, the ribbon of the Cincinnatus, and the
favor of some weak women. Proud of their great advantage, these
self-styled heroes visited Franklin, but instead of treating him
with due veneration for his age and wisdom, they appeared before him with the airs of protectors and liberators and the irri-
tating insolent manners of the French nobility. Franklin's philosophical malice led him to retaliate in the delicate raillery of the
above passage.

Franklin's theories concerning a single legislature are even
more important because their influence upon particular leaders
in the French Revolution can be directly traced and because
they represented virtually a single cause. Many other writers and
statesmen condemned a hereditary aristocracy, but none but
Franklin and his personal disciples championed a single legislature.

The first state constitution of Pennsylvania, incorporating
Franklin's unicameral theories, was widely known and widely
circulated in France because Franklin was thought to be the
principal framer. A French translation, first published in *Affaires
de l'Angleterre et de l'Amérique,* in March, 1777,[30] was printed
again as a supplement to an edition of *La Science du Bonhomme
Richard,* 1777,[31] again in the next year in *Recueil des Loix Constitutives des Colonies Anglaises,*[32] and in 1783 in *Constitutions
des Treize Etats-Unis.*[33] The latter volume was reviewed August
24 in the *Journal de Paris* with the remark that the translator
was the duc de La Rochefoucauld.

It was probably from studying the constitution of Pennsylvania
that La Rochefoucauld acquired his interest in unicameralism.
In an address presented as a tribute to Franklin in 1790—two
months after his death—La Rochefoucauld explained his own
adherence and his proposals for France. He visualized unicameralism as an example of Franklin's talent for discovering the
simplest methods in mechanical operations. A single house he
called the maximum of simplicity in political economy.

Franklin was the first to propose to put this idea into practice; the
respect the Pennsylvanians bore him made them adopt it, but it
alarmed the other states, and even the constitution of Pennsylvania

has since been changed. In Europe this opinion has had more success, but it required a certain amount of time. When I had the
honor to present to Franklin the translation of the constitutions of
America, public opinion was hardly better disposed on this side
than on the other side of the Atlantic, and if we except Doctor
Price in England and Turgot and Condorcet in France, nearly
everyone who was then occupied with political ideas had a contrary opinion to the American philosopher. I dare admit that I
was one of the small number of those who were struck by the beauty
of the simple plan which he had delineated and that I did not need
to change my opinion when the judgment of the profound thinkers
and eloquent orators who have treated the subject before the National Assembly led that body to establish as a principle of the
French constitution *that the legislation shall be entrusted to a single
body of representatives.* Perhaps I shall be forgiven for having once
spoken of myself at a time when the honor I have of being a
public servant enforces upon me the duty of explaining to my fellow citizens the issue of my opinions. France will not retrogress
toward a more complicated system, and doubtless she will have the
glory of maintaining the one she has established.[34]

Two years later, La Rochefoucauld addressed the National
Assembly at the head of the delegation from Paris, on the subject
of Franklin and the single legislature.

Your most important debt perhaps is to justify your predecessors
in the bold resolution they have taken for the nation in confiding
the law-making authority to a single body. Franklin is the first to
have proposed it and the citizens of Pennsylvania listened to his
voice—but since that time, the sentiment of certain inconveniences
and, perhaps most important of all, the powerful influence of ancient habits—have made them return to the complications of the
British system of government. The National Constituent Assembly
has seized upon this great idea; it has seen, moreover, in its adop-
tion the inestimable advantage of cementing the principles of
equality; and the law-making power has received no other limits
than those of the royal sanction. Messieurs, you will prove to France,
to Europe, to the entire universe by the wisdom of your deliberations that in the moral world as in the physical the simple methods
are always those which best and most surely produce the effect
desired.[35]

La Rochefoucauld had his wish. The Assembly retained the unicameral system, the system, which many authorities maintain,
permitted the excesses of the Reign of Terror. John Adams, for
example, argued that the doctrine had been directly responsible

for the deaths of La Rochefoucauld and of Condorcet, another close friend of Franklin's who espoused unicameralism. In 1809 Adams wrote to a friend:

> In 1775 and 1776 there had been great disputes, in Congress and in the several States, concerning a proper constitution for the several States to adopt for their government. A Convention in Pennsylvania had adopted a government in one representative assembly, and Dr. Franklin was the President of that Convention. The Doctor, when he went to France in 1776, carried with him the printed copy of that Constitution, and it was immediately propagated through France that this was the plan of government of Mr. Franklin. In truth, it was not Franklin, but Timothy Matlack, James Cannon, Thomas Young, and Thomas Paine, who were the authors of it. Mr. Turgot, the Duke de la Rochefoucauld, Mr. Condorcet, and many others, became enamored with the Constitution of Mr. Franklin. And in my opinion, the two last owed their final and fatal catastrophe to this blind love.[36]

James Cheetham, an American journalist who quoted Adams' letter in a notoriously denigratory biography of Thomas Paine, was also under the impression that Paine, not Franklin, was the author of the Pennsylvania Constitution. He remarked, therefore, "Condorcet became an advocate of a single representative assembly. He was gratified. The convention was established, and it is to the uncontrouled fury and tyranny of the convention that his death is attributable. May not Paine's constitution of Pennsylvania have been the cause of the tyranny of Robespierre?" [37] Adams and Cheetham were in error on the subject of both Paine's participation and Franklin's influence. Paine, who was not a man to hide his light under a bushel, specifically declared that he had held no correspondence with the framers of the constitution, that he "had no hand in forming any part of it, nor knew anything of its contents" until he saw it published.[38] Paine is authority also for the anecdote that Franklin gave his opinion to the Pennsylvania Convention of 1776 that a system of two houses is "like putting one horse before a cart and the other behind it, and whipping them both. If the horses are of equal strength, the wheels of the cart, like the wheels of government, will stand still; and if the horses are strong enough, the cart will be torn to pieces." [39] In a Pennsylvania newspaper, the *Federal Gazette*, November 3, 1789, Franklin made use of a similar analogy: "the

famous political fable of the snake, with two heads and one body.
. . . She was going to a Brook to drink, and in her Way was to
pass thro' a Hedge, a Twig of which opposed her direct Course;
one Head chose to go on the right side of the Twig, the other on
the left; so that time was spent in the Contest, and, before the
Decision was completed, the poor Snake died with thirst." [40]
Recent scholars have been inclined to minimize Franklin's personal importance in the unicameralism of the Pennsylvania constitution, pointing out that in colonial times the legislature had
only one house.[41] From his later writings, however, it is obvious
that he was an ardent supporter of a single legislature.

In France, friends and foes alike of the single legislature argued
that the system was Franklin's brain-child. An author opposed to
the French Constitution of 1793, but afraid to attack it openly,
leveled all his criticism against the constitution of Pennsylvania,
which he described as the model on which the French system
had been flagrantly tailored. He drew, in an imaginary dialogue
between himself, Samuel Adams, and Franklin, a pointed contrast between the constitution of Massachusetts, founded on the
division of the legislature, and that of Pennsylvania, founded on
the unity of the legislature.[42] Although Franklin is the patron
of the detested single legislature, the author treats him with respect and affection, attacking only his political views. The French
author has allegedly toured several of the American states in the
company of Adams, when one day on the outskirts of Boston they
encounter Franklin. Adams confesses that he had said of the
constitution of Pennsylvania that it would be the best in the
world if all the citizens of the state were Franklins, adding, however, that he is even here mistaken, since governments would be
useless to men who know how to govern themselves. As the nation becomes more populous and riches become a stronger force
than virtue, the republic, lacking stronger checks on individual
freedom, will degenerate into a tyranny. Returning to the present,
the author points out that of the thirteen states with an equal
degree of liberty, eleven enjoy calm and tranquility—"two only
are incessantly agitated . . . Georgia and Pennsylvania, the only
two in which the legislature is composed of a single body."

At this point the anonymous author allows Franklin to escape
without further criticism. "This is enough," Franklin replies to

Adams with an angelic softness, "let us leave the glory of criticism to those who do not possess that of creation."

By and large Franklin's political opinions were favorably received in the French press, with one important exception, a letter of comment on the French Revolution. In his first communication on the subject to a French citizen, Franklin prudently wrote (September 5, 1789), "I make no Remarks to you concerning your Public Affairs, being too remote to form just Opinions concerning them." [43] Two months later he wrote to Jean Baptiste Le Roy, however, making some very uncomplimentary remarks about the Revolution. Although he probably considered his comments in part facetious, they were of a nature to give offense to a partisan of the social upheaval. This letter is one of the most frequently quoted in America—but not because of interest in the French Revolution but because it contains Franklin's saying on death and taxes.

> It is now more than a year, since I have heard from my dear friend Le Roy. What can be the reason? Are you still living? Or have the mob of Paris mistaken the head of a monopolizer of knowledge, for a monopolizer of corn, and paraded it about the streets upon a pole.
>
> Great part of the news we have had from Paris, for near a year past, has been very afflicting. I sincerely wish and pray it may all end well and happy, both for the King and the nation. The voice of *Philosophy* I apprehend can hardly be heard among those tumults. If any thing material in that way had occurred, I am persuaded you would have acquainted me with it. However, pray let me hear from you a little oftener; for, though the distance is great, and the means of conveying letters not very regular, a year's silence between friends must needs give uneasiness.
>
> Our new Constitution is now established, and has an appearance that promises permanency; but in this world nothing can be said to be certain, except death and taxes.[44]

It was published immediately after its receipt in the *Gazette Universelle* (December 30, 1789) with the following comment:

> This letter is interesting in every sense since it tells us that the constitution of the United States has been completely established and that M. Franklin sees his country as free and happy as he could wish. One should also notice the date of this letter and agree that one could hardly expect to have fresher news from North America.

This editor, we see, passes over Franklin's remarks on the Revolution to discuss the date of the letter, which in the *Gazette Universelle* is given as November 23, but in *The Private Correspondence of Benjamin Franklin*, 1817, its first printing in English, is November 13, a significant difference of almost two weeks.[45] Probably the letter required forty-seven rather than thirty-seven days to cross the ocean, but without the original manuscript we cannot be sure. At any rate the French editor's comments on its rapid publication reveal the avidity with which news of Franklin was awaited.

The letter was reprinted three days later in Brissot's *Le Patriote François*—but Brissot, or his spokesman, reprimanded Franklin severely for his unkind remarks on the Revolution.[46]

> We cannot keep from noticing that certain expressions reflect Dr. Franklin's long sojourn close to the court and his intimacy with the ministers. It was there, no doubt, that he learned to repeat this word *populace,* and to consider as distressing the news of a revolution which returned to a people its liberty because it was tinged with a little blood. It is doubtless not at all from this point of view that the American people regard this Revolution. They paid too dearly for their own liberty to be afflicted by the sacrifices which ours cost.

Oddly enough only four weeks before these remarks were penned, Franklin himself expressed almost identical sentiments in a letter to David Hartley.

> The Convulsions in France are attended with some disagreeable Circumstances; but if by the Struggle she obtains and secures for the Nation its future Liberty, and a good Constitution, a few Years' Enjoyment of those Blessings will amply repair all the Damages their Acquisition may have occasioned.[47]

An anecdote, which circulated during the following year, attributes to Franklin very much the same reaction. When a number of his visitors pestered him by inquiring whether he did not consider the Revolution a singular circumstance, he replied with his customary wit, "Why I see nothing singular in all this, but on the contrary, what might naturally be expected; the French have served an *apprenticeship* to *Liberty* in this country, and now that they are out of their time, they *have set up for themselves.*" [48]

The leaders of the French Revolution almost unanimously considered Franklin both a personal inspiration and a historical precursor of the principles they espoused. He appears, for example, in Luchet's *Les contemporains de 1789 et 1790* (1790) as an apostle of liberty.[49]

> FRANKLIN. It is impossible to give the tableau of a revolution without including this immortal name. This philosophical republican enlightened the heroes of liberty. Before him the majority of publicists had reasoned like educated slaves of their masters; like Montesquieu they had used all their wit to justify the status quo and to coat our institutions with a deceptive poison; he alone, studying the natural rights of man, sweeping away the dust and sand, that is, the external circumstances of weakness and poverty, of inequality, of all kinds of aristocracy, discovered the foundations of society; he demonstrated that the edifice was unsound wherever it was not based on the common accord of men and reciprocal agreements. No, one may never speak of liberty without paying a tribute of homage to this immortal defender of human nature.

In subsequent chapters we shall see further evidence of the evolution of Franklin as a symbol of liberty in two worlds, how in various literary genres he became with Rousseau and Voltaire an exemplum of the devotion of reason to political freedom.

Part
Two

FRANKLIN
AS A LEGENDARY FIGURE

In Belles Lettres

---

6. POLLY BAKER

French men of letters enshrined Franklin as a literary character in three separate genres: fiction, poetry, and drama. In addition, a work of his own, *The Speech of Polly Baker,* which several French authors translated or paraphrased, helped to establish the legendary personality of Franklin. The French variations of this story may be considered a portrayal of Franklin himself in French letters, not because they present his physical traits or personality, but because they embody a complex of notions associated in French thought with Franklin and with America. The French who accepted Polly Baker as a model of feminine reason strayed as far from reality as those who accepted Father Abraham as a depiction of Franklin's own primitivistic virtues.

The Speech of Polly Baker is Franklin's most famous literary hoax. His success in mystifying authors of three nations gave rise to Balzac's phrase, "Le canard est une trouvaille de Franklin, qui a inventé le paratonnerre, le canard, et la république." [1] Franklin's French contemporaries, however, who by and large were not aware of his literary pranks, would have been more likely to declare him a master in the art of morality rather than in the art of the literary hoax.

Modern readers are familiar with the account of the discomfiture of the Abbé Raynal on learning from Franklin's mouth that the story of Polly Baker was a hoax. Having incorporated it as an authentic incident in his *Histoire philosophique et politique des . . . deux Indes,* 1770,[2] Raynal had been ridiculed for his gullibility by Silas Deane, Franklin's fellow commissioner at the Court of Louis XVI. The *locus classicus* for this anecdote is a communication by Thomas Jefferson in 1818,[3] though a version by Jefferson's friend and fellow Virginian, Phillipi Mazzei, antedates Jefferson's by thirty years.

> Toward the end of 1777 or the beginning of 1778, the abbé Raynal going one evening to visit Doctor Franklin, found Silas Deane

Notes to this chapter begin on page 245.

at Franklin's home. "We were just speaking of your work," Deane remarked, "and we said that you had been poorly served by those who gave you information concerning America, and particularly my country."

As the abbé did not wish to admit the fact, Deane cited several passages in which there was not a word of truth. Finally, they came to speak of the tale of Polly Baker. This subject brought on the most serious controversy since the abbé maintained that he had taken it from an authentic document. Dr. Franklin, after enjoying himself listening to the debate for a time, broke the silence and addressed himself to the abbé. "I am going to set you straight," he said. "When I was young and printed a newspaper, it sometimes happened that when I was short of material that I would amuse myself by making up stories and that of Polly Baker is one of the number."

"My word," replied the abbé Raynal, giving up the dispute, "I am more pleased to have included your tales in my work than the truths of others."

This anecdote appears in Mazzei's *Recherches historiques et politiques sur les Etats-Unis,* 1788, a work of four volumes, of which the entire third volume is given over to a refutation of Raynal's remarks on the United States.[4] Mazzei gives no indication of his source for the anecdote; whereas Jefferson says that his version was communicated verbally by Franklin himself. Although it is possible that Mazzei obtained the story from Jefferson, it is just as likely that he drew it from one of the originals involved in the incident. A third possibility is that the conversation never took place at all, but is merely the substance of a good anecdote—a hoax by Mazzei or someone who told the tale to him. Jefferson may have read Mazzei's account of the episode, may have later forgotten the source, and then in 1818 may have thought he had heard it directly from Franklin.

Scholarship on the affair has been complicated by the fact that it has been affirmed and accepted that Voltaire pointed out in 1774 in *Questions sur l'Encyclopédie* that the story of Polly Baker was "une plaisanterie, un pamphlet de l'illustre Franklin." [5] In truth this passage does not appear in the 1774 edition of *Questions sur l'Encyclopédie* nor in any other edition published during Voltaire's lifetime. It appeared for the first time in the Kehl edition of Voltaire's works in 1784, and one cannot be absolutely certain that it is by Voltaire himself.[6] Even so, we must add, this is still the earliest known attribution of the piece to Franklin.

It makes little difference whether or not Raynal knew of Franklin's connection with Polly's speech; the important consideration is the use he made of it in his own work. Although one cannot be sure of his motives, Franklin probably told the story of Polly Baker for the sake of the humor in certain passages, a humor so refined and subtle that he probably felt a personal satisfaction in the hope that gullible persons would not perceive his levity but would accept the entire narrative as true. The only serious theme in the story is that which I shall refer to as philoprogenitiveness—the typically eighteenth-century fondness for fecundity and procreation as such. Franklin throughout his life, both humorously and seriously, in bagatelles, in works on economic theory, in personal letters, and in practice consistently stressed the value of an augmented population. Raynal, however, is only incidentally concerned with procreation. On the surface he uses the speech of Polly Baker to illustrate the harsh laws of the New England colonies, an example of the rigorous morality of puritanism, but his version of the story has little more to do with this theme than it has to do with Franklin's philoprogenitiveness. The fact is that Raynal's text is not a literal translation of Franklin's but a very loose paraphrase with fundamental alterations and additions designed to inculcate principles of deism and feminine equalitarianism—concepts completely nonexistent in Franklin's original. Not only does Raynal take liberties with Franklin's text, he is not even true to his own. His text of Polly Baker in the revised 1774 edition of the *Histoire philosophique* eliminates an important passage found in the 1770 text and presents several sections of the speech in a reverse order.

In Franklin's original, the three most forceful passages, strategically placed in the second quarter, the middle, and the very end of the speech, defend the principle of procreation at any cost. "Can it be a crime (in the nature of things, I mean)," Polly asks rhetorically, "to add to the king's subjects, in a new country, that really wants people? I own, I should think it rather a praiseworthy than a punishable action." [7] Appealing to the religious convictions of her judges, she argues that heaven is not angry at her having children since "to the little done by me towards it, God has been pleased to add his divine skill and admirable workmanship in the

formation of their bodies, and crowned the whole by furnishing
them with rational and immortal souls." Finally, she appeals to
"the first and great command of nature and nature's God, *encrease
and multiply;* a duty from the steady performance of which nothing has been able to deter me."

Raynal loosely translates the first two of these passages, and
in the last passage shifts the emphasis from the duty of augment-
ing population to the pleasure in the sexual act itself. Considering
the human male almost an opponent or enemy of the female,
Raynal's Polly complains of masculine injustice in condemning
the female partner from whom the male derives pleasure and
companionship. "Let him not crush with opprobrium a sex which
he has himself corrupted; let him not infuse shame and misery
into the pleasure which thou hast given him as the consolation
of his affliction; let him not be ungrateful and cruel to the very
seat of happiness in delivering to torture the victim of his vo-
luptuousness." This sentimental feminism is completely alien to
Franklin.

Raynal actually adds to the narrative more elements than he
adopts from the original. Of the other high points in Franklin's
version, Raynal repeats only his humorous reflections on the
cupidity of lawyers and ministers (the only members of the community with a legitimate grievance against Polly because she has
perhaps deprived them of a fee) and his serious advocacy of the
separation of civil and religious powers. "If mine is a religious
offense," Polly declaims, "leave it to religious punishments."
Raynal was apparently indifferent to Polly's argument that bachelors who fail to marry and produce offspring out of fear of the
expense of domestic life are guilty of a far greater crime than
her own. She advocates that they be legally compelled either to
marry or to pay double the fine of fornication every year. This
scheme, rather widely advocated as a serious economic and political measure in England during the eighteenth century, Raynal
included in his 1770 translation but dropped from his revised
version in 1774, indicating that he cared little more for Franklin's economics than for his philoprogenitiveness. Rationalistic religion and sociological perfectibility, primary themes of his ten-
volume history, are also the chief themes of his version of Polly
Baker.

By and large Raynal transforms Franklin's sprightly discourse into a deistical homily; the humor of the original is either overlooked or subordinated to deistical presuppositions. In her introductory remarks, for example, Raynal's Polly independently acknowledges reason as her guide and arbiter. "I am going to make Reason speak. As she alone has the right to dictate the laws, she can examine them all." In speaking of the education she has given to her illegitimate offspring, an extension of the situation that had not occurred to Franklin, she again praises reason as her moving principle. "I have formed them to virtue, which is merely reason. They already love their country as I do. They will be citizens as yourselves unless you take away from them by new fines the basis of their maintenance and force them to flee a region which has spurned them from the cradle."

Franklin's Polly complains of the severity of the laws, but argues merely that their rigidity should sometimes be relaxed in particular circumstances, that "there is left a power somewhere to dispense with the execution of them." Raynal's Polly unequivocally sets forth the Rousseauistic precept of the supremacy of conscience over law. "I defy my enemies, if I have any which I have not merited, to accuse me of the least injustice. I examine my conscience and my conduct; the one and the other, I say it boldly, both appear pure as the day which gives me light, and when I look for my crime, I find it only in the law."

Franklin was a lover and friend of the female sex, but in none of his works does he appear as an outspoken feminist like Condorcet, Godwin, or Mary Wollstonecraft. Certainly his Polly Baker does not suggest that the female sex itself is discriminated against in human institutions, nor does he present the male sex as the persecutor of the female. Raynal's Polly, on the other hand, does exactly this in a forthright denunciation of the double standard in sexual relations. "Who was the barbarous legislator, who pronouncing on the two sexes, favored the stronger and raged against the weaker—against this unfortunate sex which for a single brief pleasure must reckon with a thousand dangers and a thousand infirmities—against this sex to whom nature sells at a price capable of appalling the wildest passions these pleasures which she gives to you so freely."

Franklin's Polly is not a prude in sexual matters; yet she justifies her cohabitation solely on the grounds of procreation. Raynal's Polly frankly admits strong sexual urges and, perhaps because of her Gallic provenance, justifies them as part of the nature of things. "In order not to betray nature, I do not fear to expose myself to unjust dishonor, to shameful punishments. I should prefer to suffer everything than to forswear the vows of propagation, than to suppress my children either before or after conceiving them. I have not been able, I admit it, after losing my virginity, to remain celibate in a secret and sterile prostitution, and I ask for the punishment which awaits me rather than to hide the fruits of the fecundity which heaven has given to man and woman as its principal benediction."

Raynal's alterations are not limited to the intellectual content of the original text; they embrace also a fundamental change in the integral form or structure of the narrative. Where Franklin's original piece consists entirely of Polly's speech directed to her judges and accusers, Raynal's version contains an additional dramatic peroration addressed to the divine being himself. After repeating Franklin's argument that God could not be angry at her deed since he had endowed her progeny with an immortal soul, she turns from her accuser to address God directly.

> God, just and good; God, corrector of evils and injustices, it is to thee to whom I appeal the sentence of my judges; do not avenge me; do not punish them, but condescend to enlighten and to soften them. If thou hast given woman to man as companion on this earth covered with thorns, let him not crush with opprobrium a sex which he has himself corrupted; let him not infuse shame and misery into the pleasure which thou hast given him as the consolation of his affliction; let him not be ungrateful and cruel to the very seat of happiness in delivering to torture the victim of his voluptuousness. Make him respect in his desires the modesty which he honors, or after having violated it in his pleasures make him pity it at least instead of injuring it. Or let him not convert to crimes the actions which thou hast permitted or commanded when thou commanded his race to increase and multiply.

This enterprising young lady may bear the name Polly Baker, but she is certainly not the character Franklin created.

Some of Polly's deistical philosophy may have been inspired by Diderot, for, according to Anacharsis Cloots, Thomas Paine's colleague in the French National Convention, "All the great tirades against superstition and despotism which have made the fortune of the *Histoire philosophique* and which one can estimate at four volumes are the work of Diderot." [8] La Harpe in his *Correspondance littéraire* also attributes to Diderot responsibility for a large share of the philosophy of Raynal's work.[9] Raynal's original translation in 1770 is probably his own work, however, since Diderot used an entirely different translation as a feature of his *Supplément au voyage de Bougainville* written subsequently to the *Histoire philosophique* and published for the first time in 1796.[10] But as Raynal's revisions seem consistently to bring the Polly of the *Histoire philosophique* more in line with Diderot's version, it has been suggested that Diderot had some hand in the subsequent version of the story, if not actually in that of the 1770 edition.[11] Notable divergences in Diderot's translation from Franklin's text include suppression of the accusation that failing to have children is a crime of the same nature as assassination, of the proposal to tax bachelors, and of Polly's claim to have deserved a monument for her procreating activities. Added is a denunciation of unmarried men who seduce virtuous women and start them on the road to prostitution.

Raynal may have had his own motives—esthetic or intellectual—for changing his interpretation of Polly Baker, or he may have been under Diderot's influence. There would seem to be some significance in the fact that in addition to reversing the order of events in the narrative (the address to the divinity being shifted from a position near the middle of the speech to the very end), Raynal omitted four consecutive sentences from his previous text, sentences embodying exactly the same concepts that Diderot omits from his translation. This may show direct influence or it may be entirely coincidental. It may be said against the theory of Diderot's influence that the 1774 version is much less deistical than that of 1770. Since Diderot is usually considered to be responsible for the bold philosophical touches in the *Histoire philosophique,* it is inconsistent to portray him as leading Raynal away from deism.

The 1780 edition, last to appear during Raynal's lifetime, has a further change not made in any earlier edition, which seems definitely attributable to Diderot. The last sentence of the speech incorporates a phrase from the subtitle of the *Supplément au voyage de Bougainville,* an addition that gives the speech an emphasis entirely different from that of the previous versions. The subtitle of Diderot's work, "Dialogue entre A. et B. sur l'inconvénient d'attacher des idées morales à certaines actions physiques qui n'en comportent pas," seems to have little bearing on the speech of Polly Baker. As we have seen, Raynal used the narrative, ostensibly to condemn the rigorous moral harshness of puritanism, but actually to promote deism and feminine equalitarianism. Yet he concluded his 1780 version with the phrase, "ce discours, qu'on entendroit souvent dans nos contrées & partout où l'on a attaché des idées morales à des actions physiques qui n'en comportent point. . . ."

Nothing that goes beyond the realm of conjecture can be said about Diderot's influence. The most important conclusion to be drawn from both authors' treatment of Polly Baker is that the narrative was used to present concepts even more extensive than the wide variety already woven into it by Franklin.

Those critics who are aware that the original publication of Franklin's Polly Baker hoax has still not been located (that the earliest versions now known appeared concurrently in the *London Magazine* and *Gentleman's Magazine* in April, 1747) might argue that perhaps Raynal's translation goes back to the original version. Or it might be contended also that Raynal copied his version from some other previous French translation. Both hypotheses are unlikely. Raynal certainly had no firsthand access to colonial American newspapers, and other French translations of the Polly Baker speech follow closely the version in the *Gentleman's Magazine.* One of these in the gazette, *Le Courrier de l'Europe,* 1777, is almost a literal translation except that the heroine's name is changed to Marie Baker.[12] Another translation, published by Brissot de Warville in his *Bibliothèque philosophique du législature,* 1782, as an example of one of the world's best discourses on criminal legislation, is somewhat shortened, but otherwise almost a literal translation.[13]

As we have already seen, both Raynal and Diderot eliminate from their texts of Polly Baker the peroration in which she maintains that she has actually merited reward instead of punishment. Franklin's Polly appeals to "the duty of the first and great command of nature and nature's God. . . . For its sake I have hazarded the loss of publick esteem, and have frequently endured publick disgrace and punishment; and therefore ought, in my humble opinion, instead of a whipping to have a statue erected to my memory." Professor Chinard believes that the exaggeration implicit in this self-vindication should have put the translators on guard.[14] Both Brissot and the translator in the *Courrier de l'Europe,* however, gave this passage in full without apparently being any the wiser. It is not surprising that they should have been deceived. Even in America the story continued to be published and accepted as an actual occurrence as late as 1813.

In the same year the story reappeared in France as an example of the progress in human relations wrought by the American Revolution. In a collection of anecdotes concerning Anglo-American relations, the speech is said to have been delivered in 1775—just at the moment when the royal courts had been replaced by native judges chosen by the people.[15] Until this moment maids accused of violating sexual codes had not dared to speak out but had accepted their punishment as inevitable destiny. Polly was the first with the courage to condemn the law. This she did "with a modesty which gave added force to her protests and added éclat to her innocence. All America was moved to pity for her situation. In Europe all other concerns were momentarily suspended by the sensation which this story created. All recitals of brigandage and murders were interrupted in the gazettes of the time in order to give place to the discourse which an unknown creature, feeble and unfortunate, had delivered in her own defense."

After this introduction, notable as much for exaggeration as for anachronism, the editor strangely enough prints Mazzei's account of the source of the speech and adds his own interpretation of its significance as a moral tale: "how a simple woman, without other guide than nature, can display reason, courage and eloquence, and despite involuntary errors, may succeed in becoming a good mother and attaining the respect of the community." In contrast he presents another tale, illustrating the dangers of an education too refined, a tale of the spoiled daughter of a wealthy English man of affairs, who has learned little but impertinence and affectation at boarding school.

So successful has been Franklin's hoax that even in modern times scholars have been taken in by it. John Morley, the emi-

nent English critic of Diderot, in discussing the influence of the
great encyclopaedist on Raynal, remarked that Polly Baker seems
to have been written "in the vein and almost the words of
Diderot." [16] Later scholarly works in German and in Swedish
have repeated the view that the narrative of Polly Baker is entirely a product of the eloquence of Diderot, the only contribution of Franklin having been the bare situation. Actually,
as we have seen, Diderot's version is virtually a literal translation except for a few excisions. Raynal's version, which goes
to the other extreme of elaboration and rhetorical sensationalism,
is much further from Franklin's original.

Raynal, viewing his version as an example of the sublime power
of natural reason, probably felt justified in changing Franklin's
emphasis. His alterations, which he undoubtedly considered improvements, were designed to demonstrate how much "the voice
of reason is above the prestige of a studied eloquence." Of the
application of this principle to Polly Baker, Mazzei tartly observed, "he does too much honor to the talents of our poor
American maidens in supposing that they speak as Dr. Franklin
writes. If eloquence consists in declamation, it is certain that this
discourse is anything but a morsel of eloquence; but if it consists
in the force of reason, in the choice of expressions, in precision
etc., in this case I dare assert that it is." [17] Whatever may be said
of Franklin's original, it is obvious that the voice of reason has
very little in common with the rhetorical eloquence of Raynal's
Polly Baker.

7. FICTION

We have hitherto discussed the reception in France of Franklin's
various literary works and the consideration accorded to certain
of his opinions. We now turn to those French authors who used
Franklin as a subject for original literary productions, in other
words, those who perpetuated the Franklin legend. As has been
noted, Franklin was celebrated in three primary categories, fic-

Notes to this chapter begin on page 245.

tion, poetry, and drama. To these might be added formal eulogies and collections of anecdotes, souvenirs, and scandal—although the latter groups present Franklin primarily as a human being rather than as a legendary figure.

In his first fictional representation, Franklin appears in the role of scientist rather than statesman. Because of his friendship for Dr. Dubourg and Dr. Vicq d'Azyr, Franklin became embroiled in a heated dispute between the Faculté de Médecine and the newly-formed Société Royale de Médecine. Franklin appears to have taken no active part in the actual controversy in which Dubourg was one of the primary figures. For Dubourg, conten-tion between rival medical societies was nothing new. Early in his career when the School of Surgery was hotly embattled against the Faculty of Medicine, Dubourg wrote two pamphlets ardently defending the latter, one in 1743, the other in 1744.[1] As an out-come of his determined support, he was admitted in 1748 as doctor of the faculty, and he became known as one of the most zealous advocates of that body. The Faculty remained the most distinguished medical organization in France until the Royal Society of Medicine was established, and, as Dubourg was pained to see, dissension developed between the two organizations over their respective functions. The members of the Faculty were apparently resentful of the prestige accorded to the new society, which admitted many foreigners and excluded prominent mem-bers of the Faculty. In 1778 a partisan of the Faculty, Le Roux des Tillets, let loose a vitriolic attack on the Royal Society, ridi-culing its best-known members. At about the same time Dubourg published a *Lettre d'un Médecin de la Faculté,* ostensibly defend-ing the other side, but actually attempting to mediate between the two groups in proposing an arrangement whereby one group would specialize in medical theory, the other in practice.

In the satire of Le Roux against the Royal Society, Franklin plays the principal role. The work, entitled *Dialogue entre Pasquin & Marforio,* is a series of symbolic allegorical descrip-tions rather than a dramatic dialogue,[2] in a setting that is, appro-priately enough, the residence of the Secretary of the Society, Vicq d'Azyr, where the earliest gatherings had been held before Louis XVI had granted a meeting place at the Louvre. Pasquin, wishing to become a doctor, visits the Royal Society and discovers that the reception hall is adorned with an emblematic painting on each side and an altar at the far end. One of the paintings represents the young king extending his benevolent patronage toward medicine, personified as stretching a hand toward suffering humanity; on the opposite side are depicted courageous scientists, who expose themselves to disease in order to save their fellow men and even the lower animals from death. The altar at the rear is hidden by a symbolic representation of sound doctrine, the destruction of charlatanism, and the advance of medical knowledge—an emblem that the reader is expected to identify with the Faculty.

Franklin, playing the role of a wise magician, now appears on the scene to dispel false illusions and to portray the truth concerning the medical profession. Seated on a throne of ivory in his customary guise of a respectable old man, he is supported by Science and Virtue trampling chained leopards underfoot. On his forehead, encompassed by a halo of light, is figured the single word Liberty.

This vision gives place to a series of satirical emblems portraying the members of the Royal Society on the basis of scandalous anecdotes of their lives. The curtain is raised, revealing a large wooden idol surrounded by allegorical symbols such as ambition, artifice, favoritism, authority, ingratitude, intrigue, self-interest, and calumny. This idol, the reader is expected to identify with the Royal Society.

Vicq d'Azyr then pronounces a discourse summarizing the successful efforts of the Society in having labeled the Faculty as rebellious and imprudent for wishing to retain its privileges. He calls upon his auditors to renew their efforts to have the meetings of the Faculty forbidden, to have its decrees suspended, and to prevent the establishment of its committee of doctrine. Finally, he exhorts his colleagues to exterminate their enemies in order to fit themselves to sacrifice at the altar of medicine.

At this moment Franklin intervenes; amid peals of thunder, the altar is shaken and the idol overturned. Franklin with his magic wand transforms each member of the society into an animal analogous to his character.

Of this curious apocalypse, we might inquire as did the *Mémoires secrets* (February 13, 1779) why Franklin was cast in

the principal role. It may be, as the editors suggested, because
he was both scientist and republican and, therefore, in theory
opposed to the privileged exclusiveness of the Royal Society.
More likely, the author, seeing in Franklin a symbol of scientific
boldness and moral integrity, felt that his cause would be advanced if he were to associate Franklin with it, correctly or in-
correctly. From the standpoint of propaganda, Le Roux was probably indifferent to the fact that a few months later Franklin accepted membership in the Royal Society. The members of the
Faculty, however, probably felt a certain chagrin. According to
the *Mémoires secrets* (June 7, 1779) they lamented grievously
when Dubourg, too, went over to the rival Society—a defection
they considered the more shameful since he had previously been
one of its most outspoken opponents. One wonders whether
Franklin had any influence upon his change of attitude.

Although in the *Dialogue* Franklin was required to play a
somewhat ambiguous part, he was still treated with respect; in
other works of fiction, particularly those with political overtones,
he was sometimes made to look ridiculous. A licentious piece of
scandal entitled *Le Vicomte de Barjac,* 1784 [3] (attributed to the
Marquis de Luchet), for example, calls him "a very poor statesman," "a mediocre physician," and "a driveller." Perhaps the
most ludicrous description of Franklin in any literature is an
account of his dining at the home of a noble lady in the spurious
Mémoires de la Marquise de Créquy.[4] These alleged memoirs,
although not published until the nineteenth century, were probably written by a contemporary or near-contemporary of Franklin, and while the information they contain is not literally exact,
every word is written with an eye to verisimilitude. Among the
varied contents are two very interesting anecdotes of Franklin,
one concerning his religious opinions, the other concerning his
table manners. The first, presumed to have been communicated
by the abbé Galiani, reports that when Franklin and d'Alembert
were one day together at the home of Mme. Necker, "D'Alembert
began to cry out with his voice of an Abyssinian eunuch that
the reign of Christianity was at an end. Franklin replied that the
revolution which menaced the world was, on the contrary, the
application of primitive Christianity—a state of affairs which
would inevitably come to pass after a half century of infidelity.

This American maintained that the return to primitive institutions would have deplorable results and that he had great fear of the anabaptists." [5] Although this encounter itself is purely imaginary, Franklin held religious opinions very close to the view here attributed to him.

The second anecdote, presumed to be from the Marquise de Créquy herself, is an account of the only time she saw Franklin— at a dinner given by Madame de Tessé, who had amused herself at her friend's expense by placing her without warning next to Franklin. The Marquise decided to turn the tables on the company by refusing to address a single word to her companion. But even without this malicious decision, she adds, she would not have known what to say to the erstwhile printer at her side.

He had long hair like a diocesan of Quimper; he had a brown habit, brown coat, and breeches of the same cloth and hands of the same color; he had a cravate striped with red. What I noticed as most remarkable about him was his method of preparing fresh eggs. This consists in emptying them into his glass, adding butter with salt, pepper and mustard. He uses five or six to prepare this pretty Philadelphia stew, which he consumes in small spoonfuls. You should know also that he does not use a spoon and that he cuts with a knife the morsels of food he wishes to eat. He bites into the asparagus instead of cutting off the tips with his knife on the plate and eating them properly with his fork. You see that he was a kind of savage. But, nevertheless, my friend, as each people has its institutions, its climate, its foods, its habits and its own customs, each nation must have its moral delicacies and its physical crudities, with the refinements of politeness that are peculiar to it and habitual negligencies that another does not have. What made me pay attention to the actions and behavior of this American philosopher was the ennui of hearing him spoken of as a social paragon and a marvel of cosmopolitan civilization.

Even though the real Marquise de Créquy had nothing to do with this passage, it must be remembered that somebody in France wrote it and had this unfavorable opinion of Franklin. It is a far cry indeed from the blandishments of his actual friends Mmes. Brillon and Helvétius. The satire may not be softened by the explanation that the author was indulging political or social prejudices. The *Mémoires* had no propaganda purpose; they are nothing more profound than a literary hoax designed to exploit the scandal and rich personalities of the period.

This fictitious account of Franklin at dinner may be balanced by the actual impressions of the Duke of Croÿ, who was an invited guest at Franklin's apartment in Passy, March 1, 1779.

I ate a frugal dinner, which consisted of a single service at a time and no soup. I found, among others, two dishes of hot fish, an excellent pudding, and pastry for dessert. At the table were two young men, one of whom was his grandson (still in boarding school) and the other a taciturn Englishman. Franklin was recovering from an attack of gout, for which he had been taking baths. He was changed and weakened and going into a decline. As he ate only this single meal every day, he ate large slices of cold meat and drank two or three bumpers of good wine. He was tranquil and spoke little. Everything in his surroundings reflected simplicity and economy. The domestic staff consisted of three persons.[6]

Elkanah Watson, an ingenuous fellow American invited to a formal dinner in the same year amid the same surroundings, felt that Franklin's domestic establishment breathed grace and luxury.

At the hour of dinner he conducted me, across a spacious garden of several acres, to the princely residence of M. Le Ray de Chaumont. . . . We entered a spacious room; I following the Doctor, where several well-dressed persons (to my unsophisticated eyes, gentlemen) bowed to us profoundly. These were servants. A folding-door opened at our approach, and presented to my view a brilliant assembly, who all greeted the wise old man, in the most cordial and affectionate manner. He introduced me as a young American, just arrived. One of the young ladies approached him with the familiarity of a daughter, tapped him kindly on the cheek, and called him "Papa Franklin." I was enraptured, with the ease and freedom exhibited in the table intercourse in France. . . . Some were waltzing; and others gathered in little groups in conversation. At the table, the ladies and gentlemen were joined together, and joined in cheerful conversation, each selecting the delicacies of various courses, and drinking of delicious light wines, but with neither toasts nor healths.[7]

Another collection of eighteenth-century memoirs—partly authentic, partly fictitious—presenting an inaccurate portrayal of one phase of Franklin's official career in France, is the colorful *Life of Baron Frederic Trenck,* published originally in German in 1786-1787. Franklin in a letter to his sister (December 17, 1789) affirmed that

what he says, as having past in France, between the Ministers of
that Country, himself & me . . . is founded on Falsehood. . . . I
never saw in that Country, nor ever knew or heard of him, any
where 'till I met with the mentioned History in Print, in the German Language, in which he ventured to relate it as a Fact, that I
had with those Ministers solicited him to enter into the American
Service.—A Translation of that Book into French has since been
printed, but the translator has omitted that pretended Fact, probably from an Apprehension that its being, in that Country, known
not to be true, might hurt the Credit & Sale of the Translation.[8]

Shortly after Franklin's death, one of his French acquaintances,
St. John de Crèvecoeur, reported in a book of travels three interviews with Franklin that never took place, probably in order
to shine in the reflected glory of Franklin's reputation and to
ensure a favorable reception for *Le Voyage dans la Haute Pensylvanie et dans l'état de New York*, 1801.[9] In one passage Franklin explains to Crèvecoeur the effects of the northwest winter
winds on the eastern states; in another he discourses on the
Gulf Stream. The former passage is actually a reworking of materials from Jonathan Carver's *Travels*, 1796, and the latter is
a paraphrase of Franklin's own *Maritime Observations*, 1785. In
the third passage, Crèvecoeur describes a journey he allegedly
made in Franklin's company to Lancaster, Pennsylvania, in 1787
to attend the dedication of Franklin College. As part of the ceremonies Franklin is supposed to have delivered an address on
the origins of the North American Indians and on some newly-
discovered Indian antiquities. Franklin College actually was dedicated at this time—indeed Franklin sent the abbé Morellet a
pamphlet describing the ceremonies that the latter translated for
the *Mercure de France*—but Franklin himself did not attend the
ceremonies nor did he, of course, deliver a speech. At the time
he and Crèvecoeur were supposedly in Lancaster, Franklin was
attending to his official duties in Philadelphia, and Crèvecoeur
was on a ship en route from France to America. The materials
for Franklin's speech Crèvecoeur drew mainly from Gilbert Im-
lay's *A Topographical Description of the Western Territory of
North America*, 1792. The entire episode is fictitious, although
highly plausible. Crèvecoeur's imaginary interviews were presented so convincingly that a number of Franklin's early biogra-
phers took them as genuine.

Most French anecdotes concerning Franklin appropriately limited themselves to his sojourn in France. Those, like Crève-coeur's, which take Franklin's life in America for their province, are rare and usually based on imagination rather than fact. One of the most fantastic of these presents him as the editor of the *Pennsylvania Gazette* at the same period of his life when Rush, Hancock, and Washington were among his friends.[10] According to this tale, some time after Franklin had established his newspaper, a subscriber objected to the vivacity with which he defended American interests and thereupon cancelled his subscription. Franklin expressed his regrets and some weeks later invited him to dinner. The erstwhile subscriber was ushered into a small apartment, modestly furnished, but extremely neat. A servant placed on a white cloth some cucumbers, a lettuce, a dish of leeks, a jug of water, a pitcher of small beer, some butter and some cheese. This was the entire supper. Soon after, Rush, Hancock, and Washington entered and regaled themselves with good humor and merriment at the humble table until midnight. The next day the invited guest thanked Franklin warmly for the lesson he had been given, remarking, "A man who can invite the principal citizens of the community to share a dish of cucumbers and lettuce can do nothing but honestly follow his political principles." The story is apocryphal, but the ingredients are traditional in both France and America: Franklin's thrift, his integrity, and his practical diplomacy.

A similar story circulated in America—perhaps the true one and the source of the legendary account.[11] Early in his journalistic career a number of Franklin's friends grew alarmed at the freedom and force with which he had been treating in the *Gazette* "some of the men & measures of the day, which no one ever before had the moral courage thus to put to the bar of public inquiry. This produced a political concussion in the primitive country not less startling than the shocks which were afterwards imparted by his original experiment with the electrick fluid." When his well-meaning friends suggested greater moderation, Franklin invited them to dinner at which his wife served nothing but pudding and water. After they had all concluded their meagre fare, Franklin thanked them for their advice, but explained that "he who can subsist upon saw dust pudding &

water, as can Benjamin Franklin, needs not the patronage of any one."

In several works of pure fiction Franklin is portrayed in a ridiculous light. Most obvious of the satires against French participation in the American Revolution is a British production by William Playfair, *Joseph and Benjamin, a conversation. Translated from a French manuscript*, London, 1787. The claim that it is translated from a French document—the only reason for mentioning the work here—is completely devoid of foundation, even though the book, consisting of an imaginary conversation on economic theory between Franklin and the Emperor of Austria, is said to be a genuine record. A similar work, attributed to Richard Tickell, *La cassette verte de Monsieur de Sartine*, 1777, may be either French or British in origin; texts of so-called fifth and sixth editions in French exist, but there may never have been any prior editions. Chief target of this satire is the tremendous amount of money given to Franklin for the American Revolution. The title refers to the reputed repository of Sartine's private papers that the editor ransacks while the hero is engaged in making love to Mlle. du Thé. The papers, all extremely ludicrous, emphasize the inconsistency of an alliance between the French monarchy and the American republic. Franklin is portrayed as a highly-skilled confidence man. An anonymous pamphlet attacking Vergennes in 1788 says of *La cassette verte*, "In it all is not true, all is not false. One may find therein an account of the profits and losses of Messrs. de Sartine, Vergennes & Franklin, which gave place at the time to many conjectures." [12]

A work in similar vein by an anonymous French isolationist satirizes not only America and England, but also Spain and Holland and, to a certain extent, even France. Although the main target of personal satire is the American naval hero, John Paul Jones, Franklin plays the secondary role, as revealed by the title: *Paul-Jones, ou prophéties sur l'Amérique, l'Angleterre, la France, l'Espagne, la Hollande, &c. par Paul-Jones, Corsaire, Prophète & Sorcier comme il n'en fut jamais. Y joint le rêve d'un Suisse sur la révolution de l'Amérique, dédié à son excellence M^{gneur} l'Ambassadeur Franklin. . . . De l'ère de l'indépendance de l'Amérique l'an V*. The main work, a pretended prophecy delivered by

Jones under the inspiration of the Grand Tonnant (a title apparently devoid of symbolic meaning) is a parody of Biblical language, particularly the Old Testament prophets, the Song of Solomon, and the Apocalypse. The satire on the political ambitions of the United States is much more amusing than the rather ambiguous dedication to Franklin. It is prophesied of America, for example:

> Thou wilt become a power, one such as has never before existed. Thou wilt harass all the emperors and all the kings, all the sultans and caesars of the earth. The Pope himself mayhap will go one day to Boston to kiss thy slippers.

Personified as a lover, America receives the following address:

> Thou art like a young maiden who has fled thy paternal abode since thy Papa and thy Mama do not grant thee all thy whims.

The dedication to Franklin, composed by a supposed matchdealer (representing Switzerland), asks Franklin to deliver a letter to Congress proposing a treaty of commerce advantageous to both and concluding with the capital intelligence that in addition to the vital match trade, the writer could promise that of Swiss cheese, which is excellent in soup.

The most detailed satirical portrait of Franklin in France appears in a colorful collection of scandal, *Histoire d'un pou françois; ou l'espion d'une nouvelle espèce, tant en France, qu'en Angleterre. Contenant les portraits de personnages intéressans dans ces deux Royaumes, & donnant la Clef des principaux événemens de l'An 1779, & de ceux qui doivent arriver en 1780.*[13] The so-called fourth edition appeared in 1779, printed with "approbation and privilege," but there is no evidence of any prior edition. The fact that it was printed with royal approval shows that official policy was willing to see Franklin portrayed in a less favorable role than that of primitive philosopher or of scientific wizard. The work, attributed to someone named Delauney, who may be none other than the printer, belongs to the literary tradition of the personified trifle, developed to perfection in England by Charles Johnstone (*Chrysal, or the Adventures of a Guinea,* 1760-65) and Tobias Smollett (*The Adventures of an Atom,* 1769). Delauney's satire cannot be considered in any sense British propaganda since the highest praise is accorded to the

French King and Queen. A strong pro-monarchist and anti-republican sentiment pervades the entire narrative.

The hero of the tale, an enterprising louse, is born upon the head of a lady of pleasure. After his marriage and the birth of several children, he embarks upon his travels, enjoying many temporary habitations, among them the persons of a countess, the Queen, a soldier, and a laundress. Eventually he establishes himself upon the notorious Mlle. d'Eon, Chevalier de St. Louis and former Captain of Dragoons, the soldier-diplomat who at the end of his career took to wearing female costumes and maintained that he had actually changed sex. In the narrative he is strongly condemned—accused of cowardice, of brawling in public, and of consorting with low company. On a visit to Franklin, who had invited Mlle. d'Eon to dinner, the French louse makes the following observations concerning Franklin's appearance.

> I avow that I could not keep myself from bursting into laughter on contemplating the grotesque countenance of this original, who, clad in the coarsest garb, from time to time affected the tone and gestures of a dandy. A complexion bronzed by the sun, a furrowed brow, warts all over his face, which upon him one would say are as attractive as are the patches which characterise the pretty features of Madame la Comtesse du Barry; a heavy and wide chin like those one describes as turned-up; a flat nose, and teeth which one would have taken for clout nails, if one had not seen them thrust into a thick jaw. Such is by and large the portrait to the life of His Excellency. As for his eyes, I have not been able to distinguish them because, as I have said, I was opposite to him, and he had spectacles hooked upon his temples which concealed a good third of his face.

One will notice that this portrayal of Franklin with the manners of a dandy is just the opposite of that in the *Mémoires de la Marquise de Créquy*, which presents him with the manners of a savage. Parenthetically it might be remarked that this is caricature, not description.

Perhaps the most precise and accurate information concerning Franklin's actual appearance is furnished by the Duke de Croÿ, who pictured Franklin as "a large man with the most handsome features with long white hair, wearing everywhere outdoors a large fur cap and having the style of a Quaker—moreover, he wore nearly always a kind of spectacles without which he would never have been able to see. . . . The resemblance is perfect in the beautiful print at the head of the quarto translation of his works on electricity." [14]

An even more flattering word-portrait is that of Franklin's intimate friend du Pont de Nemours.

It is not enough to say that Franklin is handsome; one must say that he was one of the most handsome men of the world and that one does not know any one of his age to equal him. All his proportions proclaim the vigor of Hercules, and at the age of 75 years he still has the suppleness and nimbleness of his character. His eyes reveal a perfect equanimity and his lips the smile of an unalterable serenity. It does not appear that labor has ever tired his nerves. He has wrinkles that are gay; others that are tender and proud, but there is not one that reflects a laborious existence. One sees that he has conceived more than he has studied; that he has amused himself with science, with men, and with public affairs. And while still amusing himself nearly at the end of his days, he worked to establish the most imposing republic of the world. Below his portrait this laconic inscription has been placed: *Vir*. There is not a feature of his physiognomy or his life which belies it. [15]

Again in parentheses, we might remark that this is eulogy, not description.

Returning to the imaginary meal of Franklin and Mlle. d'Eon, we find that they drink thirteen toasts, one in honor of each of the thirteen colonies. The lady approaches close to Franklin and sings to him several lines of her own composition, which had not seemed extraordinary when she composed them, but which Franklin applauds warmly. To show his gratitude, he embraces Mlle. d'Eon with ardor, but without taking off his glasses, and whispers in her ear, "Until this evening, my divine one."

After this episode, the louse leaves the Chevalier d'Eon and takes refuge with the *valet de chambre* of the playwright Beaumarchais. The servant, who hates the master, maliciously transfers his fleas to his master's person as a vindictive gesture. The hero is then in a position to overhear a dialogue between Beaumarchais and Franklin, when the latter comes to call. In this interview Franklin is made to appear as the dupe of Beaumarchais, and the military and political strategy of the American conflict are made to seem the result of Beaumarchais' intrigues.

In a further adventure the louse finds himself in a wig-maker's establishment where a very humbly-dressed friend of the proprietor engages in conversation with one of the workmen. The ensuing dialogue is a brilliant satire on Franklin's habits of frugality and his advice for attaining success. The impecunious friend of the proprietor, appropriately named Benjamin le Franc, reveals himself as a disciple of Franklin's policies, boasting first of all that he is able to live on a sparse income of only 119 pounds 10 sous per year, spending but six sous per day. Since he has developed the knack of being content with very little, his six sous provide him with a life of ease; even his mite makes him one-third more rich than Franklin had been during several years of his early life.[16] After a detailed exposition of his mentor's example of thrift, the question naturally arises, how did Franklin pass from an existence based upon the expenditure of four sous per day to his present high station. The answer is: by gradual means.

> This gentleman became very skilled in electricity. He forced the thunder to fall where he ordered it; he commanded it to withdraw and it withdrew. He did surprising things. He electrified a dog on the opposite bank of a river, making him howl like a martyr without having the least suspicion of the author of his sufferings. It was by his rare and marvellous talents that he acquired the appointment as collector of the royal revenue at Philadelphia, a post which brought him a yearly 500 pounds sterling (around 1200 in French pounds).

But how could a man of his frugal antecedents spend such a vast sum?

> He acquitted himself to perfection: he acquired a wife, children, stocked excellent wine, rum and brandy in his cellar, and kept a fine table. He was then an excellent royalist because it was his advantage to be one. He procured for his son a post in His Majesty's service. This same son is now Royal Governor of New Jersey, firm in his duty and attachment to His Britannic Majesty. As for his own interests, Franklin looked after them very well, perhaps too well, if one can judge by subsequent events, since after a certain time he was thanked very politely and his place given to another.

What had Franklin done to bring about this situation?

> Having seen in electricity that there is fire in every thing and in every place, he decided that he might turn his knowledge to account in maintaining his high standard of living. Consequently he electrified the minds of all the Americans and made them believe

that all the pain they suffered came directly from the Palace of Saint James in London, that in this Palace it had been decided to treat them as a nation in bondage and to make them pay arbitrarily all the taxes and duties that caprice and interest could conceive. Nothing else was needed to stimulate these poor sufferers to revolt. Franklin was sent to London to make propositions on their behalf, which seemed too imperious and even insulting to the Majesty of the Throne. They were rejected, as the electrician was sure that they would be. Returning to his own country, he represented wrongs of the British government which did not exist at all. He inflamed spirits, advising his countrymen to throw off the chimerical yoke of the mother country. He promised them a liberty which would provide happiness for them and their children. He indeed wished to become their legislator; he established a form of republican government and put them under the despotism of Congress.

Delauney's satire is not primarily political. Franklin's parsimony rather than his republicanism is the major target. This is apparent in the conclusion of the portrait. Benjamin le Franc, the French disciple, makes it perfectly clear that he does not propose to imitate Franklin's political career by seeking to turn his countrymen from their love and duty toward their King. He proposes to follow his mentor only in the first phase of his life, that is, by contenting himself with little and applying himself to improving some superior talent by means of which he may rise to a post in the government service.

The youth of Franklin serves admirably as a target of satire; his old age is better adapted to eulogy. We find among the *Contes Moraux,* printed in the *Mercure de France* under the title "Les Souvenirs du Coin du Feu," a sketch of the pleasures of old age in which Franklin plays the principal role. Doubtless this portrait, like most of the *Contes Moraux* in the *Mercure,* is from the pen of Marmontel, nephew of the abbé Morellet.[17] Nucleus of the narrative is a remedy against the vexations of growing old, which Franklin describes one evening to a group of white-haired dinner guests just before returning to America to die in the bosom of his native land. Touched by the realization that he would never again see his friends, he asks that they keep his memory alive, and, glass in hand, he bids them farewell. One of the guests, similarly touched, expresses regret that they could not accompany their friend to finish out their lives in a country where old age is honored. "Where is it not honored," Franklin replies, "where it knows to be what nature intended that it should be, peaceable, calm, moderate, indulgent and, above all, preceded by an honest and praiseworthy life?" All too frequently, the guest replies, old people who have led useful lives and who have neither the crotchets nor the gloom attributed to age are still abandoned to solitude. France has given up the custom, still prevalent in Pennsylvania, of bringing together all the members of a family on holidays and anniversaries, occasions on which great-grand-parents may see their descendants of three generations gathered around the same table or family hearth. Now instead of receiving the reverence of their families, the old are treated with neglect and indifference. Domestic dissensions prevail, and even fathers and mothers are forsaken by their children. Franklin advises his friends not to exaggerate the evils that have inevitably come from the internal corruption of a mixed and multiplied society; he urges them to pardon the new age for faults that were not unknown in ancient times.

> Doubtless it would be pleasant for the old men to preside over the activities of youth—at their dances and feasts as in Sparta and in the imaginary Republic of Plato; it would be even more useful for youth to be admitted to the conversation of virtuous old men, as in the ancient banquets; they would profit by the example of cordiality and openness; they would be taught prudence and honesty. It must be admitted, however, that youth has interests and occupations which are not ours; and in a world where pleasure has acquired such great vogue and favor, it is not astonishing that the young flocks should detach themselves from us, for whom the same allurement does not provide the same impulse.

Franklin's friend, somewhat more stern and gloomy, finds in the relaxing of family ties a parallel to the decreased attention to religion, arguing that it has been a mistake to abandon the concept of an eternal moral order. Franklin agrees that the recognition of a god, a system of worship, and an infallible and invariable morality are as much a need as a duty. Moral speculations do not serve to make the lot of old age less difficult, however, and Franklin thereupon offers a suggestion for the dear friends whom he is soon to leave.

> You have in yourselves the means of keeping yourselves from the ennui of solitude and of making yourselves happy. Young people live together. In that only imitate them. Form a circle of the best

and most estimable citizens of your age; and then, your eyes turned toward your best years, let your thoughts go back over your tracks, and your hearts will be rejuvenated in breathing again the air of your springtime. You will no longer hear so much talk of horse-races, of shows, of balls, of new attire, but in compensation you will recall interesting memories, and the past will distract you from the present and the future.

Although this is a purely fictitious account of Franklin, it is of some interest to notice that the real Franklin, even in his youth, was interested enough in the problems of old age to print a translation of Cato's *Moral Distiches,* 1735, for which he wrote an introduction. The translation by Franklin's friend James Logan was the first translation of a classic author to be written and printed in the colonies.

In Marmontel's account, Franklin appears merely as the symbol of a distinguished old gentleman. The broad outlines of his political career appear in another French work, in which his principles of liberty and democracy are praised with the same enthusiasm they had earlier aroused in Dubourg and the editors of the *Ephémérides.* An extended allegory by the abbé Gabriel Brizard entitled *Fragment de Xénophon, nouvellement trouvé dans les ruines de Palmyre, par un Anglois; & déposé au Museum Britannicum, à Londres,* 1783, depicts the principles and main events of the American Revolution. The work is based upon a document that the English poet and jurist Sir William Jones had composed and shown to Franklin in 1779 in an effort to bring about peace between Britain and the colonies. Jones's allegory, *A Fragment of Polybius, From his Treatise on the Athenian Government,* is a temperate plea for an accommodation of differences.[18] Describing England as "a republic with a perpetual administrator of its laws," Jones offers the colonies satisfaction of all their grievances short of absolute independence, for the logical basis of an enduring peace, he feels, can be found in strengthening the natural union between England and the colonies. In this allegory England is given the designation of Athens, and Franklin that of Eleutherion, presumably after Jupiter Eleutherius, the asserter of liberty. Although some attention is paid to the causes of the conflict, the allegory is limited by and large to the semi-official peace proposals made by Jones, a private citizen, to Franklin, the delegated spokesman of Congress. Brizard's *Fragment,* a much more comprehensive work, presents in capsule form the entire history of the American conflict with characterizations of the major personalities. Franklin is designated as Thales de Milet after the scientist-philosopher of Miletus, Thales. Other famous personalities are represented by anagrams, such as Erugenes (Vergennes), Tusingonas (Washington), and Fylaatete (Lafayette).

The style of the work, like that of Jones's *Polybius,* emulates classic simplicity. It has some resemblance to the style of Franklin's own *contes,* and it would not be amiss to point out that Franklin himself once wrote an essay for his *Pennsylvania Gazette* based upon quotations from Xenophon (September 3, 1730).

Brizard's *Fragment* seems to have been written to celebrate the treaty of peace. It is not propaganda in any sense of the word, but rather a commemorative tribute, parallel to the erection of a statue or bust or the celebration of Olympic Games, which are mentioned in the work. Praise is accorded to both France and America, but particularly to Franklin as the hero of the struggle against tyranny.

The author plays out the farce that the fragment is actually an ancient Greek manuscript. With delicate irony he cites an Oxford professor to whom it had been entrusted. The latter, arguing that it is not in the pure style of Xenophon, who has justly been named the Attic Honey Bee and the Athenian Muse, had accordingly written an elaborate commentary exposing the errors and anachronisms. The French translator, despite these learned demonstrations, persists in regarding his author as the most perfect in antiquity and the fragment as the most beautiful of his works. If it does not seem worthy of the great reputation of Xenophon, "this is due entirely to the poverty of the French language, that idiom which all learned authorities agree is completely devoid of grace, harmony and expression, a truth borne out by the writings of Racine, Fenelon, Bossuet, Rousseau, Buffon and Voltaire."

He proposes to allow the public to settle the question by means of a future edition of the original Greek text, which, he is sure, will be favorably received, especially if it is printed in a de luxe edition. Rich collectors will then be able to buy it without under-

standing it, and scholars able to read it will be unable to buy it.
By this simple method no one will have anything adverse to say
and everyone will be contented.

In the allegory, the revolted states are portrayed as Greek
colonies on the coast of Asia Minor, flourishing under a mild
climate and just and pacific laws. A veritable Golden Age seems
to have been attained; the natives have escaped dissension and
war, under the protection of the wide ocean and their primitive
morality. Like Dubourg, Montesquieu, and many other French
authors, Brizard attributes to the generality of Americans the
behavior of Quakers, who, it should be remembered, were then
a minority group even in Pennsylvania.

> Calm and simple as nature herself, these virtuous mortals abhor
> murder and war; they refrain even from swearing by the gods (for
> they believe that they should not mingle the names of the gods
> with the actions of mortals), but their word is more sacred than all
> the oaths.

Even Polly Baker seems to have had some influence.

> Happy and fruitful marriages were the safeguard of the morals and
> resources of the state, and in all this enormous country one does
> not find a single citizen who dreams of avoiding the dear and sacred
> bond of Hymen.

Since France (portrayed as Athens) had at one time established
colonies in North America, the author does not consider the revolted colonies as offshoots of Great Britain, but of all Europe.
Britain (Carthage), he suggests, gained control of the colonies
by dominating the seas, and according to this interpretation, the
Revolution developed entirely as a result of British maritime
policies. The questions of taxation and representation, which the
colonists stated as their chief grievances, are not even mentioned.
In the allegory the colonists are represented as taking up arms
to maintain the freedom of the seas. Since they needed allies in
their efforts, they inevitably turned to Athens, selecting as their
representative at the Athenian court the citizen most likely to
succeed in the delicate negotiations.

> This was Thales of Miletus, the glory and ornament of his nation.
> It was he who had first lighted the torch of art in this part of the
> world. He had opened an academy, where men were instructed in
> science and citizens, in virtue. He had been one of the most ardent

promoters of liberty as he had been one of the most zealous votaries of philosophy. For him, nature had no mysteries and wisdom, no veil. Some maintained indeed that he had inherited the secret of Prometheus and that when he wished, he forced the celestial fire to descend upon the altars of the gods. Also he had been named by the oracle as one of the seven sages of Greece.

Thales then had the approbation of all his fellow-citizens. Although of an advanced age, he was not afraid to entrust himself to the dangers of a long and perilous crossing, during which he had equally to fear the perfidy of the elements and the jealousy of the Carthaginians [British].

His reputation had preceded him to Athens. The Athenians had admired his wisdom and his virtue, but his physical characteristics had been until then unknown. His demeanor at the same time calm and venerable, the noble and majestic character of his face, his features, which breathed candor and virtue, his locks silvered by age and honorable labor, everything, even including his costume, the simplicity of which contrasted singularly with the elegance, the finery, and the affected manners of the Athenians, attracted notice and fixed attention. Everywhere he appeared, he was eagerly followed. Everywhere flattering applause announced his presence. Women, who are particularly susceptible to strong feelings, pointed him out as a model to their sons in order to inspire a notion of the heroism of virtue. A young child, believing that he had caught sight of the old man's features, said to his mother, "Mother, is this Nestor?" "Yes, my son, it is Nestor," she said. "Remember all your life the moment when you saw this great man." [19]

This dramatic incident seems reminiscent of Franklin's presentation of his grandson to Voltaire, with the latter playing the role of Nestor. One wonders how Franklin felt when it was read aloud with himself in the audience at the Musée de Paris.

In subsequent passages, Thales, admitted to the Areopagus, addresses the Athenians, declaring that he has been attracted to their city, not by their arts, their buildings, and their magnificence, but by the reputation of their justice and generosity. He appeals for their aid, therefore, not on the ground of the advantages that might accrue to them by helping to defeat Carthage, but solely on the ground that it is the nature of the generous Athenians to repair injustice as soon as it is revealed to them. These wise and diplomatic words are hailed by both the people and the monarch, with the latter immediately announcing himself to be a defender of the liberties of the colonies.

There ensues in the narrative a description of the exploits of

the noble French, including d'Estaing and Lafayette, who have
joined in the struggle. Particular notice is given to the military
genius of Washington, described as "the prodigy of his century
and his nation," and the political sagacity of Vergennes. Even
the English are credited with a valiant defense and a patriotism
greater than had ever before existed in their land.

Finally, peace is declared. Joyful feasts and frivolities take place
at Paris; monuments, including a national theater, are dedicated.
The crowning event is the holding of Olympic Games, during
the progress of which eulogies are made of the fallen brave and
of the political reforms of the Athenian monarch.

> Thales appeared at these games and experienced the fullness of
> his glory. All eyes were turned upon him. He was named the Liber-
> ator and Legislator of Asia [America]. The code of laws which he
> had designed for the new republic [the Constitution of Pennsyl-
> vania] was placed beside his immortal writings. His statue was
> borne in triumph to the acclamation of all the assemblage. It was
> crowned with an olive-branch, symbol of peace, and a laurel wreath,
> symbol of genius. He was represented holding with one hand the
> torch of Prometheus and with the other the sacred banner of lib-
> erty. At the foot of his statue is inscribed the celebrated line of
> Sophocles, the sense of which is

> He wrenched with a bold hand the thunder from the skies and
> the sceptre from the tyrants.

Similar symbols to pay tribute to Franklin had been used at
the outset of the American Revolution by Beaumarchais in dedi-
cating to Franklin a little-known work, *Le Voeu de toutes les
nations, et l'intérêt de toutes les puissances dans l'abaissement
et l'humiliation de la Grande-Bretagne* . . . 1778. In his dedication, Beaumarchais drew upon his highly-accomplished talents
in an effort to praise Franklin in a manner that Franklin would
find fresh and novel. To this purpose he introduced symbols of
antiquity.

> The heroes of Greece and Rome served their country in order to
> have a statue, to obtain a triumph. They believed that glory was
> the only recompense that the gods and men of virtue should expect
> from the gratitude of men. Rome erected statues and bestowed the
> honors of the triumph upon the victor of Numantia and Carthage,
> but Athens gave only two sprigs of laurel to the one who had de-
> livered her from the thirty tyrants. The seven heroes of Persia who

exterminated the Magi-usurpers wanted for themselves and their posterity only the privilege of wearing a peaked cap on the front of their heads because this peaked bonnet had been the mark of their fortunate enterprise. For you, Monsieur, above the statues and triumphs of Rome, the laurels of Greece, and the cap of Persia, there is nothing great enough in the world to be the reward of the signal services that you have rendered your country.

Beaumarchais further attributes to Franklin's noble influence the freedom of the New World and the dawn of the fortunate revolution in America. In the text of his work, Beaumarchais, like the author of the *Fragment of Xenophon,* finds the chief danger to world security in the British monopoly of the seas. All nations should defend themselves, he maintains, against the pretensions of a single power to universal monarchy of the seas.

8. POETRY

The *Fragment of Xenophon,* which we discussed in the last chapter, ends with the inscription

Il arracha d'une main hardie, au ciel sa foudre et le sceptre aux tyrans.

This is, of course, a translation of the most famous line ever written about Franklin, the Latin epigram attributed to Turgot. It appeared originally as the first line of a six-line stanza of which the other five were in French.[1]

Eripuit coelo fulmen, sceptrumque tyrannis
Le voilà, ce mortel dont l'heureuse industrie
Sut enchaîner la foudre et lui donner des lois,
Dont la sagesse active et l'éloquente voix
D'un pouvoir oppresseur affranchit sa patrie,
Qui désarma les Dieux, qui réprima les Rois.

In 1778 the epigram appeared under the famous bust of Franklin by Houdon [2] and also upon a terra-cotta medallion of Franklin by Jean Baptiste Nini, who is supposed to have been the first to use

Notes to this chapter begin on page 246.

the epigram in a work of art.[3] In the same year Fragonard designed an allegorical engraving to illustrate the Latin line,[4] and knowing that Franklin was to visit the Louvre, he prepared a plate in advance and printed it in Franklin's presence, in order to present him with the first impression. The conceit in the epigram based upon the electricity discovery had been exploited many years before in the abbé Mangin's *Histoire générale et particulière de l'électricité,* 1752, without special reference to Franklin. Mangin wrote that "one must acknowledge that if Prometheus acquired such a great reputation for having stolen fire from the gods, the heroes of electricity deserve to be crowned with an immortal glory, for not content to imitate their thunderbolts and lightning, they dared to try to seize them out of their hands." [5] Turgot by adding the political parallel rendered the conceit the exclusive property of Franklin.

The grandeur and magnitude—indeed the panegyric sublimity of the epigram—seem to be unparalleled. We may perhaps attain an idea of its grandeur through the aid of a renowned legal authority, who, speaking before the Academy of Lyon in 1781, developed the essence of the epigram to portray Franklin's contribution to human knowledge.

> Jupiter who disposed of the thunder at his pleasure was a fable in Greece, and in our day it has become a reality in America. Franklin said to the thunder, "fall," and the thunder fell. But whereas the god of Greece governed the thunder like a man to seek revenge and to destroy, the man of America governed it like a god; he ended its destruction and annulled it by diverting it from human beings.[6]

The Latin epigram and the French verses that follow are generally attributed to Turgot although none of his letters or other documents extant conclusively prove his authorship. After Franklin's death, the infamous Baron Trenck argued in court that he had written the Latin epigram.[7] Turgot on June 5, 1776, alluded to the verses in his correspondence without compromising himself by admitting authorship. "On the subject of America," he wrote to du Pont de Nemours, "here are some Latin and French inscriptions for the portrait of Franklin by an anonymous writer. Copy them with your own hand and burn the original." [8] Since Turgot occupied a high government position, this injunction may have been motivated by caution rather than literary modesty.

John Adams, who was visibly irked by the French adulation of Franklin, expressed two different theories attributing the Latin epigram to sources other than Turgot. On December 15, 1809, he wrote to F. A. Vanderkemp: [9]

> . . . When I was in Leyden, a gentleman was introduced to me, I know not by whom, who presented me with a small volume of Latin poetry of his own composition. In it was the famous compliment to Dr. Franklin,—
>
> > Eripuit coelo fulmen, sceptrumque tyrannis,
>
> and I always understood that gentleman to be the author of it. Can you tell me his name? It has been, in France and the world, attributed to Mr. Turgot; but I have always understood that Mr. Turgot took it from that volume, and only altered it to *"Eripuit coelo fulmen; mox sceptrum tyrannis."* Pray, tell me, if you can, the name and character of that Leyden Latin poet, and whether my memory has not deceived me.

Apparently Adams' correspondent had no knowledge of a Latin poet, for two years later Adams had a new theory. His exposition of it in the *Boston Patriot*, May 15, 1811, is notable, not for its clues to authorship, but for its statement of the significance of the epigram as a measure of Franklin's celebrity.[10]

> . . . To condense all the rays of this glory to a focus, to sum it up in a single line, to impress it on every mind and transmit it to all posterity, a motto was devised for his picture, and soon became familiar to the memory of every school-boy who understood a word of Latin:—
>
> > "Eripuit coelo fulmen sceptrumque tyrannis."
>
> Thus it appeared at first, and the author of it was held in a mysterious obscurity. But, after some time, M. Turgot altered it to
>
> > "Eripuit coelo fulmen; mox sceptra tyrannis."
>
> By the first line, the rulers of Great Britain and their arbitrary oppressions of the Colonies were alone understood. By the second was intimated that Mr. Franklin was soon to destroy or at least to dethrone all kings and abolish all monarchical governments. This, it cannot be disguised, flattered at that time the ruling popular passion of all Europe. It was at first hinted that it was written in Holland; but I have long entertained a suspicion, from many circumstances, that Sir William Jones, who undoubtedly furnished Mr. Franklin with his motto,
>
> > "Non sine Diis animosus infans,"

sent him the *Eripuit coelo,* and that M. Turgot only added the *mox sceptra.*

We see that Adams himself gave up the theory of Dutch authorship, and there is no evidence to associate Sir William Jones in any way with the epigram. It is possible, as Adams suggests, that Turgot found the epigram in some obscure author and adapted it to his own purposes by adding the adverb *mox.* All evidence, however, indicates that the reverse is what actually took place—that the original version utilized *mox* and that it was eliminated in subsequent printings. Condorcet states unequivocally in his *Vie de Turgot* that Turgot was the author and prints the version with *mox.*[11]

Franklin gave his opinion of the verses in two of his letters that have since been published. John Jay, minister plenipotentiary to Spain in 1780, had written to him requesting a print of his portrait, and Franklin sent him one bearing Turgot's verses, modestly explaining that the extravagance of the praise was due to the contemporary French tendency to exaggerate (June 13, 1780).[12] Later when the French poet Félix Nogaret sent Franklin a translation of the epigrammatic first line into French and asked his opinion of it, Franklin replied (March 8, 1781) that modesty kept him from making any observation—"except that it ascribes too much to me, especially in what relates to the Tyrant; the Revolution having been the work of many able and brave Men, wherein it is sufficient Honour for me if I am allowed a small Share."[13]

Franklin is said to have written in almost identical terms to Turgot: "I shall draw your attention merely to two inexactitudes in the original line. In spite of my experiments with electricity, thunder continues to strike at our noses and beards, and, as for the tyrant, we have been more than a million men occupied in taking away his scepter."[14]

As soon as the Latin epigram began to circulate, d'Alembert wrote the following interesting letter to Jean Baptiste Antoine Suard:[15]

You are aware of the line about Franklin:

Eripuit coelo fulmen, mox sceptra tyrannis.

I should agree with La Harpe that *sceptrumque* is more appropriate, first since *mox sceptra* is a little harsh, and also because *mox,* according to the dictionary of Gessner, which gives examples, signifies equally *statim* or *deinde,* which leads to an equivocation *mox eripuit* or *mox eripiet.*

Be that as it may, I have tried to translate this line for Franklin's portrait.

> Tu vois le sage courageux
> Dont l'heureux et mâle génie
> Arracha le tonnerre aux dieux,
> Et le sceptre à la tyrannie.

If you find these lines tolerable enough so that I shall not be ridiculed for them, you may put them in the Paris paper, even with my name; I shall be honored for this homage paid to Franklin, but still only on the condition that you find them printable; as I am not pretentious about them, I shall be quite content if you reject them as bad.

One might also write for the third line: *a ravi le tonnerre aux cieux,* or *aux dieux.* I prefer the other, but you may choose.

Here are some other lines which I have written this night for the same portrait, for you see that I am at the moment like Mascarille, *incommodé de la veine poétique.* You may make use of them in the same manner and under the same conditions.

> Sa vertu, son courage et sa simplicité,
> De Rome ont retracé le caractère antique;
> Et cher à la raison, cher à l'humanité,
> Il éclaira l'Europe, et sauva l'Amérique.

Would you prefer the first line like this:

> Son généreux courage et sa simplicité.

Or would you prefer the first two lines in this way:

> Par son noble courage et sa simplicité,
> De Rome il retraça le caractère antique.

The latter are linked a little more smoothly with the two following; but the others contain the additional quality of *vertu,* which is perhaps not a matter of indifference.

I wrote the third line at first,

> Et cher à la raison comme à l'humanité.

It is less poetic than the other, but it seems to me that there is something more interesting conveyed by the simplicity of the turn. However I lean toward the other; you may choose.

But in the four lines of the second group, do you not prefer *Sparta* to *Rome?* It seems to me that Sparta is more valuable since there has always been but a single characteristic associated with Sparta, whereas Rome has frequently changed. Nevertheless, the word *antique* may indicate ancient Rome.

D'Alembert must have seen an early version of the Latin epigram since he quotes the second hemistich as *mox sceptra tyrannis.* The majority of printed versions read, *sceptrumque tyrannis,* the emendation that d'Alembert and La Harpe favored.

D'Alembert's translation together with his emendation was forthwith published in *Le Courrier de l'Europe,*[16] where he is described as one of the greatest geometricians of Europe, one who joins to the profundity of the sciences all the graces of the subject. Two years later his own verses were likewise printed in *Le Courrier* in the following form: [17]

> Sa vertu, son courage & sa simplicité,
> De Sparta ont retracé le caractère antique;
> Et cher à la raison, cher à l'humanité,
> Il éclaira l'Europe & sauva l'Amérique.

One notices that in this version the editor (or the author) has substituted *Sparta* for *Rome,* but otherwise none of d'Alembert's second choices have been incorporated.

Of the various critics, both French and American, who have noted Latin parallels to Turgot's epigram, Grimm seems to have been the first. In his *Correspondance littéraire* (April, 1778) he pointed out that the first hemistich derives from the *Astronomicon* of Manilius (I, 104).[18] Here the poet is speaking of Epicurus.

> Eripuit Jovi fulmen, viresque tonandi.

It has also been compared to the *Anti-Lucretius* of the Cardinal Polignac (I, 1747).[19]

> Eripuitque Jovi fulmen, Phoeboque sagittas.

The most pointed tribute to Turgot's epigram appeared after the death of both Turgot and Franklin in a review of Franklin's *Memoirs* in *Le Mercure de France* (juin 1791).[20] The author, Chamfort, contrasts Turgot's epigram with the most famous English verses about Franklin, verses that had been paraphrased in France among the additions to the Buisson edition of Franklin's *Mémoires.* These English verses, which the French critic justly describes as a malicious eulogy (éloge malin), were actually written many years before Franklin's death by an enemy of Franklin and the American Revolution, an American Loyalist Jonathan

Odell. The lines are not a funeral elegy as they have sometimes been interpreted, but a subtle attack on Franklin's political career disguised as a tribute to his scientific genius. The ingenuity of the lines consists in a play on the word *urn,* used to suggest a funeral urn, but describing a stove in a similar shape. The complete title is "Inscription for a Curious Chamber-Stove, in the Form of an Urn, so contrived as to make the Flame descend, instead of rise, from the Fire: Invented by Doctor Franklin."

Many manuscript copies of these verses circulated widely throughout the colonies. As a result of their anonymity, they were attributed to several Philadelphians, among them the wife of Franklin's most jealous critic, William Smith, the man who by one of the least fortunate choices in American history was chosen after Franklin's death to deliver the official panegyric of Franklin in America. The sincerity of Smith's performance can be judged from the fact that he warmly praised the following lines in a memorandum concerning his eulogium of Franklin.[21]

> Like Newton sublimely he soared
> To a summit before unattained;
> New regions of science explored,
> And the palm of philosophy gained.
>
> With a spark which he caught from the skies,
> He displayed an unparalleled wonder;
> And we saw with delight and surprise,
> That his rod could secure us from thunder.
>
> Oh! had he been more wise to pursue
> The track for his talents designed,
> What a tribute of praise had been due
> To the teacher and friend of mankind.
>
> But to covet political fame
> Was in him a degrading ambition;
> The spark that from Lucifer came
> Enkindled the blaze of sedition.
>
> Let candor then write on his urn,
> "Here lies the renowned inventor,
> Whose flame to the skies ought to burn,
> But inverted, descends to the centre." [22]

The enemies of Franklin highly admired the final stanza, a judgment revealing at least as much partiality as esthetic penetration.

In truth the lines are ambiguous; one cannot be sure whether they mean that Franklin's political views were self-centered or merely that they were not divinely inspired.

The French reviewer of Franklin's *Memoirs* saw these verses only in translation, the last part of which I shall print along with his pertinent and just comparison of these lines to Turgot's epigram.

". . . Thus sincerity will write on his urn: Here rests the renowned inventor. His genius, like the flame, should have raised itself toward the skies, but forced and perverted, it descends towards the earth, and the spark reenters the somber abode from which it came."

One cannot deny that this comparison is ingenious. And here is one of a more beautiful kind:

> *Eripuit coelo fulmen, sceptrumque tyrannis.*

A minister of France, M. Turgot, when he was in office wrote this line for the bust of Franklin, while a simple private citizen of England put together the rhymes we have read in translation. Here is a contrast which is not at all to the advantage of the English versifier. Perhaps it even betokens a marked change in the spirit of the two peoples.

It seems to me that this is one of the most penetrating comments ever made concerning Franklin's literary reputation. Although Odell was a Tory and an enemy of Franklin, his verses are the best in English ever to be written about him, and during Franklin's lifetime they enjoyed great vogue throughout Franklin's own state of Pennsylvania. The contrast in the verses of Odell and of Turgot symbolizes not only the difference between the French and the English national spirit, but also the reception and recognition accorded to Franklin in his native America and in his adopted home France. This same contrast is further illustrated by the eulogies after the death of Franklin, which I shall discuss in a subsequent chapter.

There is more to be said about the translation of Turgot's epigram. Masson, who had seen d'Alembert's translation in *Le Courrier de l'Europe,* sent Franklin his own attempt (June 22, 1778).[23]

> Il arracha par ses rares talens
> La foudre aux dieux, le sceptre aux tyrans.

Du Pont rendered it: [24]

> Il a, par ses travaux, toujours plus étonnans,
> Ravi la foudre aux Dieux, et le sceptre aux Tyrans.

Félix Nogaret not only translated Turgot's epigram, but sent Franklin critical remarks on the difficulty of making an adequate translation in as few words as the original Latin (March 2, 1781).[25] Every previous French translation had required at least one additional line. Nogaret took for illustration a version that had appeared during the previous year in *l'Almanach des Muses*.

> Cet homme que tu vois, sublime en tous les tems,
> Dérobe aux dieux la foudre et le sceptre aux tyrans.

The first line, Nogaret felt, was supererogatory. He suggested as an improvement *arrache* for *dérobe*, but even with this change he felt that this single line would fail to comprise the full meaning. A noun or pronoun would have to be added, but to make such an addition would overburden the meter. He suggested as a compromise, therefore, a line supplying the pronoun but eliminating the images of *foudre* and *sceptre*.

> On l'a vu désarmer les tyrans et les dieux.

The omission of *foudre* and *sceptre* he justified on the grounds that they were implied by the sense. To disarm Jupiter is to take away his thunder; to disarm a tyrant is to take away his sceptre. The Latin *coelo*, Nogaret felt, was a concept more embracing than the French *cieux*. He substituted, therefore, the word *dieux*, which refers specifically to beings. Of his translation he concluded, "I do not say that the matter gains, but the poetry does not lose."

Translations of the epigram found their way into a number of quite different literary genres. Billardon de Sauvigny, for example, worked a version into an American battlefield scene in his drama *Vashington, ou la liberté du nouveau monde*, 1791. The French ambassador is addressing Washington.

> Ce génie immortel, l'homme de tous les tems,
> Qui dirigea la foudre et chassa les tyrans,
> Politique profond et philosophe austère,
> Franklin, cher aux Français.

Abbé Morellet used the idea of the first hemistich as one stanza of a long drinking song in honor of his friend.[26]

> Comme un aigle audacieux,
> Il a volé jusqu'aux cieux,
> Et dérobé le tonnerre
> Dont ils effrayaient la terre,
>   Heureux larcin
> De l'habile Benjamin.

Abbé Louis Gabriel Bourdon in a verse dialogue *Voyage d'Amérique,* 1786, refurbished the concept as evidence of intellectual life in America.[27]

> Ce n'est point cependant qu'en ce Monde nouveau,
> Comme le vil Sauvage admiré par Rousseau,
> Des Sciences, les Arts, dédaignant la culture,
> L'homme soit insensible à leur volupté pure.
> Par leurs talens divers servant tous deux l'Etat,
> Francklin & Washington brillent du même éclat.
> Tandis que de Passy le sage politique,
> Bienfaiteur des humains en morale, en physique,
> Par-tout victorieux, triomphoit à la fois
> De la foudre des Dieux & de celle des Rois.

The most ingenious version of all is that of the Comte d'Estaing, a famous naval hero who participated in the American Revolution. In his version, which appeared on the title page of a political essay, he cleverly combines the tribute to Franklin with the proud statement that Franklin had corrected his essay, *Apperçu hazardé sur l'exportation dans les colonies,* 1790, dedicated to Franklin.[28]

> Toi qui corrigeas tout, le tonnerre, & les Rois,
> Nos foyers trop brûlants, les exclusives loix,
> Peuples, discours, & sons; & même mon ouvrage;
> Revis, & par tes traits fais valoir cet hommage.

A note by the editor on the verso explains the meaning of these lines. Franklin had corrected overheated living rooms by his Pennsylvania fireplace—and had corrected the laws of Pennsylvania by abrogating restrictions on public office based on religious affiliation. He had corrected sound by his Harmonica—and had corrected literary works when he read proof for his own printing press. There is no reason to wonder, therefore, that he should have corrected a work by d'Estaing when he was at Passy.

D'Estaing's essay is a defense of transporting vagrants to the colonies as a salutary social principle. When we remember Franklin's vigorous protests against the same system in America in his *Exporting of Felons to the Colonies*, 1751, it is hard to believe that he could have sanctioned the arguments of d'Estaing. Even though the latter's scheme concerns primarily beggars and volunteers rather than hardened criminals, it is antithetical in sentiments to Franklin's earlier essay.

Because of the tremendous vogue of Turgot's epigram, scores of other aspiring poets tried their hand at composing verses for Franklin's portrait. Even before Turgot's epigram, French verses had appeared under Franklin's portrait—in 1773 on the frontispiece of Dubourg's edition of Franklin's *Œuvres*.

> Il a ravi le feu des Cieux
> Il fait fleurir les Arts en des Climats sauvages
> L'Amérique le place à la tête des Sages
> La Grèce l'auroit mis au nombre de ses Dieux.

An English admirer, perhaps Franklin himself, translated them for the English press.[29]

> To steal from Heaven its sacred fire he taught,
> The arts to thrive in savage Climes he brought:
> In the New World the first of Men esteem'd;
> Among the Greeks a God he had been deem'd.

Four years later, in the midst of the American Revolution, Dubourg wrote a quatrain much more incendiary.[30]

> C'est l'honneur et l'appui du nouvel hémisphère
> Les flots de l'océan débordent à sa voix.
> Il réprime, ou dirige à son gré le tonnerre,
> Qui désarme les dieux put-il craindre des rois.

Grimm reported in his *Correspondance littéraire* (October, 1777) that these verses were made expressly for the portrait of Franklin designed by Cochin and engraved by Saint-Aubin, but the censor considered himself obliged to suppress them as blasphemous.[31] For this reason Dubourg's lines do not appear on any of the Saint-Aubin portraits now in existence.

The verses from Franklin's *Œuvres* were apparently known in manuscript as well as in print. La Harpe circulated them in his

Correspondance littéraire (Lettre LXIII) along with another quatrain by M. Target, described as one of the best lawyers of the bar, who was also a personal friend of Franklin.[32]

> Le voilà ce mortel, dont l'heureuse industrie
>   Au tonnerre imposa des loix.
> Il est beau d'asservir la nature au génie:
>   Il est plus beau de triompher des rois.

Du Pont de Nemours apparently sent the following variant to an English friend of Franklin for criticism:

> C'est Franklin, ce mortel dont l'heureuse industrie
> Sut enchaîner la foudre et lui donner des Loix.
> C'est lui dont la raison affermissant la voix
> Du joug de l'Injustice affranchit sa Patrie;
> Il désarma les Dieux, Il réprime les Rois.

The friend replied, September 5, 1775, a time when Americans uniformly attributed their grievances to Parliament, not to the Crown, that "The last line is too strong, might have pass'd when Plurality of Gods were in fashion, and when Kings were Tyrants and were not pesterd with bad ministers." [33]

When Franklin in 1781 asked an engraver to cast some special types for his press at Passy, the engraver, Fournier, printed off a sample sheet with other verses for Franklin's portrait.[34]

> Honneur du nouveau Monde & de l'Humanité,
> Ce Sage aimable & vrai les guide & les éclaire;
> Comme un autre Mentor, il cache à l'oeil vulgaire,
> Sous les traits d'un Mortel, une Divinité.

These verses may be identified as the work of Aimé Ambroise Joseph Feutry, a member of the American Philosophical Society, published originally in his *Nouveaux opuscules,* 1779, along with several other verse tributes to Franklin.[35]

After the sensational balloon ascents of Montgolfier, one of Franklin's fellow Masons, Hilliard d'Auberteuil, compared Montgolfier to Franklin as a kindred conqueror of the skies. His lines appeared in the *Mémoires secrets,* December 24, 1784.

> Si Jupiter veut nous réduire en poudre,
> Sage Franklin, tu lui précis tes loix,
> Et Montgolfier, plus hardi mille fois,
> Va jusqu'au ciel lui disputer la foudre.

Several similar epigrammatic tributes to Franklin exist in manuscript form in the American Philosophical Society, but a printing of them would add little to the story of Franklin's reputation. The verses that enjoyed contemporary vogue were those of Turgot, Dubourg, and d'Alembert, of which the first two at least were in great measure a labor of love. All three, it should be noted, expressed advanced political concepts. The epigram of Turgot, which attained international fame, undoubtedly had some effect in preparing public opinion for the ideals of the French Revolution.

As we have seen in our survey of works of fiction, not everyone in France was a partisan of Franklin or of the American Revolution. In verse also, a satirical portrait has survived under the title *Stances sur les Insurgens.*[36]

Entre nous, ces fameux athlètes
Que vous accablez de lauriers,
Leurs vertus sont dans les gazettes,
Leurs vues sont dans leurs foyers.

Vous voyez leur mobile unique,
Ce vieux Docteur *in partibus*
Dont l'insidieuse rubrique
Vous échauffe de ses rébus.

Sur l'Amérique consternée
Plaçant le bout d'un conducteur,
De l'autre à l'Europe étonnée
Il lance le feu destructeur.

Caméléon octogénaire,
Son esprit se ploye aisément;
De la France & de l'Angleterre,
Le fourbe rit également.

La haine dont son coeur regorge
Fait qu'en ses propos inouïs,
Si Louis lui répond de George,
George lui répond de Louis.

Ce Hancock qu'il tient en tutelle,
Aux dehors plats, aux sens grossiers,
Peut fournir un riche modèle
A nos délicats financiers.

Franklin de l'or du fanatique
Ebauche son hardi projet,
Et dans cette farce héroïque
Il en fit son milord Huyzet.

Many longer poems were written in praise of Franklin, a large number of which served merely as a pretext for asking him favors, usually monetary. The number of these now existing in manuscript form shows either that Franklin liked to save scraps of paper or that he was tolerant of bad poetry if it had something to do with idealistic political concepts. The poems that found their way into print, however, are of a different character. Each had some independent quality besides the merely occasional feature of celebrating Franklin.

Franklin himself printed one of these on his Passy press—a light piece written to accompany a gold-headed walking stick, emblematic of the crown of liberty, when it was presented to Franklin by Madame de Forbach, Comtesse Douairière de Deux Ponts.[37] According to the progress theme of the poem, the wood of the cane had been seized on the plains of Marathon by the Goddess of Liberty before abandoning Greece. It had been transported to Switzerland, where the valiant mountaineers fought against the invading Austrians, and more recently to Trenton, where Washington defeated the British. The poet assures Franklin that his possession of this symbol of victory will assure him of a place in the Temple of Memory. Probably this tribute led Franklin later to dedicate the walking stick to Washington in his will.

An even lighter effusion was inspired by a minor poetess, resident of Nîmes, Madame de Bourdic, who became acquainted with Franklin during a sojourn in Paris in 1783-1784. On her return to the provinces, an anonymous admirer twitted her in "Epître à Madame la Baronne de Bourdic, sur ses relations avec le Docteur Franklin," which appeared both in the *Journal de Paris*, July 5, 1784, and in the *Almanach des Muses*, 1785. What a spectacle, wrote the poet, to see this elegant lady abandon the ballroom and the theater for a philosophic Quaker! Grudgingly he granted that the Nestor of Philadelphia was adored on two continents, that his bold hand had snatched the thunder from the gods, the sceptre from the tyrants, but he argued that Franklin had honors enough without monopolizing the lovely de Bourdic. Playfully he suggested that if Franklin were her own age, they would have enjoyed less incorporeal relations.

Franklin's scientific exploits were celebrated in the spirit of Turgot's epigram in an ode by M. Paris of the Oratory, entitled *Le Fluide Electrique*.[38] In the passage devoted to Franklin, the poet addresses the American philosopher as one who knows how to decompose the fire that animates us and to lay expiring thunderbolts at our feet. The poet then considers Franklin as a symbol of his age. The eighteenth century, he affirms, will live because of Franklin's accomplishments and will receive the homage of all other ages whenever the name of Franklin is uttered to posterity.

One of Franklin's fellow Masons, Joseph François Michaud, read before the Lodge of the Nine Sisters, July 14, 1791, a long poetic tribute entitled *Franklin législateur du nouveau monde*. It was printed in an anthology of pieces read before the society and also as a separate work.[39] In the opening stanza Michaud gives an idyllic picture of America, favored in climate, virtue, and freedom, the latter won through the wisdom of Franklin, who was considered as a tutelary god. The second stanza describes the philosophical calm of his death. Franklin awaits the end without fear; he stems the tears of his friends by assuring them that he abandons his life to God, confident of his virtue and patriotism. Succeeding stanzas, rich in poetic imagination, have little relation to actual truth. In a deserted and tranquil valley, not far from the Potomac River, Franklin's ashes repose on a simple and majestic altar to which his friends repair to sing his praise. Among them, John Adams, who in real life had very little affection for Franklin, delivers a speech lauding Franklin's virtue, his leadership during the Revolution and his subsequent law-making, his economic theories and his electrical discoveries. As the skies become brighter, Franklin himself descends from heaven in a cloud of light to depict the glories of his celestial habitation. In paradise he had seen Solon and the heroes of the Tiber, jealous of the liberty of the American people, and Cato, who was now no longer so proud of being a Roman. Finally, Franklin heralds the demise of the Iron Age and the birth of the Golden Age under the laws of Liberty: the sun is purer, nature is more beautiful, and society returns to happiness and man to virtue.

A dramatic poet and early romanticist, Billardon de Sauvigny, portrayed Franklin in two apologues in verse. "L'heureux fruit de l'instruction" traces Franklin's gradual political progress from wit to rebel.[40] In a prior prose paragraph the English court is described immediately after the War of 1756, when the ministers, taking cognizance of the enormous colonial sacrifices in men and materials, realize that the colonies have become extremely powerful. They decide to incite them to insurrection in order to deprive them of their charters and treat them as an enslaved nation. The poem presents Franklin's behavior in the face of this situation. At first he writes satirical pamphlets to instruct the people and show the need for reforming, but by degrees he realizes that open resistance is the only means of procuring liberty.

In a longer poem, "Les derniers adieux de Francklin [sic] aux français," Sauvigny describes the farewell scene,[41] in which Franklin himself speaks words of consolation to enable his friends to endure the pain of separation. His friends, tears in their eyes, assure him that the French people also are rising to expel tyrants and regain supreme authority. Franklin, congratulating them, reviews his own experiences. Hoping to remedy colonial grievances at the British court, he had found there only egotism and corruption, but in France as soon as he had acquainted the people with the patriotic ideals of the Americans, they had responded with sympathetic warmth. He praises their courage in espousing the same cause of human rights and predicts they will be an example for the whole universe. Although he warns that the united weight of monarchs will be pitted against the Revolution, he assures them that he has cast their horoscope and has read their eventual triumph. Finally, Franklin prophesies that the new, freed French nation will have as its boundaries those that nature prescribed, the Pyrenees, the Alps, the seas, and the Rhine.

Most interesting, most finished, and most original of all the poems on Franklin is a dramatic narrative of brisk, ringing verse with the simple title *Le Docteur Franklin, Poëme.*[42] The author of this work of twenty-six pages, divided into four chants, is M. le Manissier, professor of humanities at the Collège du Mont in Caen. In the opening chant, after an invocation to the amiable Goddess Liberty, Franklin is seen crossing the ocean en route to France with a retinue of 100 warriors. The elements favor these new argonauts; the splendor of the sea and the myriads of stars in the sky inspire Franklin's companions to pour out praise for the magnificence of heaven. Franklin agrees with them that they should be grateful for divine blessings, but warns them against the error of assuming that God exists for their benefit rather than the reverse. He points out that the suns of the universe are not created exclusively for our world, that God does not limit his works to those that concern human beings. Each world indeed has its own sun—or rather, each sun has many worlds, for a single sun can give light to twenty planets. After a long description of the sun's influence upon the seasons and climates of the world, Franklin utters his own hymn of praise on the theme that the sun itself confounds atheism.

> O Soleil! que ton cours me paraît merveilleux!
> Que tu m'annonces bien la sagesse des Cieux!
> Quand tu brilles sur nous serait-il des Athées?
> Et des humains leurs voix sont-elles écoutées?

Arrived in France, Franklin addresses the French monarch, imploring his supreme goodness to aid the people of Boston. The former enemies of the French king are now beseeching his aid to free them from the English yoke, and Louis, in reply, compliments Franklin for his active prudence.

> FRANKLIN ne voit sur lui s'élever que les Dieux.

In the second chant, Franklin outlines the causes of the American war. The English had violated the peaceful economy of America by imposing tributes so onerous that its prosperity had been converted to desolation. Franklin says that until that moment he had lived apart from political affairs in devotion to philosophy. He loved peace, hated war, but seeing the carnage of the English, suddenly realized that he must dedicate himself to the salvation of his country. Kept by age from bearing arms, his only means of serving was to appeal to Louis for aid. He proceeds to praise the august French monarch, viewing him as the destined rampart of liberty in Boston. Louis responds with compliments:

La Vertu de FRANKLIN ne m'est pas inconnue;
Sa réputation jusqu'à nous est venue.
La Justice elle-même emprunte votre voix;
Oracle des humains, vous leur dictez ces loix.

Louis promises French aid as an ally against England and fore-
casts the defeat of the English fleet by the French forces under
d'Estaing.

In the third chant, Franklin returns to America by way of Cuba
and Santo Domingo, colonies of Spain. Here he sheds tears over
the ravages of the Spanish, who have destroyed ancient cultures
and overthrown the native agricultural prosperity. He laments
the fate of Montezuma and condemns the ferocious Cortez. Describing the mines where miserable Negroes and Indians are re-
duced to perpetual slavery, he scores the perversion of nature
by which the advantages of fertile soil and beneficent climate are
neglected for mineral wealth. He contrasts these scenes of desolation with the utopian city of Philadelphia and the benevolent
laws of Pennsylvania, to which he returns after passing the coasts
of Florida and Carolina.

The fourth chant is partly allegorical. In it, Washington, van-
quisher of tyranny and servitude, erects a Temple of Liberty, containing pictorial representations of the peaceful prosperity of
America. But there are two enemies of liberty, Pride and Avarice,
which stand guard, allowing only Christians to enter, excluding
Negroes and Indians. The latter protest that since they also are
human and children of God they should have the same rights as
others. Washington, in the name of the All-Powerful Supreme
Being, suggests that they be allowed to enter the Temple, but
makes no forthright statement; instead he expresses gratitude for
the aid of Louis XVI in helping to break the bondage of slavery.
Franklin in similar strains recites his interviews with Louis and
his ministers and celebrates the victory over the English with the
aid of d'Estaing. But, he urges, it was primarily Liberty that delivered Boston, and Liberty is incompatible with Negro slavery.
He concludes, therefore, with an impassioned plea for the freeing
of all slaves in America, Indian and Negro.

Obviously this author had very little knowledge of Franklin
and even less about America. His poem should be considered less
a personal tribute to Franklin than an imaginative defense of the

principles for which Franklin stood. Perhaps even better than an open panegyric of Franklin's virtues, this narrative of Franklin as a champion of human rights is evidence of the enviable reputation he enjoyed in contemporary France.

9. DRAMA

The French theater also served as a means of paying tribute to Franklin. While he did not figure as the protagonist of any major dramatic work during the eighteenth century, he did play an important role in a number of works dramatic in form. First of these is the allegorical tableau of Le Roux, *Dialogue entre Pasquin & Marforio,* 1779, which we have already discussed.[1] Although never intended for stage presentation, it has certain dramatic features— to be sure those of a masque rather than of a comedy of situation, but there is indubitably movement in the dialogue.

The decade immediately after Franklin's death—the era of the French Revolution—brought with it a number of plays on the theme of the reception of departed heroes in the afterworld, dramatic counterparts of the popular dialogues of the dead of the preceding century. The same spirit that led to the substitution of the heroes of the Pantheon for the saints of the church apparently brought about a revived interest in the pagan shades as a compensation for the loss of the Christian heaven. In *Le journaliste des ombres,* 1790, by Aude, a newspaper man descends to the nether regions to interview the philosophic mentors of the Revolution concerning their opinions of the events that their works had helped to initiate.[2] Rousseau, Voltaire, the abbé de Saint Pierre, and others are praising the new constitution, when Franklin appears as a passenger in Charon's boat.

> Rhadamante le voit, court, l'embrasse & s'écrie,
> C'est le rival des Dieux, le Dieu de sa patrie,
> Le Vengeur de l'humanité

Notes to this chapter begin on page 248.

L'Apôtre de la liberté
Le Sage de Philadelphie.

Voltaire, Rousseau, and the others welcome Franklin effusively. To Voltaire's question as to why he left the earth at the very moment that liberty and justice are beginning to triumph, Franklin replies that when he saw his dearest wishes accomplished on two continents, he realized that he was at last ready to retire.

> Qu'avois-je à voir sous le ciel qui l'éclaire?
> Tout avoit de mon coeur rempli les voeux ardens.
> J'ai vu l'égalité, ce supplice des grands,
> Jeter dans l'univers ses racines profondes.
> J'ai vu la chute des tyrans
> Et la liberté des deux mondes.

Both Voltaire and Rousseau laud Franklin for his service to universal liberty, and Franklin returns the compliment to France by honoring Lafayette's role in the American Revolution.

In a similar piece, *L'ombre de Mirabeau*, 1791, Franklin joins with Voltaire, Rousseau, and a number of the ancients in honoring Mirabeau as he enters the Elysian Fields. When Voltaire's remains were taken to the Pantheon, a play celebrating the event, *Le panthéon français*, 1791, brought together a number of departed notables including Voltaire, Rousseau, and Franklin. In a poem on the same theme (in *Les Sabates Jacobites*, Nos. 33-34, 1791), Rousseau and his friends in the Elysian Fields encounter Franklin in the company of Solon, Lycurgus, and Plato.

The second play in which Franklin plays a major role is a dramatization of a commemorative ceremony in honor of Franklin held by the printers of Paris, August 10, 1790. The play, *L'imprimeur ou la fête de Franklin,* which was staged eight months later, has as its hero Germeuil, a fellow-printer and ardent admirer of Franklin.[3] The scene is his printing shop where a bust of Franklin is to be dedicated. On the day of the celebration Germeuil addresses a gathering of soldiers and printers, pointing out that no man could serve them as a better model than Franklin to teach them regard for liberty. Born poor and obscure, he became the preceptor of nations, the savior of America, the patriarch of liberty. Following closely the address delivered on the occasion of the actual ceremony, Germeuil pledges himself to follow Franklin's example. "Like us, my friends, Franklin began as an apprentice printer—and while he followed the trade not an obscene line appeared on his presses—he employed his types exclusively for works sanctioned by the government, by morals, by law, and by truth." At the actual ceremonies, a speaker had urged the printers to serve as self-censors in the service of reason and truth; apparently at this time the printers were suspected of seditious or anti-revolutionary activities and were being exhorted by the government to remain loyal.

In the finale of the play, Franklin is praised by verses such as the following:

> Si vous voulés au vrai civisme
> décerner l'immortalité
> offrir à qui l'a mérité
> l'hommage du patriotisme;
> Ah! c'est toujours, toujours francklin
> que nommera notre refrain.

> *Choeur*
> oui, chaque jour, couronne, et gloire
> Chantons célébrons sans fin
> la mémoire
> de francklin

Diderot in a one-act play, "La pièce et le prologue," composed about 1772 and retouched in 1777, alluded briefly to Franklin as "un acuto quakero," probably to give a contemporary air to the work.[4] And in a German translation, 1793, of Diderot's *Les bijoux indiscrets,* the name of a character, Charron, is converted to Franklin.[5]

Franklin appeared as the symbol of liberty also in *L'époux ré-publicain* by Maurin de Pompigny, presented in 1794. This is a species of heroic play in which the principal character denounces his wife and son to the authorities for anti-revolutionary activity. The protagonist has renounced his aristocratic name "Leroi" in favor of the name "Franklin," which he has taken as a symbol of republicanism. Newly-named, he explains to his friends, "as soon as it was permissible to change one's patron, J took Franklin for mine, and I love to bear his name. It reflects the sincerity of his character and the liberty of his country."

Finally, a dramatic author, A. Sérieys, presented a dialogue between Franklin and Mirabeau in the same volume with his

tragedy in three acts, *La Mort de Robespierre,* 1801.[6] Employing
the form of a dialogue of the dead—a genre that we have seen
was not far removed from actual dramatic works of the time—
Sérieys considers Franklin as an emblem of constitutional reform
and contrasts him with the demagogues Mirabeau and Marat. In
the opening speech of the dialogue Franklin asserts that he had
predicted the French Revolution—a fact by no means certain—
and he presents an interesting comparison between the revolutions in France and America.

> Yes, monsieur, I had predicted everything which has happened
> to the French people in consequence of a revolution poorly con-
> ceived and even less well carried out. They wanted to ape us Amer-
> icans, but they failed to understand that above all it is necessary
> to have that purity of behavior, that love of law, without which
> there cannot exist true liberty. You advanced some excellent prin-
> ciples—but the ambition of some individuals spoiled everything and
> you were not yourself far removed from serving a man who, under
> the name of Equality, carried in his heart the thirst for the throne
> and supreme power.

To these words Mirabeau replies that it is unfair to judge his
motives, which must remain concealed because of his premature
death, adding that he should be judged instead by his writings,
his discourse, and his actions. Franklin delivers a scorching in-
dictment of the latter—an appraisal of great interest in view of
the literary relations between the two men in real life.

> Do you believe that because you made my eulogy at the tribunal of
> your assembly and brought about my funeral honors, that you have
> the right to impose upon me. I am not your fellow-citizen, Monsieur
> the Count, and since I must say it, I do not like you at all. Your
> life is a tissue of perfidies and atrocities. Not content with tortur-
> ing your wife, you brought shame upon two women whom you ab-
> ducted and whose husbands you robbed. . . . And the enormous
> debts you never ceased to contract; and the false money you put into
> circulation; and the writers, the friends, whose reputation you stole
> by passing off their compositions as your own & promising to repay
> them, which you have never done; and the spirit of libertinism
> which dishonored your whole life and led you to a premature
> grave; and the reckless ambition which forced you to attempt all,
> betray all, and sacrifice all—were these minor errors of youth?

Instead of answering these accusations, Mirabeau cleverly turns
the subject to Franklin's own life.

Doctor, if we were both living you would not speak to me in this language. It is not in my character to use reprisals in the form of calumnies. Do you think, however, that your own conduct is irreproachable? Each step that you made—was it not a step toward honors or employments? Reveal, if you dare, your whole heart; explain how from a profound obscurity you attained the highest degree of elevation.

This, of course, is exactly what Franklin had done in writing his memoirs; in fact, he was the first in the history of western literature to analyze in detail his rise from obscurity to eminence. One wonders whether Sérieys was thinking of Franklin's autobiography when he wrote this passage; if so, he seems to suggest by the parallel with Mirabeau that everything in Franklin's life was not as honorable as public opinion assumed. Was Sérieys in effect an early critic of Franklin's opportunism? There is no further light on this point in the dialogue, for Franklin makes no reply to the implied slurs upon his life. He merely makes the concession to Mirabeau that he was somewhat less villainous than his successor.

Whether or not Sérieys intended his dialogue as a reflection upon Franklin's moral career, contemporary readers would probably have made the association with his *Memoirs,* which, as we shall see in the next chapter, enjoyed a considerable vogue at the time.

Part
Three

———◆———

FRANKLIN
AS A HUMAN BEING

His Own and His Friends'
Recollections and
Conversation Pieces

———◆———

Franklin's *Memoirs,* his most important literary work, is connected with France in two important ways. Franklin sent a revised copy to Passy to be read by his friends Le Veillard and La Rochefoucauld, and three of the four parts into which the autobiography is divided were first printed in French translations on French presses.[1] The second part, moreover, was written at Passy in 1784.

From the latter circumstance it might be assumed that this part would reflect the interests and perhaps the influence of Franklin's French circle. Although there is evidence to show that Franklin discussed the content of this section with his French friends, there is no reason at all for believing that his sojourn in France influenced this or the other parts of his memoirs. The section written at Passy concerns primarily his Art of Virtue or scheme for attaining moral perfection, which he included as part of his memoirs at the instigation of two of his friends who wrote to him from America and from England while he was residing at Passy. Franklin inserted their letters in the text of his memoirs as an introduction to the second part. His American friend, Abel James, exhorted him to complete his autobiography so that when published it would lead young men "to equal the industry and temperance of thy early youth." His English friend, Benjamin Vaughan, remarked on "the chance which your life will give for the forming of future great men; and in conjunction with your Art of Virtue (which you design to publish) of improving the features of private character, and consequently of aiding all happiness, both public and domestic." Franklin never published his Art of Virtue separately, but included it as the major element of the second part of his autobiography. It is obvious then that the inspiration for this section came from afar and not from Passy, where it was written.

While composing or planning his work, however, Franklin

Notes to this chapter begin on page 249.

discussed it with the abbé Morellet and with Cabanis. As we shall see in a subsequent chapter, the former sent to *Le Moniteur* Franklin's anecdote of a speckled axe before it appeared in print in the *Memoirs*,[2] and Cabanis recorded conversations with Franklin on three of the subjects in the section of the *Memoirs* written in Passy.[3] These comprise the industry and frugality of his wife, a proverb from the Bible, and the little notebook that Franklin had devised as part of his system to correct his moral faults. This little notebook he allowed Cabanis to hold and examine.

Although Franklin's French sojourn had little influence on the contents of his *Memoirs,* it had a tremendous influence on the subsequent history of the manuscripts of the work, which made their way to France as a result of the friendships Franklin had made in Passy. The story of the composition and publication of Franklin's *Memoirs* is one of the most complicated in any literature, and the work presents the most perplexing textual problems to be encountered anywhere in American letters. The reason for these problems is that Franklin wrote his *Memoirs* in three separate sections, then had two copies made that incorporated a number of changes, and later wrote a fourth section. At present the manuscript of the original version is still in existence, but only printed texts of the revised versions exist. No one can be sure whether Franklin would have wished the original or the revised version to be considered as the authoritative text. The differences, chiefly in phrasing rather than ideas, are fundamental enough to give each version a distinctive character.

We are not concerned with these textual variants, however, but with the history of the publication of the *Memoirs* in France. To explain this it is first necessary to outline the four parts:

Part I, comprising 44 per cent of the entire work, was written at Twyford, England, in 1771. It concerns Franklin's life to 1730.

Part II, comprising 9 per cent of the entire work, was written at Passy in 1784. It contains Franklin's scheme for moral perfection.

Part III, comprising 40 per cent of the entire work, was written at Philadelphia in 1788. It continues the narrative to Franklin's arrival in London, July, 1757.

Part IV, comprising 7 per cent of the entire work, was presumably written at Philadelphia between November, 1789, and Franklin's death, April, 1790.

The first part, Franklin says, was written primarily for his family; the other three for the public.

In 1789, Franklin's grandson, Benjamin Franklin Bache, made two copies of the first three parts. Franklin sent one copy to England to be read and criticized by his friends Benjamin Vaughan and Richard Price and the other to France to be read by Le Veillard and La Rochefoucauld. These two copies embodied the revisions already alluded to. Franklin retained in his own possession the original manuscript and later added to it Part IV. This manuscript is now in existence at the Huntington Library in California. At the time of his death, Franklin willed the original manuscript to his grandson William Temple Franklin; the copy sent to England remained in the hands of Vaughan and that sent to France remained in the hands of either La Rochefoucauld or Le Veillard.

The last trace of Vaughan's copy is found in a letter that he wrote to La Rochefoucauld (June 4, 1790) announcing Franklin's death, extracts from which are now printed for the first time.[4]

It is with much concern that I inform your grace, that about the beginning of April last, Dr. Franklin was seized with an imposthume in his lungs, which was attended with pain & difficulty of breathing for 10 days & was succeeded with some days of ease, but finally carried him off about the 16: day. He was sensible, as usual, excepting a part of the last day.

He died in affluence, leaving some lands to Mr. W. T. Franklin, & the rest of his fortune chiefly to the family of his daughter Mrs. Beach. Mr. Jay & four others are his Executors.

I do not find that he continued his memoirs beyond the year 1757, but the American Philosophical Society at Philadelphia have resolved upon an Eloge, which will probably include many particulars of his life. I am told that Dr. Rush is to send me some anecdotes & papers respecting him.

The copy of his memoirs which he sent to me is still in my hands, unseen by any one excepting Dr. Price & myself, to whose opinions he was pleased to submit it. We have accordingly made some remarks, & forwarded them to America. It is probable that his Executors, or his family, or whoever shall have power herein, will not refuse to adopt the little that is proposed by us; and if similar requests have been made by Dr. Franklin to those persons at Paris to whom he transmitted another copy, it will be kind in them not to suffer his representatives in America to rest without the communication of such observations as may have occurred to them. In the meantime, every thing here will remain in its present state till we are further instructed by those who have direction concerning these papers; which rule, I presume, will be observed at Paris.

This letter tells us among other things that Vaughan and La Rochefoucauld were good friends and that Vaughan and Price had written out their opinions of Franklin's work and had suggested further changes. Unfortunately, their observations have not been preserved.

In 1791 an enterprising but unscrupulous printer, Buisson, published a French translation of Part I of the *Memoirs* together with a collection of other pieces by and about Franklin.[5] No one knows where Buisson obtained the manuscript from which this translation was made nor why he apparently had access only to Part I. That he did not see the copy in the possession of Le Veillard is apparent from a letter Le Veillard sent to *Le Moniteur*, March 2, 1791, condemning Buisson for printing Franklin's work without authorization, but admitting that Buisson's text was essentially the same as the manuscript in his possession.[6]

A short time before his death, Franklin sent me the memoirs of his life written by himself. I have translated them, and I have deferred publication only out of regard for his family and for Mr. W. T. Franklin, his grandson, to whom his ancestor willed all his manuscripts, and who proposes to make a complete edition of them, both in English and in French, in which he will insert my translation. He is at this moment in England where he is occupied with this subject, and in a few days he will return to France to complete it.

There has just been published at the establishment of Mr. Buisson a volume in octavo entitled, Mémoires de la vie privée de Benjamin Franklin, écrits par lui-même, et adressés à son fils. The first 156 pages of this volume contain indeed the beginning of Franklin's memoirs, entirely conformable to the manuscript which I possess. I do not know how the translator has been able to procure it, but I declare, and I believe it necessary to make it known, that he did not receive it from me, that I had nothing to do with the translation, that this part, which ends at 1730, is hardly a third of that which I have, which goes to 1757, and which consequently does not complete the work, and that the rest is in the hands of Mr. W. T. Franklin, who will arrange his edition in such a way that the memoirs will form one, or at most two, volumes, which may be procured separately.

Le Veillard felt obliged to make this public statement since William Temple had previously pledged him not to publish his copy nor to show it to anyone—except possibly to the member of the Academy who was to write Franklin's eulogy. William Temple made this request in a letter (May 22, 1790) shortly after Franklin's death, explaining that a publication of any part of Franklin's *Memoirs* would be prejudicial to a complete edition that he was himself preparing for publication.[7]

Condorcet, the member of the Academy chosen to write Franklin's eulogy, seems not to have seen Le Veillard's manuscript, but apparently contented himself with a paraphrase of high points of the narrative prepared expressly for him by Le Veillard. The evolution of Condorcet's oration may be traced through four separate manuscript drafts still in existence.[8] Le Veillard, in sending his paraphrase under the title "Notices tirées des mémoires de monsieur Franklin," wrote to Condorcet,

> . . . I shall not hide from you that I should be flattered if, without making the slightest eulogy of me, you could, however, make known in that of Monsieur Franklin the warm friendship which he had for me.

In response to this request Condorcet inserted the following sentence concerning Franklin's return to America: "He embarked at an English port, where he was accompanied by M. Le Veillard, who during his residence at Passy had lavished upon him all the concerns of a filial tenderness, and who wished to defer the melancholy instant of an eternal separation."[9]

It has been suggested that the Buisson translation, which appeared during the same year as Condorcet's éloge, was based upon Vaughan's copy, but there is no evidence to support this conjecture; nor does this supposition explain why the Buisson version should be confined to Part I. Another hypothesis is that when Franklin returned to America in 1785, he found Part I among his papers, revised it, and sent a copy to La Rochefoucauld before proceeding to write Part III. Then in 1789 he may have sent to France another copy of all three parts. This hypothesis is suggested by the draft of a letter among the papers of the abbé de la Roche designed to point out some of the errors in the Castéra edition of 1798.[10]

> . . . his Memoirs which go as far as 1757 had been written at this period in America. In France he said to his friends that he believed them lost in the pillage of all his papers by the English, but that he had conserved all of his notes concerning his political career and that he would complete putting them in order as soon as he returned to America. Returned to his home, he rediscovered the first part of his life conserved by one of his friends, and he immediately passed it on to the Duke de La Rochefoucauld.

This communication is not absolutely reliable. The statement that Franklin wrote part of his *Memoirs* in America about 1757 is completely inaccurate. It is quite true, however, that when he returned to America he found Part I, which he had left there in 1776, preserved by his friend Abel James. It has been established that practically all variations between the original manuscript and the revised copy exist in Part I. It is quite possible that Franklin returned to Philadelphia, bearing with him Part II, which he had composed in Passy; then rereading Part I, which he had not seen for nine years, he revised it to conform to the style of Part II, and then made two copies of his revision, retaining one for himself and sending the other to La Rochefoucauld.

Sometime between 1790 and 1792, William Temple Franklin exchanged his manuscript (the original) for the revised version in Le Veillard's hands, an exchange that may have already taken place when Le Veillard wrote his letter to *Le Moniteur*. It is not certain why William Temple Franklin wished to trade manuscripts, nor why Le Veillard was willing to cooperate. Perhaps William Temple knew that Franklin had made revisions and wished to have his grandfather's final word in his possession. Le Veillard had begun his translation with the revised copy, and after procuring the original manuscript, he changed several passages of his translation in an effort to restore the original wording. The manuscript of his translation, covering all parts, which was not printed until a few years ago, is now in the Library of Congress.[11]

The Buisson text was translated into English and published by a London printer, Robinson, in 1793. Then in 1798, Buisson brought out a fuller edition of the *Memoirs* translated by Castéra, an edition comprising a retranslation into French of Part I from the Robinson edition and a fresh translation of Part II made in Philadelphia from a manuscript loaned to the citizen Delessert. The latter had previously communicated this translation to *La Décade Philosophique*.[12]

William Temple Franklin, with the revised copy in his possession, continued gathering materials for a complete edition of Franklin's works, which he finally published in London in 1818. This edition included the revised copy of the *Memoirs* (Parts I, II and III) and marked the first publication of Part III, the only one of the four parts not to appear originally in French.

In 1828 another French publisher, Renouard, brought out a translation of the William Temple edition, with an additional feature—a translation of Part IV based on the original manuscript then in the hands of the Le Veillard family. Part IV did not appear in English until 1868, when John Bigelow printed the entire original manuscript, which he had obtained from the last descendant of the Le Veillards.

French readers of Franklin's autobiography naturally looked for resemblances to the *Confessions* of Rousseau, which had appeared in 1782. Castéra in his edition of 1798 declared that Franklin and his friends were appalled by Rousseau's *Confessions* and that Franklin's *Memoirs* was designed to offset its baneful effect.[13] It is more plausible to say that Franklin's work is a contrast to the *Confessions* than to consider it an imitation, but probably Franklin did not even consider the author of *Emile* in writing his own autobiography, particularly since he wrote Part I in 1771, eleven years before the publication of Part I of Rousseau's *Confessions*. This does not rule out the possibility that he may have given some thought to the *Confessions* in writing the later sections. Although there is no evidence that Franklin ever read Rousseau's outpourings, some of his friends had been intimates of Rousseau, particularly the Comtesse d'Houdetot, the Sophie of the *Confessions,* who once held a famous fete in Franklin's honor.[14] A communication among the papers of the abbé de la Roche, however, a companion piece to the one already quoted, forthrightly asserts that Franklin wrote quite independently of Rousseau.[15]

If the estimable editor of Mémoires sur la Vie de Franklin printed by Buisson had consulted some of the friends whom this great man had left in France and who lived with him in the greatest familiarity, he would have been able to gather interesting anecdotes and avoid the errors of fact too lightly advanced in his preface and in his notes. He would not have said that Franklin wrote his Memoirs on account of the Confessions of J. J. Rousseau. Because of the solicitation of his friends, he designed them 20 years previously and left them in America in his home, which was pillaged by the English. One of his friends saved them. They were continued at his return to Philadelphia and sent in France to the Duke de La Rochefoucauld.

Franklin read little, and his type of mind would not have appreciated the works of Rousseau, least of all his Confessions. He attached more importance to a fact well observed than to all abstract reasoning not founded either on nature or on the truth of experience. His sound reason made him prefer solidity of thought and everything which the examples and lessons of an everyday morality offer to man to the embellishments and refinements of style. His tastes of wisdom and study were based upon a groundwork of happiness and general utility. Concern for the welfare of his fellow men is revealed in all the conduct of his life and even in the most minor bagatelles which came from his pen.

Other critics might observe that Franklin and Rousseau had much more in common than is here represented. Each intended to accomplish what had never before been attempted in English or French literature—to reveal to his fellow creatures the writer's own character in all the truth of nature. Whether the autobiographies of the sages of Philadelphia and Geneva are remarkable primarily for contrasts or similarities, it was only natural for literary critics to consider them jointly.

Chamfort pointed out a significant parallel in the rise of both men from poverty to eminence: [16]

Here is something which would have appeared impossible at the beginning of the century and which is merely to be admired at the end. It is a pleasure to imagine the astonishment of the high and mighty of Europe about the year 1730, if a prophetic spirit, announcing the destinies of Franklin and Jean-Jacques Rousseau, had said to them: "Two men of the class of those whom you designate the common people, poor, destitute to the point of sleeping in the open air; the one, after establishing liberty in his nation; the other, after establishing the first foundations of social organizations, would

have the honor of having beside . . . each other a statue in the
Temple of Liberty . . . at Paris."

Chamfort was particularly impressed by Franklin's ability to see
the relations between small things and great, particularly "the
influence of minor events in youth upon character, upon the ideas
which determine the habits of a lifetime, and upon principles
which eventually decide the role one plays in the most important
circumstances."

A reviewer for *Le Moniteur* remarked that no other of the
distinguished men of the century was accorded a more universal
veneration by the French nation than was Franklin.[17] No one
else of this period who had passed upon the theater of the world
had revealed such perfect harmony between his practice and
principles, "had done so many great things with a more simple
air, had offered in his demeanor, patriarchal and venerable, a
more striking or useful contrast with our futile and corrupt manners, had more greatly advanced, although indirectly, our political regeneration." Franklin's principal claims to glory and to
the gratitude of the French people, according to this reviewer,
were his contributions to American liberty, and by indirection
to French, the influence of his presence and conversation, and
the popularity and concreteness he had given to truths that others
had rendered remote and abstract. This critic believed that the
story of his private life gives more than a sterile pleasure; by
tracing the development of his reason and his fortune, it fur-
nishes valuable lessons for all posterity.

The reviewer for the *Journal de Paris* said little about the
literary aspects of Franklin's *Memoirs,* but quoted the description
of Franklin's personal appearance from Hilliard d'Auberteuil
and discussed his influence on the French Revolution.[18] This
writer considered it incontestable that the American Revolution
had produced the French, but was not sure whether its example
would be baleful or salutary. The chief value of Franklin's work,
in his opinion, was the light it might shed on the fundamental
political question confronting the French people, whether it is
possible for an old, corrupted nation to cultivate true liberty.

The most enthusiastic of French comments on Franklin's
Memoirs was appropriately that of La Rochefoucauld, who de-

scribed the work in a eulogy of Franklin before any part of the *Memoirs* had been published.[19]

> In it, he speaks of himself as he would have spoken of another. He traces his thoughts, his actions, and even his errors and his faults. He portrays the development of his genius and of his talents with the sentiment of a clear conscience which has never had to reproach itself.
>
> In fact, Franklin's entire life, his meditations, his labors—all have been directed toward public good; but this great object that he had always in view did not close his heart toward private sentiments. He was beneficent; the charms of his society were inexpressible. He spoke little, but he did not refuse to speak; and his conversation, always interesting, was always instructive.

We see then that indirectly as a result of the friendship of La Rochefoucauld and Le Veillard, Franklin's autobiography became widely known and appreciated in France before it was even printed elsewhere.

Although French and American readers have been enjoying the *Memoirs* for over a century, there are still many unsolved problems connected with the circumstances of publication. Did Franklin send a copy of Part I alone to La Rochefoucauld? If not, how can the Buisson translation be explained? When Franklin made the two revised copies that were sent to England and France, did he make another copy for his own use? If he did not, why would he make changes—which he apparently considered improvements—and then let all copies incorporating these improvements leave his own possession? If he did make a copy for himself, why did he not add Part IV to his improved copy rather than to the original version? Unfortunately, documentary evidence that might have answered these questions seems to have disappeared.

Contemporary French readers were, of course, not concerned with these problems, of whose existence they were not even aware. So far as they were concerned, the *Memoirs* were in a sense a biographical commentary on *Bonhomme Richard,* a further opportunity of making acquaintance with the founder of American liberty.

11. BAGATELLES

As we have seen, *The Way to Wealth* is fundamentally a very miscellaneous production that Franklin himself never took very seriously, but that many of his readers loaded with moral significance. There exists in Franklin's works a related category of facetious writing, produced primarily for self-amusement, a series of humorous sallies united in spirit only by a slight overtone of didacticism. Franklin was at heart a moralist, and he found amusement in moral reflections even when combined with absurd situations or bawdy allusions. A number of minor works combining these characteristics have been jointly discussed by various critics as Franklin's bagatelles. In some, the moral overwhelms the ludicrous; in others, the ludicrous overwhelms the moral. Most critics in treating them have emphasized ethical concerns. Actually these should be considered secondary. The important thing to be said is that Franklin wrote most of these light pieces not for the effect that they would have on readers—potential or actual—but for his own amusement in composing them.

Franklin began writing bagatelles in his youth and continued throughout his life. The most famous are those composed during his sojourn in Paris—famous primarily because Franklin printed them on his own printing press for distribution to a closed circle of friends, and because bibliophiles have exaggerated their literary merit in deference to their extreme value as typographical rarities. Because of this combination of circumstances the definitions associated with Franklin's bagatelles have been highly artificial and arbitrary. One critic considers them to comprise only those lighthearted essays or jeux d'esprit, printed at Franklin's Passy press, and intended for the amusement of himself and his friends.[7] W. T. Franklin maintains that they make up a collection written for an intimate society in both London and Paris, a collection that Franklin himself gathered together and left in a

Notes to this chapter begin on page 250.

portfolio and that W. T. Franklin published in his edition of
Franklin's works.[2] Since these and other current schemes of classi-
fication fail to provide a consistent or homogeneous list, it might
be more useful to apply the same definition in describing Franklin's bagatelles that would be used in connection with the facetious minor works of any other author. Accordingly, the term
would include all light and short works written at any time during the author's career for the conscious amusement of the author
himself. Polly Baker and William Henry would obviously be
included in the group of Franklin's bagatelles. Franklin wrote
many other light pieces before coming to France, but we shall
here be concerned only with those written after his arrival or
those that gained some renown in France.

We cannot say for certain that he printed all these pieces on
his own press installed at Passy since Passy imprints do not exist
for at least two of his French bagatelles ("An Economical Project"
and "Petition of the Left Hand"), which were published in
periodicals. He may very well have printed them privately as
well, but no evidence exists that he did. The question of whether
the bagatelles reflect, in the words of one critic, an "exquisite
French," rather than a "solid Saxon or English quality," is a
tenuous one.[3] If it is possible to contrast English with French
fun-making, perhaps it may be said that the English excel in delineating "humor" characters or types (Ben Jonson), in describing
by means of exaggeration and irony (Jonathan Swift), and in
perpetrating literary hoaxes (Swift again). The French may be
said to excel in apparent infantine simplicity or *naïveté* (La Fontaine), in grace, precision, and conciseness (Voltaire), in whimsy
or delicate fantasy (Marivaux), and in a certain charm that comes
from an assumed aloofness of the narrator (La Bruyère). Common
to both French and English styles are burlesque, intellectual
gymnastics, such as puns, and comedy of situation. Four or five of
Franklin's bagatelles have the delicacy of touch associated with
the French mode, but others exhibit typically Anglo-Saxon blunt-
ness—a result either of excessive didacticism ("The Whistle") or
heavy-handed ribaldry ("Letter to the Royal Academy of Brussels"). Against the last identifying characteristic of Anglo-Saxon
comedy, one might say that Rabelais is sometimes considered to

be characteristic of the Gallic spirit, but even so, Franklin in the last-mentioned piece outdoes Rabelais.

Certainly the bagatelles were intended for an audience vastly more sophisticated than the general public that, even before Franklin's French sojourn, had known his moral and political propaganda. The bagatelles were intended for a select circle, composed of a few very close friends with whom Franklin passed his leisure hours in Passy. As might be expected, considering Franklin's acknowledged amorous disposition and the reputed attractiveness of French women, the most intimate of Franklin's associates were priests and ladies. At the moment of his arrival in France, he was introduced into the homes of Turgot, Helvétius, La Rochefoucauld, and d'Holbach. Here "he formed several liaisons which he cultivated with much care. He loved to cite and to practice faithfully the proverb of his friends the American Indians, 'Keep the chain of friendship bright and shining.' " [4] Two of Franklin's most shining links in France were Mme. Helvétius, widow of the philosopher, and Mme. Brillon, the young wife of an apparently indifferent husband twenty-four years her senior.

Mme. Helvétius kept a famous salon in her home in Auteuil, which came to be known as The Academy, in honor of the more than thirty members of that society who frequented it. Her more intimate associates were two priests and a medical student, who actually resided on her estate more or less permanently. All three came to be intimate friends of Franklin also, and joined him in paying homage to Notre Dame d'Auteuil, the name that they had given to Mme. Helvétius. All three, moreover, wrote very informative memoirs concerning Franklin after his death. One of them, the abbé Morellet, an economist, political writer, and translator of many works in English, gives the following account of domestic relations *chez* Mme. Helvétius.[5]

> The society of Mme. Helvétius was then formed, in addition to myself, of two men of letters residing in her house and living with her in a great intimacy. One of them, the abbé de la Roche, was an ex-Benedictine, whom Helvétius had after a fashion secularized, . . . a man of sense and moderated wit, attached to Helvétius by gratitude. . . . The other man of letters . . . was M. de Cabanis, a young man of between twenty-one and twenty-two years when she became acquainted with him. He was the son of a bourgeois of

Brives-la-Gaillarde, for whom Turgot had conceived esteem and confidence. The young man, gifted with a pleasing countenance and much spirit and talent, had also won Turgot's esteem. Mme. Helvétius had seen him at Turgot's home and participated in the interest he caused everyone to evince. . . . The abbé, Cabanis and I lived together under the same roof for more than fifteen years without having the slightest altercation. I loved them both, the abbé de la Roche less than Cabanis, but I had for the latter a real esteem and a tender friendship. If the difference of age did not allow him to share this sentiment, he discharged it at least, I believe, with some benevolence and even some esteem. We lived very peaceably with the same friend, who did not exhibit for any one of the three, a preference which would have displeased the other two.

The household must indeed have enjoyed an idyllic existence, especially when Franklin came to visit. The abbé de la Roche, in a letter to Franklin after the latter's return to America, revived nostalgic memories. "We were indeed happy when we found ourselves together around a good luncheon table; we discoursed of morality, of politics, and of philosophy; our Lady of Auteuil excited your coquetry, and the abbé Morellet wrangled over the cream, and ushered his arguments in order to prove what we did not believe; then we would have gladly renounced the other paradise in order to conserve this one and live as we were during all of an eternity." [6]

In explaining the attraction that Mme. Helvétius exerted over "statesmen, philosophers, historians, poets, and men of learning of all sorts," Franklin remarked in a letter to that lady, "we find in your sweet society that charming benevolence, that amiable attention to oblige, that disposition to please and be pleased, which we do not always find in the society of one another. It springs from you; it has its influence on us all, and in your company we are not only pleased with you, but better pleased with one another and with ourselves." [7] This was presumably written early in their acquaintance. Franklin eventually grew bolder, for shortly before the writing of his first bagatelle to Mme. Helvétius, he sent her a brief message by Cabanis in which he remarked in the third person: "If that Lady likes to pass her Days with him; he in turn would like to pass his Nights with her; & as he has already given her many of his days, though he has so few left to give, she appears ungrateful never to have given him a single one of her nights, which steadily pass as a pure loss, without giving happiness to anyone except Poupon." [8]

The same impartiality that Mme. Helvétius exhibited toward her house guests, she revealed in regard to Franklin and Turgot, both of whom became seriously enamored and proposed marriage. The two bagatelles that Franklin addressed to Mme. Helvétius concern his matrimonial proposal. The light facetious tone in which they are composed creates the impression that Franklin was only semi-serious in his propositions—that they had been extended in a spirit of gallantry, but a letter from Turgot to du Pont de Nemours suggests that Franklin wrote them in order to allay the emotional turbulences to which his declaration had given rise and to pass off his own declaration as a form of complimentary address that he had no reason to conceal from the world. Turgot, although a rival for the hand of the same lady, with whom he enjoyed no greater romantic success than had Franklin, succeeded in remaining on closest terms of friendship with both Franklin and Mme. Helvétius. His main concern was to restore harmony, exactly what Franklin was attempting to do with his bagatelles. "I have seen," Turgot wrote to du Pont de Nemours, "one of our friends [Mme. Helvétius] whom I have found in a rather bad condition. Her tranquillity has been constantly disturbed and always by the same follies. I shall tell you all that when I see you again. She has decided to leave to spend the summer with a relative at Tours and to take her eldest daughter. She will establish herself in the country in order to occupy herself exclusively with her daughter in order to forget, if she can, all the worry with which she has been tormented. I find this resolution very reasonable and very proper, not only for her own tranquillity, but also to reestablish it in the other head [Franklin's] which is agitated so improperly." [9]

Franklin's proposal of marriage probably caused Mme. Helvétius' agitation. On the evening following an earlier proposal, Franklin had written a letter to Mme. Helvétius, which he later printed as a bagatelle with the title, "The Elysian Fields." [10] After hearing her "barbarous resolution" to remain single for the rest of her life, Franklin returned to his home and dreamed that he was in the Elysian Fields. Learning that Socrates and

Helvétius were close at hand, he asked to be allowed to speak to the latter, who, delighted to see his old friend, asked a host of questions concerning politics and social life, but said not a word about his former wife. Noticing Franklin's surprise, Helvétius explained that in order to find happiness in paradise one must forget the past; he had, therefore, taken another wife, one closely resembling his former spouse. Franklin then remarked that Mme. Helvétius possessed a much more faithful spirit since she had been known to refuse many offers, including his own. Helvétius expressed regret for Franklin's lack of success and suggested that the lady might change her mind if Franklin could persuade the abbé Morellet to speak in his behalf and the abbé de la Roche to speak against him. At that moment the new Mme. Helvétius entered upon the scene, and Franklin recognized her as his own former American wife. When Franklin advanced to greet her, she responded coolly, "I was a good wife to you for nearly fifty years—be satisfied with that. I have now found a new connection which will last throughout eternity." Indignant at this refusal, Franklin resolved to return to earth and again to seek out Mme. Helvétius. Cryptically he ended his tale, "Here I am. Let us avenge ourselves." ⏋

It is hardly likely that Franklin intended this for general circulation, yet in April, 1780, presumably just after its composition, Grimm included the work without comment in his *Correspondance littéraire,* giving it the title "Lettre de M. Franklin à Madame Helvétius." [11] It was printed again by the abbé Morellet in his *Mémoires.* [12] The second bagatelle addressed to Mme. Helvétius, an address of the flies in Franklin's apartment to those in the apartment of Mme. Helvétius, in which they suggest among other things that the two societies be made into one household, was not published until modern times. [13]

Presumably these letters or other influences softened Mme. Helvétius, for in 1784 she shocked Mrs. John Adams by her amorous behavior. The latter's description of Mme. Helvétius and Franklin has become a classic. [14]

She entered the room with a careless, jaunty air; upon seeing ladies who were strangers to her, she bawled out, "Ah! mon Dieu, where is Franklin? Why did you not tell me there were ladies here?" You must suppose her speaking all this in French. "How I look!" said she, taking hold of a chemise made of tiffany, which she had on over a blue lutestring, and which looked as much upon the decay as her beauty, for she was once a handsome woman; her hair was frizzled; over it she had a small straw hat, with a dirty gauze half-handkerchief behind. She had a black gauze scarf thrown over her shoulders. She ran out of the room; when she returned, the Doctor entered at one door, she at the other; upon which she ran forward to him, caught him by the hand, "Helas! Franklin"; then gave him a double kiss one upon each cheek, and another upon his forehead. When we went into the room to dine, she was placed between the Doctor and Mr. Adams. She carried on the chief of the conversation at dinner, frequently locking her hand into the Doctor's, and sometimes spreading her arm upon the backs of both the gentlemen's chairs, then throwing her arm carelessly upon the Doctor's neck.

I should have been greatly astonished at this conduct, if the good Doctor had not told me that in this lady I should see a genuine Frenchwoman, wholly free from affectation of stiffness of behavior, and one of the best women in the world. For this I must take the Doctor's word; but I should have set her down for a very bad one, although sixty years of age, and a widow. I own I was highly disgusted, and never wish for an acquaintance with ladies of this cast. After dinner she threw herself on a settee, where she showed more than her feet. She had a little lap-dog, who was, next to the Doctor, her favorite. This she kissed, and when he wet the floor she wiped it up with her chemise. This is one of the Doctor's most intimate friends, with whom he dines once every week, and she with him.

Mme. Brillon also engaged in public exhibitions of affection toward Franklin. Even her compatriots, she wrote to Franklin, had "the audacity to criticize my pleasant habit of sitting upon your knees, and yours of always asking me for what I refuse." [15] At the time of their meeting, Mme. Brillon was thirty-six years old. In writing about her to a friend, Franklin explained that he spent one evening twice a week at her home. "She has, among other elegant accomplishments, that of an excellent musician; and, with her daughters who sing prettily, and some friends who play, she kindly entertains me and my grandson with little concerts, a cup of tea, and a game of chess. I call this *my Opera*, for I rarely go to the Opera at Paris." [16]

Most of the bagatelles for Mme. Brillon, like the two sent to Mme. Helvétius, were written in French, and both Mme. Brillon and the abbé Morellet corrected Franklin's grammar. Some of the bagatelles may actually be considered exercises in writing a foreign tongue. Mme. Brillon, to encourage her pupil, often praised the sparkle and fluency of his French phrases. Referring to his "Dialogue between the Gout and Mr. Franklin" she wrote, "the corrector of your French spoiled your work. Believe me, leave your works as they are, use words that say things, and laugh at grammarians, who by their purity, weaken all your sentences. If I had a good enough head, I would compose a terrible diatribe against those who dare to re-touch you, were it l'Abbé de la Roche, my neighbor Veillard, etc. etc. etc." [17] Franklin, in a letter to Mme. Brillon of which only a manuscript abstract remains today, thanked Mme. Brillon for her encouragement, but complained of his difficulties in composition.[18] "Vous m'enhardissez tant par l'accueil favorable que vous accordez à mes Epitres si mal écrites, qu'il me prend envie de vous en envoyer une que j'ai esquissée il y a deux semaines; mais que je n'ai pas finie, parce que je n'avoit pas le tems de chercher le dictionnaire pour regler les masculines et les feminins & ni la Grammaire pour les modes et les tens. il y a 60 ans que les choses masculines et feminines (hors des modes et des tems) m'ont donné beaucoup d'embaras. j'esperoit autrefois qu'à 80, je pouvois en être delivré. me voici à 4 fois 19, ce qui en est bien près. néanmoins ces feminines françaises me tracassent encore. cela me doit rendre plus content d'aller en Paradis, où l'on dit que ces distinctions seront abolies." In answer to this or a similar letter Mme. Brillon protested against his opinion that he wrote French badly.[19] "To make an academic discourse, one must be a good grammarian; but to write to our friends all we need is a heart, and you combine with the best heart, when you wish, the soundest moral teaching, a lively imagination, and that droll roguishness which shows that the wisest of men allows his wisdom to be perpetually broken against the rocks of femininity."

The correspondence between Franklin and Mme. Brillon is filled with allusions, which from one point of view may be described as those of gayety and gallantry, but from another as serious amorous proposals. No one but Franklin himself can be sure of their real intention. The bagatelles written for Mme. Brillon, however, reveal a consistently high moral tone; indeed, if they have a fault, it is in their excessive didacticism.

Since some of them are not dated, their chronology is uncer-

tain. "The Ephemera," which seems to be the earliest, was written in 1778 to ridicule the dispute then raging between the disciples of Gluck and Piccini over the relative merits of their
music.[20] In order to illustrate the insignificance of the controversy
as well as the negligible importance of all other human concerns,
Franklin ironically describes a solemn discourse delivered by an
ephemeron on the brevity of life and the vanity of moral desires.
He laments that the "present race of ephemerae will in a course
of minutes become corrupt, like those of other and older bushes,
and consequently as wretched. . . . Alas! art is long, and life is
short." In a letter to a friend about "The Ephemera," Franklin
remarked that the "thought was partly taken from a little piece
of some unknown writer, which I met with fifty years since in a
newspaper, and which the sight of the Ephemera brought to my
recollection." [21] This little piece is an essay in Franklin's *Pennsylvania Gazette* (December 4, 1735) in which an insect discourses
on his long life of twelve hours, a span longer than that of any
others of his kind. In his dying breath, he asserts that the private
misfortunes of existence have taught him that "no happiness can
be secure or lasting which is placed in things that are out of our
power." For many years students of Franklin have assumed that
he was the author of this piece, but I have recently discovered
that he took it from an English periodical published in 1719.[22]

Since the text of "The Ephemera" in every edition of Franklin's work is based on either the Passy or the W. T. Franklin
printed versions, no critics have discussed a contemporary manuscript text entitled "Lettre de M. Franklin à Mme Brillon," which
specifically names Mme. Brillon as Franklin's inspiration.[23] In the
printed texts, Franklin in his own character concludes, "To me,
after all my eager pursuits, no solid pleasures now remain, but
the reflection of a long life spent in meaning well, the sensible
conversation of a few good lady ephemerae, and now and then
a kind smile and a tune from the ever amiable Brillante." In
the French manuscript, this is rendered the "toujours aimable
Brillon." The first text given to the public (in the *Journal de
Paris*, 12 avril 1786) is neither that of Passy nor that of the manuscript. It concludes: "Pour moi, après tant de recherches actives,
il ne me reste de bien réels, que la satisfaction d'avoir passé ma
vie dans l'intention d'être utile, la conversation aimable d'un

petit nombre de bonnes dames éphémères, & de tems en tems le doux sourire & quelques accords du piano forte de Mme B . . ."

Next to love-making and moralizing, Franklin seems to have devoted his leisure time to playing chess, a pastime he often shared with Mme. Brillon. For this reason he felt that his bagatelle, "The Morals of Chess," should have been dedicated to her. The best advice that it contained, he said, had been modelled after her generous and magnanimous manner of playing, which Franklin had often witnessed.[24] The work, which is of interest to few besides devotees of the game, consists of two parts—a list of the desirable mental qualities said to be developed by the game and a list of rules to enable the participants to derive the maximum pleasure from playing. Franklin's disciple, Dr. Dubourg, dissented on the value of chess and prepared a companion piece in which he pointed out the adverse effects of the game and refuted the fallacy that the problems of chess resemble the problems of daily living. On June 28, 1779, Dubourg wrote to Franklin that he was preparing a translation of "The Morals of Chess" for publication in the *Journal de Paris* along with his own remarks, but neither piece appeared in that periodical.[25]

Mme. Brillon served as direct inspiration for another of Franklin's bagatelles, "Dialogue between Mr. Franklin and the Gout." [26] Since both Franklin and M. Brillon, a plump, agreeable gentleman, suffered from the malady, Mme. Brillon had undoubtedly endured much conversation on the subject, inspiring her to produce some brief verses dedicated to Franklin, entitled "Le Sage et la Goutte." Franklin responded with his dialogue, in which the personified gout rebukes Franklin for his sedentary habits.

Toward the end of 1779, Franklin presented to Mme. Brillon another bagatelle, "The Whistle," the theme of which he had used twenty years previously in America. This also was directly inspired by a letter from Mme. Brillon, a point that editors of the piece have strangely neglected. In a serious letter to Franklin on November 1, 1779, she developed the theme that because of the uncertainty of mortal happiness, only the thought of a future life can enable us to bear the trials of this one. This concept led to a description of the anticipated joys of paradise.[27]

We shall there live on roasted apples only; the music will be composed of Scotch airs; all parties will be given over to chess, so that no one may be disappointed; every one will speak the same language; the English will be neither unjust nor wicked there; the women will not be coquettes, the men will be neither jealous nor too gallant; "King John" will be left to eat his apples in peace; perhaps he will be decent enough to offer some to his neighbours—who knows? since we shall want for nothing in paradise! We shall never suffer from gout there nor from our nerves.

Franklin, in replying, approved of the conclusion that "we should draw all the Good we can from this world," but warned against false valuations that keep us from drawing more good and suffering less evil from life than might otherwise be our lot.[28] To illustrate these false valuations, Franklin told a story of his childhood. When only seven years old, friends of the family had filled his pockets with halfpence. Proceeding to a neighboring toy shop, he met another boy on the way who charmed him with the sound of a whistle. Franklin emptied his pockets on the spot for the whistle and returned to his home, happy over his purchase. His family then pointed out that he had paid four times as much as the whistle was worth, and taunted him by naming the good things he could otherwise have bought with the rest of the money. This served as a lesson that lasted throughout his life, for whenever he was tempted to buy an unneeded object, he said to himself, "Do not give too much for the whistle." As he grew in experience he encountered a number of men who had given too much for their whistle—court sycophants, popularity-seekers, misers, and men of pleasure. A great part of the miseries of mankind had been "brought upon them by the false estimates they had made of the value of things."

Although the letter to Mme. Brillon may have been the first version of "The Whistle" to be printed, we learn through another French source, the "Notice concerning Benjamin Franklin" by Cabanis, that he had told the story several years earlier to his son, William Franklin.[29] When the latter had solicited at the British court the post of royal governor of New Jersey, Franklin warned him against his incipient aristocratic tendencies, which later led him to embrace the Tory side during the American Revolution. "Think of what the whistle may one day cost you," Franklin said to his son. "Why not become a joiner or wheelwright, if the estate I leave you is not enough? The man who lives by his labor is at least free." In telling the story to the Passy circle, Franklin added that his son had been infatuated with the title of *excellency;* he had been ashamed to resemble his father. The abbé de la Roche remarked that Franklin himself owed to his childhood experience with the whistle his lifelong power to reject everything that does not directly lead to the true pleasure of a rational mind.[30]

The last of the bagatelles associated with Mme. Brillon is "The Handsome and the Deformed Leg," a rather heavy didactic piece of little intrinsic interest.[31] Contrasting the optimistic with the pessimistic view of life, Franklin points out that there are some people who see the good in every situation, others who see only the bad. This turn of mind, he believes, is not founded in nature, but comes from observation and imitation of others; because of it the pessimists make disagreeable companions, inconvenient associates. An old philosophical friend of Franklin's had a deformed leg that he used as an instrument to detect this unpleasing disposition in strangers—if the stranger regarded his ugly leg rather than his handsome one or made any comment on it, the philosopher decided to have nothing more to do with him. In conclusion, Franklin advises these "critical, querulous, discontented unhappy People" that, if they wish to be respected by others or gain happiness for themselves, they "should leave off looking at the ugly Leg." It may be purely coincidental, but an Italian diplomat, Caracciolo, who represented the court of Naples in London during the period of Franklin's sojourn and who resided in Paris during Franklin's residence there, possessed a sound and a deformed leg exactly as described by Franklin. The abbé Galiani, reporting the return of Caracciolo to Naples in 1781, wrote, "He is in excellent condition in his whole body with the exception of a certain left leg, which is of an extremely ungainly architecture and quite different from the right leg. Despite this faulty architecture, the edifice may still last many more years." [32] Caracciolo was known as a philosopher, and numbered many illustrious foreigners among his acquaintance, including d'Alembert and all the mathematicians of his time.[33] It is quite possible that Franklin knew him and used him as the model for his essay. Although published by Castéra in 1798, this piece seems not to have had any influence in France. Even less well known is the Rabelaisian "To the Royal Academy of Brussels," which has never been printed in French—perhaps because many of its puns cannot be translated.[34]

Two other pieces that Franklin printed on his Passy press have antecedents quite different from the other bagatelles. One of these, "Remarks concerning the Savages of North America," which grew out of a work in the *Ephémérides du citoyen*, I have discussed in the first chapter. The other, "Information to Those Who Would Remove to America," requires little comment since it has no apparent previous or subsequent French literary connections. Both tracts stem from Franklin's letter to Peter Collinson, May 9, 1753, in which he discusses the racial characteristics of Indians and Germans in Pennsylvania.[35] In the "Remarks" Franklin repeated an anecdote concerning the Indian attitude toward education; in "Information to Those Who Would Remove to America" he continued the discussion of the amount of labor required for subsistence or prosperity in America. The letter to Collinson suggests that there are a number of inherently lazy groups, who subsist with little or no labor. The "Information" makes it clear that hard work and industry are indispensable. Verbal relations are seen in his efforts to reproduce dialect in the letter to Collinson in which a Transylvania Tartar discourses on labor: "God make Man for Paradise, he make him to live Lazy; Man make God angry, God turns him Out of Paradise, and bid work. Man no love work, he want to go to Paradise again, he want to live Lazy; So all Mankind love Lazy." The "Information" presents a Negro's views: "Boccarorra (meaning the White men) make de black man workee, make de Horse workee, make de Ox workee, make ebery ting workee; only de Hog. He, de Hog, no workee; he eat, he drink, he walk about, he go to sleep when he please, he libb like a Gentleman."

This work, the theme of which is that America is a desirable habitat only for those who work hard, Franklin wrote because of the incessant demands he received in Paris for information about America—demands that were usually accompanied with requests for the granting of special rights or privileged positions or for financial assistance in making the journey. For certain periods nearly one letter in ten that Franklin received in Paris contained a request for aid in emigration. Franklin had neither the authority nor the desire to grant special concessions, and he composed his tract to discourage solicitation. As he wrote to Charles Thomson, President of Congress (March 9, 1784), "I am pestered continually with numbers of letters from people in different parts of Europe, who would go to settle in America, but who manifest very extravagant expectations, such as I can by no means encourage, and who appear otherwise to be very improper persons." [36] To save himself trouble he proposed to send out copies of his "Information" in answer to soliciting letters.

Some of the petitioners for financial aid proposed in return to serve in the American forces; others sent original poems, and one even offered his prayers. A certain prior wrote that he had recently lost a considerable sum at gambling and begged Franklin to aid him but to keep his secret and guard his reputation, his only treasure. On the letter Franklin noted, "Wants me to pay his gaming debts, and he will pray for success to our cause." [37] A lady of the court sent him a young man with the following letter of recommendation: "If you have in your country the secret of reforming a detestable creature who is the chief torment of his family, I beg of you to send over the bearer of this letter. You will be performing a miracle worthy of yourself." [38] The young man was accepted, fought courageously, and was killed in battle.

Returning to Franklin's bagatelles, we shall consider the two that seem to have attracted the greatest amount of attention in France. One of these, entitled simply "Conte," was written in French. Like the "Dialogue between Mr. Franklin and the Gout," "The Ephemera," and "The Elysian Fields," all printed English versions of the "Conte" are translations by hands other than Franklin's. The following translation is my own.

There was an officer, a man of virtue, named Montresor, who was seriously ill. His curate, believing that he was going to die, advised him to make his peace with God in order to be received in Paradise. "I have not much anxiety on this subject," said Montresor, "for last night I had a vision which has given me complete tranquillity." "What vision did you have?" asked the good priest. "I was at the gate of Heaven," replied Montresor, "with a crowd of people who wanted to enter. And St. Peter asked each one what his religious profession was. One replied, "I am Roman Catholic." "Very well," said St. Peter, "enter and take your place among the Catholics." Another said that he was of the Anglican church. "Very well," said St. Peter, "enter and take your place among the Anglicans." Another said that he was a Quaker. "Enter," said St. Peter, "and take your place among the Quakers." Finally my turn coming, he asked me what my religion was. "Alas!" I replied, "unfortunately the poor James Montresor has none." "That is too bad," said the Saint, "I do not know where to put you; but enter anyway; and find a place where you can."

The fact that this version (in French) was printed by Franklin would seem to give it authority as the accepted text. There exists, however, a manuscript version (also in French) in a contemporary hand that, in addition to a number of very minor verbal differences, has a more appropriate conclusion and may represent Franklin's second thought.[39] In this version St. Peter says at the end, "Enter anyway and take any place you wish." The ending of the Passy version actually has little point; that of the manuscript, however, forcibly presents Franklin's principle that sectarian differences have little significance in judging the virtue of a human being.

Another version, almost identical with the manuscript, except that the conclusion is amplified, had at least three separate printings in Paris during the eighteenth century. This version appeared as a note to *Les Jardins de Betz, poëme accompagné de notes instructives sur les travaux champêtres, sur les arts, les lois, les révolutions, la noblesse, le clergé, &c. fait en 1785, par M. Cerutti, et publié en 1792*. Before it appeared in book form, Cerutti printed a long section of the poem concerning the independence of America, including Franklin's apologue, in his periodical *La Feuille Villageoise* (February 9, 1792). It was then reprinted a few days later by Brissot in *Le Patriote François,* a periodical of much wider circulation.[40] It would seem, therefore, that this bagatelle had the greatest contemporary vogue of any of Franklin's French pieces printed at Passy. The amplified conclusion in the version published by Cerutti was probably the latter's own work. (We have already seen how he improved upon *Bonhomme Richard*.) His additions emphasize the principle that it was Montresor's benevolence and good works rather than religious faith that gained his admission to heaven.

Enfin il m'a demandé de quelle religion j'étois. Hélas! ai-je répondu, je n'en ai point d'autre que la loi naturelle et l'amour au genre humain: le Saint réfléchit un instant, ensuite il me dit: Entrez toujours et placez-vous où vous voudrez.

In the body of the poem, Cerutti, a former Jesuit priest, describes a benevolent inhabitant of a small village, a French equivalent of Alexander Pope's Man of Ross. The author explains in a note that after the man's death he had conversed about him with the village curate, who, after uttering some conventional phrases appropriate for a funeral elegy, began to censure the deceased humanitarian. After several questions, the author discovered that the curate's bitterness was due to the fact that the philosopher had been an atheist and the curate had failed to convert him. To confute the priest, Cerutti drew from his pocket Franklin's apologue, which he describes as "the work of Franklin, this divine man whom the oracle of Delphos would have named with Socrates as the sage of the universe." Franklin's "Conte" was published by Renouard in 1795 and again in 1798 by Castéra. The latter edition includes also an "imitation heureuse" in verse by "citoyen Parny," in which version, six men present themselves at the doors of heaven. These include a Mohammedan, a Jew, a Lutheran, a Quaker, a Catholic, and a man of no religion. According to Parny's view of the Quakers' heaven, they form a club where they smoke and wear their hats. Parny's man without a church, unlike Franklin's, specifically acknowledges belief in an immortal soul and a God who bestows recompense and punishment.

It was Cerutti who publicized in France another Franklin bagatelle on religious toleration, "A Parable Against Persecution." Although printed on the Passy press as were the works previously discussed, the "Parable" was originally written in English and published as early as 1759, many years before Franklin's residence in Passy.[41] This piece Franklin appparently used as an exercise to improve his French, since there are five separate manuscripts available in French, one of them with the notation at the end, "Exercise No. 7 / *Abraham* / corrigé." [42] It is Franklin's only in its style, for the substance of the piece had appeared a century earlier in a parable of Jeremy Taylor. In England Franklin had used the piece, a parody of Biblical language, as a literary hoax. He was accustomed to reading the "Parable" aloud from an open Bible and asking his guests to distinguish the genuine Biblical extracts from his imitation. Franklin's parable concerns the wrath of Abraham against a traveler whom he had first received into his tent and then had driven out after the stranger had refused to worship God. At midnight the Lord appeared to Abraham and rebuked him on the grounds that since He had borne with the man's obstinacy and rebellion for 198 years, Abraham should have been able to bear with him for a single night.

Cerutti considered this as an object lesson against religious fanaticism and the sectarian spirit. He told his readers in *La Feuille Villageoise,* therefore, that in Pennsylvania Franklin had struggled particularly against the prejudices of fanaticism, "which he regarded as a devouring weed which desiccated the field of public liberty and prevented the sound grain of liberty from germinating and taking root. According to Franklin, an eternal servitude will be the lot of any people which wastes time in transgressing conscience, in contending for vain differences of creed or ritual. Any man who bears malice toward his neighbor for not worshipping in the same church as he, is better equipped to be a deacon than a citizen." [43] Cerutti explained, not quite accurately, that Franklin's "Parable" arose out of the quarrels of nonconformists in Pennsylvania and that Franklin wished to show that between two sects, the more impious is the least tolerant and that God prefers a heretic to a persecutor.

While no other light pieces that Franklin printed on his Passy press have come down to the present, there are at least two others he wrote during his sojourn in France that have equal right with any of the pieces so far discussed to the title of bagatelles. The most brilliant and witty of all he sent to the *Journal de Paris,* where it was actually published under the pseudonym, *Un Abonné.* In the character of the *Journal de Paris* and its editors lies the only clue to Franklin's purpose in writing the piece.

The *Journal de Paris* had been founded in 1779 by Antoine-Alexis-François Cadet de Vaux, a well-meaning and conscientious pharmacist and chemist. Cadet mentioned Franklin frequently in the *Journal de Paris,* always with great respect. In July, 1779, he reported, for example, that Franklin had attended a lecture-demonstration of electrical principles at the College of Mazarin, describing with rapture the effect of Franklin's distinguished presence upon students and teacher. The theologian-scientist who conducted the experiments "saw in his person only the prince of natural philosophy. The enthusiasm with which he was received by the students of this college demonstrates the vivid impression which the sight of a great man can produce upon the sensitive imagination of youth."

Cadet de Vaux was a specialist in the culinary arts as well as in pharmacy, chemistry, and journalism, and he held the official title, "Professor of Baking," at an institution that he conducted with a colleague, Parmentier. The government at the time was seeking a method of substituting coal for wood as domestic fuel, and Cadet de Vaux, as part of the research effort, was conducting experiments in baking bread with the new fuel. Franklin had designed a special stove for this purpose, a diagram of which he had sent to Cadet, who hoped that he could persuade Franklin to write some observations on his experiments and an explanation of the stove, which Cadet hoped to edit. He accordingly wrote a letter to Vergennes, secretary of state (March 28, 1783), asking him to use his influence to prevail upon Franklin to undertake the project.[44] A year later Cadet was still exhorting Franklin to undertake research on the stove. Franklin wrote from Passy (February 5, 1784) to say that he could not leave Paris at the moment, but sent Cadet some bread baked on his stove.[45] The letter is here printed in full, not only because it has never before been published, but because it illustrates Franklin's ability in French composition. The manuscript shows no sign of having been corrected by another hand—and it is doubtful that Franklin would have considered this letter important enough to have made a preliminary draft.

Malgré tout le desir que J'ai, Monsieur, de faire quelque Chose qui puisse vous etre agreable ainsi qu'a M. Votre Frere, Il m'est absoluement impossible de faire le voyage de Paris dans Ce moment cy; ma Maladie, et la saison vigoureuse sont des obstacles insurmontables pour moi.

J'ai moi meme fait executer un Poele Cheminée propre à bruler le Charbon de Terre telle que M. le Noir a paru desirer que je fis connoitre dans ce Pays cy. Je serai charmé de vous le montrer quand vos Affaires vous permettront de venir à Passy: Je ne puis encore en faire un Usage habituel faute de Charbon de Terre. Si vous pouvez m'en procurer vous me ferez grand Plaisir.

J'ai reçu dans le Tems La Farine de Bled de Turquie, que vous avez eu la complaisance de me faire venir—et pour la quelle Je vous suis redevable—Je vous envoye par le Porteur un Echantillon de Pain fait en Partie avec cette Farine, mais Je crois qu'il seroit possible de le faire meilleur. Je vous envoye la Recette pour le faire—Si vous jugerez a propos d'en faire faire l'Essaye a l'Ecole du Boulangerie.

Franklin continued to correspond with Cadet on the subject of bread and the materials for baking it. On April 28, 1785, he sent him an informative essay, "Observations on Maize or Indian Corn," which Cadet published in the *Journal de Paris,* February 17, 1786, under the heading "Economie." [46] This essay gives a complete summary of the many forms in which nutriment for human consumption may be extracted from maize—eleven, to be exact, including corn bread.

From these facts we can draw the conclusion that a feature of the *Journal de Paris* was the publication of utilitarian articles on nutrition and other domestic concerns. The periodical, in addition to news and belles lettres, regularly published articles of practical usefulness and household hints, some of these appearing under the heading of "Economie." Franklin's bagatelle, which appeared in the same category, is obviously a gentle parody of this type of article. The title it bears in English, "An Economical Project," is really not a title at all, but merely a feature heading from the *Journal de Paris.* In keeping with the tone of articles on popular science, Franklin describes a gathering at which an oil lamp newly-invented by Quinquet and Lange had been introduced. Although the lamp was capable of producing a splendid light, a number of the spectators asked whether the expense of the oil it consumed might not outweigh the increased brilliance of the light. Franklin was pleased to see this general concern for economy; going home and to bed several hours after midnight, he continued thinking on the subject. He was awakened at six in the morning by an accidental noise, surprised to see the room filled with light. At first thinking that a number of the new lamps had been brought in, he discovered that the light came through the window. After looking into the almanacs, he repeated the experiment on the three following mornings and came to the

amazing conclusion that the sun rises every day at that hour and
that it gives light as soon as it rises. He then realized that if he
had not made this discovery, he would have slept six additional
hours each day during the sunlight and paid for it by six hours
of candlelight, a much more expensive form of illumination.
Motivated by his love for economy, he calculated how much of a
saving this would represent for him personally—and in keeping
with the burlesque spirit, multiplied his individual savings by
the number of families in Paris. This produced an enormous
sum, and so he suggested a number of measures to secure this
saving for the municipality, including taxing shutters that would
keep out the sun, restricting the number of candles permitted
each household, restricting the passage of coaches after sunset,
and ringing bells and setting off cannon at sunrise to awaken the
citizens to their true interest. In conclusion he anticipated jealous minds who might depreciate his discovery by charging that
it was known to the ancients. Franklin admitted that their almanacs may have indicated the early rising of the sun, but it does
not follow, he argued, "that they knew *he gave light as soon as
he rose.*" This was Franklin's contribution.

The mild satire of this combined literary parody and moral
parable resembles Swift's writings in a mellow mood. It is the
type of irony Swift would have written in place of *A Modest Proposal* if he had spent five years in the company of Mmes. Helvétius and Brillon. There is as much self-satire in the piece as
there is social criticism. Not only is it a parody of some of Franklin's scientific and economic works, but it is also a reflection on
his own habits. At Passy Franklin had been known to stay up
all night playing chess until well after sunrise.

The work appeared first in English in a periodical publication
in 1788 and later in W. T. Franklin's edition. For some reason
all modern editors, following A. H. Smyth, have given the piece
an incorrect date,[47] and Carl Van Doren, Franklin's biographer,
remarks that Franklin did not print it in France.[48] The fact is,
however, that it appeared in the *Journal de Paris,* where Franklin had sent it, April 26, 1784. Strangely enough it was reported
in a later French periodical (*La Décade Philosophique,* 30 Fructi-
dor, An III) that the letter had not been printed in the *Journal
de Paris* because of some circumstances of the time. The writer

added that since the piece suited perfectly the present epoch, he would print it from Franklin's own manuscript.

Apparently Franklin did not himself compose the French version of this bagatelle as he had composed some of the others. Castéra, who printed a translation in 1798, remarked that the version in the *Journal de Paris* was also a translation and that his own was based on the original to which Franklin had subsequently made corrections and additions.[49] Castéra's translation and that in *La Décade Philosophique,* although different, are certainly based on the same English text.

Contemporary response to Franklin's pleasantry was not uniform. Although the editors of the *Journal de Paris* felt that it had missed its mark, at least one close associate of the journal was sufficiently amused to undertake an imitation. On the day following the publication of Franklin's letter, a scholar and well-known librarian, Mercier de Saint-Léger, submitted to the *Journal de Paris* a similar humorous letter in which he observed that the *abonné* had not mentioned that the sun gives not only light but heat as well and that the *abonné* could well have made similar calculations on the amount of fuel to be saved.[50] The editors rejected this letter, which led Saint-Léger to note in a bibliography of his own works:

> Année 1784. . . . Lettre au *Journal de Paris* sur la plaisanterie de Franklin, qui avait invité les Parisiens à se lever avec le soleil. Non imprimée, parce que cette plaisanterie n'avait pas réussi, et que MM. du Journal ne voulaient pas la rappeler.

Perhaps most surprising of all, the editors of the *Journal de Paris* in 1795 read Franklin's letter in *La Décade Philosophique* and reprinted it November 30, not realizing, or forgetting, that it had already appeared in their own journal in 1784. A few days later, December 3, a subscriber protested in two columns against this posthumous publication, conjecturing that Franklin in rereading his letter had found it cold and insipid since—so far as this author knew—he had not sent it to the journal. Many people, this author affirmed, agreed with Franklin. "One is guilty of compromising the glory of illustrious men and at the same time betraying their intentions by publishing works which they themselves considered unworthy of their pens." Finally, December 9, Quinquet himself, inventor of the lamp, defended Franklin in arguing that he had been guilty neither of foolishness nor of a bad joke. Quinquet affirmed that he himself, unaware of Franklin's idea, had six months previously communicated similar views to several official bodies. Another periodical (*Journal des patriotes de 89*, December 2, 1795) jested on the date of the most recent publication of Franklin's letter. A writer who admitted that Franklin's advice might be sound felt, nevertheless, that the time of giving it had been poorly chosen. He found it incongruous "to invite people to get up early in the morning in order to save light in a season when at seven o'clock it is still dark."

The last bagatelle associated with Franklin's French period is "A Petition of the Left Hand" addressed "To Those Who Have the Superintendency of Education." In all editions of Franklin's works this piece appears with the caption "date unknown." There seems to be evidence in the *Journal de Paris*, however, to show that Franklin composed it sometime in 1785, shortly before leaving France. In the piece, the left hand appeals to the friends of youth to rescue her from the prejudices that have blighted her existence. "There are twin sisters of us"; she says, "and the two eyes of man do not more resemble, nor are capable of being upon better terms with each other, than my sister and myself, were it not for the partiality of our parents, who make the most injurious distinction between us." In short, the left hand was considered an inferior being; her sister was given training in every accomplishment whereas she was not only ignored, but rebuked or punished if she attempted to take an active part. She appeals for equal treatment, not out of vanity but out of prudence, reminding her readers that if some accident befall her sister, both must perish from distress. "It is the practice in our family, that the whole business of providing for its subsistence falls upon my sister and myself. If any indisposition should attack my sister,—and I mention it in confidence upon this occasion that she is subject to the gout, the rheumatism, and cramp, without making mention of other accidents, what would be the fate of our poor family?"

In the *Journal de Paris* of 1785 are two brief essays on exactly the same theme and written in parallel phraseology. Since the theme was not familiar or commonplace, it would seem that these essays are Franklin's source of inspiration. The first (May 31, 1785) is a serious letter without Franklin's sprightliness, but there are a number of obvious parallels.

> . . . If the working hand is wounded or becomes infirm, frequent accidents in the mechanical professions, the unfortunate workman finds himself out of work and without resources. . . . it is absurd stupidity to enforce upon children the use of one hand rather than the other; . . . the two hands have no preeminence between them; . . . they are two twin sisters to whom the same education is suited since they must face the same risks.

A letter in a later issue (June 26, 1785) that this piece inspired reflects the same facetious tone as Franklin's petition. Indeed, it could very well have been written by Franklin. It is signed *Un de vos Abonnés,* almost the same pseudonym that Franklin used for his "An Economical Project."

> . . . For a long time people have been writing against the absurd practice of requiring children to use the right hand and making them almost inept in using the other, although Nature has actually made us ambidextrous. Several mothers have so well realized the justice of these protests that they have risen above the ancient prejudice and no longer oppose this natural perfection.
>
> A lady of my acquaintance had so effectively accustomed her daughter to use her two hands indifferently that the child worked, sewed, and even wrote with the same facility with the left as with the right and without thinking that there was anything extraordinary in it. Circumstances required that this young girl be put into a boarding school for some months. She retained the use of her two hands, but her new teachers were scandalized at this deformity; to reform her they used remonstrances and even penance, and succeeded so well that not only did the child lose the facility of using her left hand, but she felt embarrassment whenever she absent-mindedly used it for some exercise exclusively reserved for the right.
>
> . . . I remember, in closing my letter, a rather amusing sally. One day a child scolded for not using the right hand exclusively, being contradicted by his governess, gave her a brisk blow. The mother, who was present, instead of punishing him, said with a note of pedantry, "Oh dear, my son, always with the left hand! you are indeed incorrigible."

Franklin's "Petition," like many of his other bagatelles, was published in France before the appearance of an English version. The first printing I have been able to trace is in an almanac of

1787, *Etrennes à l'humanité*.[51] It appeared ten years later in *La Décade Philosophique*.[52]

Franklin himself in referring to his little pieces of wit and morality used the term *bagatelles:* the French more often classified them as *opuscules moraux (moral tracts)*. One of the most flattering French descriptions, published in the year of Franklin's death, emphasizes the copious originality of Franklin's mind revealed in these pieces.[53] "It is the naiveté and finesse of La Fontaine, it is the profundity and elevation of the Holy Scriptures and the oriental moralists, it is the concealed irony of Socrates without the prolix subtlety of Plato. Finally, it is the superior and indulgent spirit of a sage, who has judged man both in the rural frankness of the pioneer and in the artificial refinements of French politeness."

A more pertinent summary of Franklin's satirical gift appears in a comment by the abbé Morellet on all the productions of the Academy of Auteuil. Not Franklin alone, but Mme. Helvétius, Mme. Brillon, and the abbé Morellet, produced bagatelles for the enjoyment of the entire circle. Morellet wrote that his own are "in your own vein of pleasantry, and somewhat I conceive, in that of Swift, with rather less of his dark misanthropy. At any rate, Dr. Jonathan and Dr. Benjamin are the models on whom I have fixed my eyes; and perhaps Nature herself has given me something of the turn of both in the art of speaking the truth in a jesting way, or without seeming to speak it. The difficulty is, that one cannot laugh outright at every thing which is truly laughable." [54] According to this view, the Franklin of the bagatelles is a good-humored Swift—a sound appraisal.

Literary critics have failed to give due attention to the strong resemblances between Franklin's satirical works and Swift's. It is well known that Franklin in the prefaces to *Poor Richard* imitated Swift's Isaac Bickerstaff hoax, but many other parallels have gone unnoticed. In a work that has never been reprinted, for example, *A Defence of the Rev. Mr. Hemphill's Observations*, 1735, Franklin paraphrases Swift's famous apologue of the spider and the bee.

Yet Franklin seldom duplicated Swift's invective and savage indignation. His early satirical works are blunt, sometimes bitter, but during his residence at Passy, his pleasantries were warm and

mellow. A bagatelle in the best tradition resembles "conversation badinante et réfléchie," a phrase applied to Franklin by one
of the young girls whom he served as moral and philosophical
mentor.[55] Whether considered as pert wisdom or sage persiflage,
Franklin's bagatelles combine delight with moral truth, the emphasis being upon delight. They are among the world's master-
pieces of light literature.

So far we have discussed the works of Franklin that have been
influential in France or that have been heralded by French men
of letters. We must add that the reverse process took place at least
twice. In other words, two literary works by French authors were
printed by Franklin because they expressed concepts that Franklin himself admired and wished to see promulgated. The first of
these, a tract on morality and deism by his old friend Dr. Dubourg, who envisaged it as a "digeste de l'humanité," grew from
a brief statement in the *Mercure de France*, 1768, concerning the
relations between the individual and the creator and the development of social relations. Because of its deistical tendency Dubourg was unable to publish an expanded version of his digest
in France; and so in 1773 Franklin saw it through the press in
London in both French and English editions. Here it bore the
title *Petit code de la raison humaine*. Later in 1782 Franklin
printed a still further enlarged version at his press in Passy.[56]
Dubourg dedicated his work to Franklin in a preface in which
he indicated that Franklin himself had been the basic source of
his ideas.

> You recognized in the first sketch of this Little Digest the simple
> and naive expression of your own heart. I have developed it as
> much as I am able, and I hope that you will perceive in it only
> the best of yourself. If I have expressed anything that is not quite
> exact, I hope you will condescend to rectify it. I have dedicated it
> to you in order to submit it to your judgment, having been for-
> tunate enough to find in you both a great master and a good friend.
> You are going to travel far away from this hemisphere, and I can-
> not follow you in the other; but the immense ocean which you must
> cross will not separate the best parts of ourselves; our spirits will
> always be united, as they always have been; I do myself honor in
> publishing it and you need not blush to acknowledge it. You may
> have some disciples who are more noble, but you have no more
> faithful servant.
>
> B. D.

If we proceed beyond this preface and analyze the moral and political maxims that constitute the *Petit code,* we cannot escape the conclusion that the work intimately reflects Franklin's wisdom and personality.

Kindred concepts appeared in the second French work published by Franklin in Passy, *Conciliateur de toutes les nations de l'Europe,* 1782, by Pierre André Gargaz. The author, an erstwhile galley slave, had arrived at his ideas, however, without any influence whatsoever from Franklin. The story of this galley slave turned author, who succeeded in obtaining Voltaire and Franklin as literary patrons, is one of the most incredible and romantic of the entire century.[57]

Gargaz, a native of Theze in the former province of Dauphiné, was condemned, March 11, 1761, to a service of twenty years in the galleys after being flogged and branded. A former schoolmaster (*régent d'école*), he had been found guilty of assassination. Since the widow of the victim had been prosecuted at the same time, it would appear that Gargaz was involved in a "crime passionnel." He stoutly protested his innocence, however, in letters to Franklin in 1779, three years before his release from the galley. At this time he begged Franklin to print two accompanying manuscripts, which Franklin later endorsed "Project of universal peace by a galley slave." Three years previously Gargaz had written similar letters to Voltaire, who at the time had done more than Franklin to encourage the unfortunate conciliator. Franklin apparently took no notice of Gargaz' letters, whereas Voltaire wrote some verse for Gargaz in which, underscoring his hatred of tyrants, he expressed the hope that their trade would soon be supplanted by Gargaz' sublime notions of peace.

Considering the cruel suffering and hardship associated with the lot of a galley slave, it is a matter of considerable astonishment that Gargaz was able to survive his twenty-year period of servitude. The distinguished historian A. Aulard has suggested that apart from the possibility that he may have had an unusually hardy physique coupled with heroic will power, Gargaz may have served as secretary to the captain of his Galley, the *Duchesse.* The latter may also have been a man of letters and Gargaz may have convinced his masters of his innocence. The mere fact that the letters of Gargaz to Franklin and Voltaire reached their destination proves that he was a privileged character—as does the fact that he had the opportunity to compose the two manuscripts he sent to Franklin and another that he actually had published in Marseilles in 1773, concerning a scheme for a phonetic alphabet.

Some time after his release Gargaz succeeded in acquiring a modest income of nearly 150 crowns annually (18 pounds sterling), and in the summer of 1782 set off from the south of France with his manuscript to visit Franklin. Since he could not afford to ride, he walked every step of the way. He was shabby in appearance; "all his dress together was not worth 5s." Franklin took Gargaz' plan and read it, apparently not recalling his earlier letters. Impressed by the honest peasant's (Franklin's phrase) zeal for peace, Franklin immediately printed the manuscript and gave Gargaz as many copies as he desired. In a letter to David Hartley, Franklin wrote, "This man aims at no profit from his pamphlet or his project, asks for nothing, expects nothing, and does not even desire to be known. . . . I honor much the character of this *véritable philosophe*."

In addition to their kindred notions of international peace, it is highly probable that in their interview the two *philosophes* discussed schemes for spelling reform and phonetic writing, a subject on which Franklin also had written. In a work composed in 1769, *A Scheme for a New Alphabet and Reformed Mode of Spelling* (published 1779), he had introduced a phonetic system very much like that of Gargaz, and as late as 1786 Franklin was still distributing copies of his reformed alphabet.

After the printing of his *Conciliateur,* Gargaz wrote to Franklin on two occasions asking for assistance in obtaining recompense from the government. The French national archives have records of a number of formal requests by Gargaz for rehabilitation, but all were refused. In 1785 and 1786 he wrote again on the subject of his peace projects to Franklin's successor in Paris, Thomas Jefferson.

A cursory survey of the eleven-page pamphlet of Gargaz will show why Franklin was willing to aid in promulgating his ingenious scheme. Basis of the plan was the establishment in Lyon, or a similar site, of a "perpetual Congress, composed of a mediator representing each sovereign of Europe and any of their neighbors who should wish to enter into this universal union."

The following general rules were to prevail: As soon as ten sovereigns have joined, provided that at least five are representatives of hereditary monarchs, they will deliberate concerning all the disputes of their sovereign. The presiding officer will always be the mediator of the oldest sovereign; whenever there is a tie in the voting, the vote of the presiding officer will be decisive. All member nations are to renounce conquest and additions of territory except those in dispute when the Congress is organized—and these will be adjudged and settled at the first meetings. Afterwards there will be permitted no other territorial aggrandizements, not even those that might result from inheritance, dowry, or settlement. If a sovereign should attempt to conquer another or to invade another nation without permission of the Congress, the latter will elect another sovereign in his place, without considering the family of the deposed. If a sovereign dies without heir, his successor will be elected by Congress.

In answer to the common objection that war is the glory of a nation, Gargaz affirms instead that the true glory is found in great public works—and he gives as examples of future projects the penetration of the Isthmuses of Panama and of Suez. To the argument that since there always have been wars there always will be, he points to the examples of the princes of Germany, Poland, and France, who at one time struggled internally, but who now meet in parliaments and superior councils—on terms of domestic tranquillity that may well serve as a model for international affairs.

This was the project that Franklin read and approved. After Franklin's death, Gargaz revised his plan to bring it in line with the principles of the French Revolution, which had just taken place. The new version, called *Contrat social surnommé union francmaçone entre tous les bons citoiens de la République françoise,* has the same essential features except that freemasons are substituted for monarchs. Each nation is to send five masonic arbiters who are over forty years of age; those nations refusing to participate will be persuaded by pressure on their merchants and clerks, who will not be allowed any contact with member nations. The refractory nations will on no account be attacked or invaded, but subjected to such absolute ostracism that even if their citizens should suffer famine, shipwreck, or holocaust, they would be given no aid, but treated as if they do not exist.

Three editions of this work were published at Toulon, one without date, another during the fifth year of the Revolutionary calendar (1797-1798). The third, the most novel version of all, is an edition of the previous year printed entirely in phonetic spelling, based on the principles of the scheme that Gargaz had presented in 1773. Not only the theme of international peace, but also the masonic overtones and the reformed spelling are reminiscent of the spirit of Franklin.

Although Franklin by no means reserved his private press for the printing of bagatelles, all the literary works he undertook to print reflected in one way or another some phase of his personality or intellectual proclivities.

12. ANECDOTES

After our survey of Franklin's literary diversions in Passy, we pass to the most entertaining aspect of his residence—the intimate details of his personal life. In eighteenth-century France, even as today, the average man was interested in celebrities, particularly in scandal and gossip and in accounts of bons mots or eccentricities. The abbé de la Roche collected a number of anecdotes concerning minor events in Franklin's life that, although seemingly trivial, had a great influence, he was convinced, upon his character and subsequent conduct. "The slightest facts in the history of a celebrated man," he argued, "become the most interesting when they bring about a new order of ideas which suddenly change the determination of his will." [1] De la Roche may have felt that he needed to justify his anecdotes by such a general principle, but the average man was only too pleased to have a good story or item of scandal for its own sake.

Franklin himself liked to be amused by the reading of collections of bons mots, especially those in which the salt of pleasantry

Notes to this chapter begin on page 252.

concealed a philosophical purpose, and for every story told to him he could reciprocate with another of the same kind.[2] Many anecdotes comprising witty retorts were attributed to Franklin, most of which included the philosophical turn that he prized. One of the best, which was never published in France, concerns his response to the abbé Raynal's "favorite theory of the degeneracy of animals, and even of man, in America."[3] At a dinner party when Raynal had been urging the doctrine with his customary eloquence, Franklin suggested that the French and the American guests rise so that they could "see on which side nature had degenerated." It happened that the American guests were "of the finest stature and form; while those of the other side were remarkably diminutive, and the Abbé himself particularly, was a mere shrimp."

Grimm reported in his *Correspondance littéraire* (July, 1778) an anecdote of Franklin's taciturnity. Throughout his sojourn in Paris he was noted for his silence in company, but especially so on his first appearance in 1776 before France became an open ally of the United States. A wit at a dinner during that time said to Franklin, hoping to bring him out in conversation, "One must admit, monsieur, that it is a great and superb spectacle which America offers us today." "Yes," replied Franklin modestly, "but the spectators do not pay."[4] Grimm also reported the most famous of Franklin's bons mots, that concerning the first balloon ascensions. "Many people who prided themselves upon remaining indifferent in the midst of the public enthusiasm did not fail to repeat, 'To what use do they expect to put these experiments? What good is this discovery that they make so much noise about?' The venerable Franklin replied with his accustomed simplicity, 'What good is a new-born baby?' "[5] One of the pioneer aerialists, Ducarne de Blaugy, hearing of this flippant allusion, wrote to Franklin in high dudgeon,[6] maintaining in great seriousness that several successful flights had been made from Calais to Dover and that, if the balloon had been invented earlier, Gibraltar could have been taken. This remonstrance did not check Franklin's levity, however, for on the occasion of the flight of the first hydrogen balloon carrying passengers, he remarked that the earliest balloon was an infant, but the latest, a giant. In similar vein he observed that the first aerostatic machine was a child, of which M. Montgolfier was the father and M. Charles the foster-mother.[7]

A few months after Franklin's death, the abbé Morellet sent a whole series of anecdotes to *Le Moniteur,* the foremost newspaper of the time,[8] each illustrating a phase of Franklin's practical good sense. The first of these is recorded also by Cabanis in a slightly expanded form.[9] In England Franklin carried out one of his experiments to calm water in a pond by pouring oil upon it. A credulous farmer, imagining some kind of supernatural influence, asked in amazement, "Tell me, what am I to believe?" "Nothing except what you see," replied Franklin. He later observed to his friends, "This man, being witness to something extraordinary was ready to believe the wildest absurdities—such is the logic of three-fourths of the human race." Morellet's next anecdote illustrates exactly the opposite characteristic in the American Indians—that they may witness a most extraordinary event without seeking to trace it back to its cause. An Indian one day saw Franklin's experiment of igniting alcohol by a spark of electricity. "Clever people, these whites," he said, without the least surprise or reflection.

Elsewhere in his literary works, Morellet reports an observation of Franklin on the subject of men who pretend to knowledge that they do not possess.[10] Franklin observed that an Englishman would readily admit "I don't know" when asked a question beyond his powers, but a Frenchman would never do so. "A Frenchman always replies as though he knows very well what you ask; but when pinned down to details and circumstances, he is frequently forced to admit that he is ignorant of the most important ones, even those which are indispensable to the giving of any kind of an answer." Condorcet also preserved one of Franklin's observations on French national character.[11] "You have in France," he said one day to Turgot, "an excellent means of making war at absolutely no cost to the nation. You have only to agree not to have your hair curled and not to use powder as long as the war shall last. Your wig-makers will form an army, and you can maintain them with the fees you will save, and the grain which would otherwise go to make powder will serve to nourish them."

Morellet repeats two stories he had heard Franklin tell several times that illustrate traits contrary to those symbolized by Franklin himself.[12] One concerns his experiences with a journeyman printer who never came to work before Wednesday. When Franklin pointed out that a full week's work would enable him to provide for the future, the workman replied: "Some people make themselves gentlemen by wholesale; I prefer doing it by retail. I should rather be idle half of every week for the next twenty years than be idle all of the week twenty years hence." Another in a similar vein is of a man who wished to sharpen a dull axe, a story Franklin included in his autobiography. The smith promised to grind it bright if the man would turn the wheel. Finding this a fatiguing business, the owner of the axe stopped his turning when the axe had just taken on a mottled shade, explaining, "I think a speckled axe is best."

After the War for Independence had broken out, Franklin commented on his earlier having been dispossessed of the office of Postmaster in the colonies. "Since the suppression of my office, I have received no further income from it, but neither has the king." In his autobiography he remarked that during his tenure it yielded three times as much clear revenue to the crown as the post office of Ireland; after his removal, "not one farthing!" [13] Speaking of the corruption in the English parliament, he once said that if the people of the United States had given him one quarter of the cost of the war to be used in bribery, he could have bought their independence for them. Cabanis reports essentially the same words,[14] and Chamfort remarks that all of Franklin's friends in Paris knew the story.[15]

On the subject of the American Revolution Franklin also confided to Cabanis that he knew how to profit by ministerial pride, the false views of British diplomacy, and the hatred of George III.[16] In the affairs of the world, he said, "it is a great advantage to inspire a passionate hatred in one's enemy." On leaving the stand after his famous examination, he said to a friend who had accompanied him, "That was a handsome discourse which the buyer has not finished paying for. It can turn out to be more expensive than he thinks." Franklin customarily ridiculed the concept of checks and balances in government and had no admiration for the English political system. To him, it was an amorphous hodgepodge of circumstances, maintained by corruption and kept in order only by public spirit and freedom of the press.

We return to the tales of Morellet: [17] When Franklin served in the Pennsylvania Assembly shortly after the Declaration of Independence, great debates took place concerning the form of government that was to be instituted. These debates extended themselves without issue for two or three months during which time life in the community continued smoothly and evenly. "You see," Franklin warned his fellow legislators, "that in the midst of our present anarchy life goes on just as before. If our disputes continue, take care lest the people realize that they can easily dispense with our services."

One day he was visiting the factories in Norwich, where a portly industrialist in showing him around boasted, "Here is cloth for Italy; this is for Germany, this for the West Indies, and this for the American continent." During this display Franklin noticed that the workers were half-naked or wearing patched and tattered clothing. He turned toward his guide and asked, "And don't you make anything for Norwich?"

This story was told also by Charles Pougens, who had heard it with some others from a Scottish family living in France, distantly related by marriage to Franklin. [18] Among his other tales, Pougens tells one of the crudest in existence concerning Franklin. It must also have been one of the most popular since Pougens regards its common vogue as its greatest fault. When Franklin was trying to demonstrate to Parliament that the colonists lacked the resources to pay the taxes required by the Stamp Act, someone objected that the colonists should at least reimburse Parliament for the expense of having the stamps printed. This reminded Franklin of a workman on the Pont-Neuf in Paris, who was heating iron rods in a bucket and who proposed to a passer-by that he insert one in his backside. When the latter refused categorically, the worker demanded, "At least pay me for my coals." The story is authentic, for Franklin had told it in a London newspaper in 1766. [19] In the original version Franklin compared the English demand for payment of the unused stamps after the repeal of the Stamp Act to this same worker—

the Frenchman that used to accost English and other Strangers on the Pont-Neuf, with many Compliments, and a red hot Iron in his

Hand; *Pray Monsieur Anglois,* says he, *Do me the Favour to let me have the Honour of thrusting this hot Iron into your Backside?* Zoons, what does the Fellow mean! Begone with your Iron or I'll break your Head! *Nay Monsieur,* replies he, *if you do not chuse it, I do not insist upon it. But at least, you will in Justice have the Goodness to pay me something for the heating of my Iron.*

Pougens also tells of Franklin's efforts to keep Barbeu Dubourg from investing in a financial enterprise, the operation of which Dubourg was completely ignorant. Franklin told him the story of a man condemned to be hanged for horse-stealing. A professional horse thief, who went to see the condemned man to find out how he came to be taken, realized after a few questions that the condemned was a novice at the trade. When the other admitted it was pure chance that led him to take the horse, the professional replied indignantly, "What the devil do you mean by stealing horses, if you are not a real horse thief?" This story also is authentic, for John Adams recorded in his diary that he heard Franklin tell it at Dubourg's home, May 20, 1778.[20]

While Franklin was in France, gossip concerning his activities circulated in the pages of the *Mémoires secrets*. Here and in *l'Espion anglois* we find an identical description of his first appearance in Paris. He is described as very proud of his country, but very reticent in public. "He said that the heavens, jealous of her beauty, had visited her with the scourge of civil war." The freethinkers who had sounded him on the subject of religion had come to the conclusion that he shared their own—that is, that he had none.[21] The latter opinion was not widespread, however, for even in the *Dictionnaire des athées anciens et modernes,* 1800, a work that includes Young, author of *Night Thoughts,* Franklin is described merely as "the Pythagoras of the new world and the second founder of American liberty." No mention is made of religious heterodoxy.

The *Mémoires* continued to report Franklin's public appearances, particularly those with a note of frivolity. During the progress of his negotiations with the French court, the *Mémoires* noticed that Franklin was showing his human side more and more by appearing at social events—even those noted for gallantry.[22] At a ball given by the wife of a financier, each of the young and beautiful women present went in turn to pay him homage and to embrace him despite his spectacles, which he wore constantly on his nose. Many were shocked by the luxury he allowed his grandsons, whose red heels and other frivolous decorations contrasted sharply with Franklin's dignified simplicity.

During the entire period of his sojourn at Passy, Franklin was active in the affairs of the Masonic lodge of the Nine Sisters, attending regular meetings and social events and for a time serving as Grand Master (Vénérable). In 1778 he was present at a festival in his own honor, and the *Mémoires,* in reporting it, expressed astonishment that a man charged with such grave responsibilities as Franklin could spend an entire day "amid a heap of youngsters and poetasters who intoxicated him with insipid and puerile incense." [23] Announcing the news that Franklin had been elected Vénérable (May 26, 1779), the *Mémoires* marvelled derisively that Franklin with all his weighty affairs could find the time "to play in the chapel and follow the assemblies of the free-masons as though he were the idlest brother." [24]

At Twelfth Night (*la veille des Rois*), Franklin decided to observe the French custom of serving consecrated bread—although as a protestant and a mere leaseholder there was ample warrant for his not doing so.[25] But he found personal satisfaction in the ceremony, for which he had ordered thirteen brioches—the number of the American colonies. Instead of placing in each cake the traditional figure of a king, he wanted to insert a banderole with the word *Liberty* inscribed on the first. Two prelates, whom he had invited to dinner on the eve of the festival, protested against his unorthodox innovations. The Chevalier d'Eon, who was also present, added a political opinion to their theological remonstrance. "Being only three leagues from Versailles," he argued, "it was not expedient to use a word which the court neither loved nor wished to be acquainted with."

At the beginning of 1783, when a victorious peace was certain for the Americans, La Musée de Paris, a social and artistic organization founded by the Lodge of the Nine Sisters, held a public assembly at which homage to the new nation was rendered to Franklin as its representative.[26] There had been interminable personal tributes in prose and verse, including a reading of abbé Brizard's *Fragment de Xénophon,* followed by a concert and magnificent supper. The journalists felt that the whole thing was a little ridiculous and that it had been carried much too far. "There *inter scyphos & pocula,* in a delightful delirium, they crowned with laurel and myrtle even the head of Franklin. It is doubtless not a spectacle devoid of philosophy to see a grave personnage like M. Franklin, burdened with the most important concerns, especially at this moment, occupying himself with literary foolishness of the kind, participating in these infantile games, and amusing himself by it."

Just a few months later the same journal printed some satirical words to a popular refrain, suggesting that Franklin affected to be tired of popular adulation, but nevertheless showed himself where he was sure to receive it.[27]

> Nestor de l'Amérique,
> Prise la voix publique
> Du monde politique
> Et du monde savant:
> Mais dédaigne l'hommage
> Dont le peuple volage,
> Sans respect pour ton âge,
> T'ennuie à chaque instant.
> Conserve bien ta tête,
> Mais sans la montrer tant.

At least two of the anecdotes in the *Mémoires secrets* are substantiated by manuscripts now existing. In 1782 Lafayette, just returned to France from America, became the father of a daughter, whom he named Virginie in honor of the new republic. The *Mémoires* reported that Franklin, to whom he had told the good news, replied good-humoredly that he wished the General a child for every state.[28] He added facetiously that the names of some were not very harmonious and that Mlle. Connecticut or Mlle. Massachusetts Bay would not be very fond of theirs. This is quite in accord with the spirit of Franklin's actual letter:

> In naming your Children I think you do well to begin with the most antient State. And as we cannot have too many of so good a Race I hope you & Mme. de la Fayette will go thro the Thirteen. But as that may be in the common Way too severe a task for her delicate Frame, and Children of Seven Months may become as Strong as those of Nine, I consent to the Abridgement of Two Months for each; and I wish her to spend the Twenty-six Months so gained, in perfect Ease, Health & Pleasure.

While you are proceeding, I hope our States will some of them
new-name themselves. Miss Virginia, Miss Carolina, and Miss
Georgiana will sound prettily enough for the Girls; but Massachusetts & Connecticut, are too harsh even for the Boys, unless
they were to be Savages.[29]

The *Mémoires secrets* found Franklin's own name subject for
amusement, reporting at length an extremely crude pun.[30] A
farmer from Normandy named Franqlin came with his genealogical records to visit Franklin and to determine whether they
belonged to the same family. After the exchange of appropriate
greetings, Franklin asked his secretary to examine his claims. The
latter, remarking on the difference in the spelling of the two
names, concocted a witticism, which cannot be translated, "Monsieur, de votre Q (cul) faites un K (cas) & vos papiers vous
serviront." Whether or not he was forced to submit to this rude
pun, there was actually a country-dweller named Franquelin who
fancied himself as Franklin's relative. A number of his letters on
the subject are still in existence, including one in which he asks
Franklin to use his illustrious name and influence to obtain for
him the position of Agent on one of the King's farms.[31] The pun
on his name must have found great favor with the Paris wits,
for six years later the entire tale reappeared in the *Mémoires
secrets* in verse form.[32] The only notable difference is that the
name is here spelled Franquelin, and he is said to come from
Brittany. This is the spelling on the letters actually sent to Franklin, but they came from Hesdin, which is in Pas-de-Calais.

> Un Breton nommé *Franquelin,*
> Se croyant le cousin-germain
> Du Savant de Philadelphie,
> Vint à Paris de Quimper-Corentin
> Pour compulser la généalogie.
> Voilà mon homme convaincu
> De son bon droit, qui déduit sa demande.
> Monsieur, dit un plaisant, la différence est grande
> Entre les noms & l'on vous a deçu.
> Le Docteur pose un K & vous posez un Q.
> La signature ainsi de tout tems fût écrite:
> Mais pour vous tirer d'embarras,
> De votre Q (cul) faites un K (cas)
> Et vos papiers vous serviront ensuite.

The court circle also found amusement in Franklin's name. One day when he was coldly received by the King, a wag said his name should be Franc-Côlin (a true rustic).[33]

A number of anecdotes concern Franklin's adaptation to the artificial manners of Parisian society. A very improbable story in the *New Hampshire Gazette*, December 22, 1778, describes Franklin in the gardens of Versailles demonstrating some of his electrical experiments for the benefit of the Queen.[34] "She asked him, in a fit of raillery, if he did not dread the fate of Prometheus, who was so severely served for stealing fire from Heaven. 'Yes, please your Majesty' (replied old Franklin, with infinite gallantry), 'if I did not behold a pair of eyes this moment, which have stolen infinitely more fire from Jove than ever I did, pass unpunished, though they do more mischief in a week than I have done in all my experiments.'"

A more probable anecdote concerns his relations with Lord Stormont, the British ambassador in Paris who, like Franklin, engaged in propaganda for his country. On one occasion he allegedly "told a French nobleman, that six battalions in Washington's army had laid down their arms. The nobleman applied to Doctor Franklin, to know whether the story was a truth (*une vérité*), to which the Doctor answered, '*Non, Monsieur, ce n'est pas vérité, c'est seulement un Stormont.* No Sir, it is not a truth, it is only a Stormont.' This answer was afterwards handed about amongst the wits of Paris, and the word Stormont has since become the court phrase for a lie." [35]

Details concerning another phase of Franklin's life at Passy—his inveterate chess playing—came from the grandson of Franklin's landlord, Donatien le Ray de Chaumont.[36] Franklin spent nearly every free evening at the latter's home in the central part of a large building of which Franklin occupied one of the wings. One evening in the apartment of Mme. de Chaumont, Franklin began a game of chess with the priest who served as tutor to the heir of the family. When the lady wished to retire, the game was transferred at Franklin's suggestion to his own quarters. There one game succeeded another, until the supply of candles became exhausted. Franklin, absorbed by the pleasures of combat, protested, "My dear abbé, it is impossible for two men such as we to give up because of the lack of illumination." The priest thereupon offered to seek a new supply of candles in his own quarters and set off with Franklin's benediction, "May the goddess of night protect you in your adventurous journey." In his absence Franklin took advantage of the last flickers of candlelight treacherously to plot a check-mate. He was still far from having arranged it when the abbé returned with a bewildered air. "What is wrong?" Franklin asked. "You look like a man who has just lost two chess-games. Has the goddess of night failed to answer my prayer or has Mercury sent one of his imps to our park?" "It is not at all a matter of night and robbers," replied the abbé. "It is Phoebus or at least Aurora with her rosy fingers who reigns at this moment." So saying, he opened the blinds and the sunlight filled the room. "You are right, it is daytime," Franklin replied calmly. "Let's go to bed."

On another occasion Franklin was playing with an important northern diplomat at the home of one of the French ministers. The room filled with public men and diplomats, but Franklin refused to give up his game. Suddenly a messenger presented Franklin with a packet from America that had just arrived at Franklin's house. This was at a time of one of the most crucial phases of the war and there had been no dispatches for some time; still Franklin pretended not to hear and went on with his game. The younger Chaumont, who had been Franklin's pupil in chess as well as in English, ventured to take the packet and present it again to Franklin, explaining that it was a dispatch from Congress. Franklin replied that it could keep until the game was over, and only then did he open the dispatch, which announced one of the most sensational triumphs of the war. Jefferson relates that Franklin frequently played with the old Duchess of Bourbon, whose game was about equal to his. "Happening once to put his king into prize, the Doctor took it. 'Ah,' says she, 'we do not take kings so.' 'We do in America,' said the Doctor." [37] Lafayette told a similar story to Fanny Wright, who in turn passed it on to Jeremy Bentham. "While Franklin was negotiating in Paris, he sometimes went into a café to play at chess. A crowd usually assembled, of course to see the man rather than the play. Upon one occasion, Franklin lost in the middle of the game, when, composedly taking the king from the board, he put him in his pocket and continued to move. The antagonist looked up. The face of

Franklin was so grave, and his gesture so much in earnest, that he began with an expostulatory, 'Sir!' 'Yes, Sir, continue,' said Franklin, 'and we shall soon see that the party without a king will win the game.' " [38]

Chaumont includes among his anecdotes a tale of Franklin's shrewd behavior at a country inn in America. Entering the tap-room one day, benumbed with cold, he found the fireplace sur-rounded and all the benches taken. No one moved, for Franklin was at the time unknown. He called out, therefore, in a stentorian voice for a basket of oysters to be taken outside to his horse. The chimney-squatters, overhearing the command, ran with curiosity to watch the oysters being opened and presented to the horse. Franklin in the meantime took his choice of the vacated seats. The company came trooping back to Franklin to explain that the horse had refused to eat the oysters. "In that case," Franklin replied, "give the horse some hay and bring the oysters to me." [39] The same story circulated in America as well, where it was turned into the following verse.[40]

> Franklin, one night, cold freezing to the skin,
> Stop'd on his journey, at a public inn;
> Rejoic'd perceives the kindling flames arise;
> But, luckless sage, perceives with distant eyes
> A blackguard crew monopolize the heat,
> . . .   .   seat.
> "Ho," cries the doctor never at a loss,
> "Landlord a peck of oysters for my horse."
> "Your horse eat oysters," cries the wondering host?
> "Give him a peck, you'll see they wont be lost."
> The croud astonish'd rush into the stall;
> "A horse eat oysters, what, and shells and all!"
> Meantime, our traveller as the rest retire,
> Picks the best seat at the deserted fire;
> A place convenient for the cunning elf,
> To roast his oysters and to warm himself.
> The herd return'd, "your horse wont eat them sir."
> "Wont eat good oysters; he's a simple cur,
> I know who will," he adds in merry mood,
> "Hand them to me, a horse don't know what's good."

The authors of all of the foregoing anecdotes were concerned primarily with telling a good story or repeating a memorable event. Two other compilers of Franklin memorabilia, the abbé de la Roche and Cabanis, used their material not primarily for its own sake, but to illustrate a general principle of morality or human behavior. De la Roche gathered together his anecdotes in order to show that minor events and apparently trivial circumstances—even those of childhood—may serve to develop the character of an extraordinary man. He considered his reminiscences of Franklin as a study in human character. In his own words, "My liaison with this great man . . . has enabled me to record the particular events which, although slight in appearance, have had in his own opinion the greatest influence on his character and on the whole conduct of his life." [41] Ironically those anecdotes of Franklin that were printed merely as morsels of gossip or samples of witty repartee and human eccentricity enjoyed a wide circulation, whereas the incidents that de la Roche selected to illustrate his principle of moral development were not published until modern times. We shall see that all of the following incidents reflect in one way or another the view that in all the occupations of his life Franklin despised anything that did not lead directly to the true enjoyment of a rational man. Doubtless the abbé would have had little respect for the opinion of Chaumont and the editors of the *Mémoires secrets* that some of Franklin's occupations represented a rather low degree of rational enjoyment.

According to the abbé, Franklin throughout his life constantly based his conduct on the maxim, "To be useful to others and to depend on them as little as possible is to approach the perfection of the all-powerful Being who does good to everything and has need of nothing." The habit of doing everything for himself led to his scientific discoveries and enabled him to devise and manufacture for himself the equipment necessary for his experiments. In whatever he did he sought simplicity and valued things only for their usefulness. His zeal for simplicity led him to ridicule the vanity of variety and multiplicity, the incommodious luxury of the handsome apartments of Parisian aristocrats. He once commented, "I see marble, porcelain and gilt squandered without utility, elegant fireplaces which smoke without heating; tables on which one cannot write without freezing with cold and then only against the light; beds and alcoves where one may sleep in good health, but where in sickness it is impossible to be cared for or to read or to write comfortably."

He had a rich Quaker friend, who lived by himself in an enormous home. Franklin, visiting him, asked in every superfluous room he entered, why his friend bothered to keep it up. The latter always answered that he did so because he had the means. Finally, Franklin asked why he had a table in his dining room large enough for twenty-five people. The answer was the same—because he had the means. "In that case," replied Franklin, "why don't you have a hat of the same size. You have the means." In the spirit of *Poor Richard* Franklin argued that by seeking to display wealth we are seeing through the eyes of others. Franklin himself, by curtailing the foolish display of vanity, was able to devote his time to making his life useful to his country and to the world. Even in the midst of his complicated diplomatic negotiations he never allowed his correspondence or other affairs to remain without attention. His health was so good that he sometimes went for eight days at a time without any rest except a few hours in his armchair. Even at the age of eighty, he taught his grandson to swim in the Seine at Passy, making the trip with him from bank to bank.

Franklin enjoyed feminine companionship and indulged himself in it even though it meant a loss of time. "He welcomed his friends of the gentler sex with a sort of amiable coquettishness which pleased every one of them. If any one of them, jealous of his preferences, demanded whether he did not love her more than the others, he replied, 'Yes, when you are nearest to me because of the force of attraction.'" He loved to tell his moral tales to young people also and to inspire them with simple and natural tastes. To a young man ready for a trip to Italy, Franklin gave a lesson in education. Discovering that the young man knew nothing of the arts and the talents of the country he was planning to visit, Franklin advised him to acquire some knowledge before setting out. "To see monuments requires only eyes, but to appreciate them requires a judgment exercised by comparisons and enlightened by study." Franklin told the young man that without prior knowledge he could hope to learn little by travel, for it is necessary to converse in order to learn. Conversation is a form of exchange, and he who contributes nothing receives nothing in return. The man who cannot even ask the right questions will not find others eager to give away information gratuitously.

His love of simplicity led him to confine himself to a single secretary, despite his voluminous correspondence, and he persuaded Vergennes to conduct all American affairs personally with him in order to spare the delays and duplications of bureaucracy. Despite his mania for economizing time, he felt himself obliged to be civil to almost everyone who importuned him. A certain member of the ancient nobility wrote, for example, to offer his services as monarch of the new country, declaring that since his title extended to William the Conqueror, he was possessed of all the qualifications. He offered to accept the title of King with a pension of fifteen thousand pounds and agreed to remain in his own province so that the Americans could govern themselves as they pleased. Thomas Paine in *The Rights of Man* tells the story with minor variations. The candidate for the American kingship introduced his proposal to the Doctor by letter, stating, that as the Americans had dismissed their king, they would need another, that he was a Norman of more ancient family than the Dukes of Normandy and that his line had never been bastardized. Receiving no reply, he wrote a second letter in which he proposed "with great dignity . . . that if his offer was not accepted, an acknowledgement of about £30,000 might be made to him for his generosity!" [42]

At the conclusion of the war, Mme. Helvétius and Franklin's other friends begged him not to return to Pennsylvania, but to undergo an operation for the stone and to finish out the remainder of his days with them. Jefferson on hearing this made the remark that if Franklin were to accept this proposal and then succumb to the operation, he would have no alternative but to seize his coffin and return it to America, convinced that the very presence of Franklin's body would consolidate the spirit of the Revolution. Franklin himself begged his friends not to make his parting more difficult by urging him to remain. "My task is not finished," he told them. "The little which remains of my life I owe to those who have entrusted me with their own. I suffer, it is true, but nature, which has treated me so well up to the present, will surely allow me the time to reply to the desires of my countrymen. If I am cured after satisfying all my duties toward my country, my greatest happiness will be to finish out my days in a country where I have enjoyed so many pleasures among the most enlightened men of Europe." A similar anecdote appeared in print the year after Franklin's death. To someone who asked why he should leave the climate of France to which he was now accustomed, he replied, "If I had no country of my own, it would be at Paris where I should like to finish out my days; but I want to enjoy for a moment the pleasure of seeing my fellow-citizens free and ready for all the happiness I wish them." [43]

Although de la Roche measured the sincerity of Franklin's regrets on the subject of his departure by the presence of tears in his eyes, he was careful to add that at all times his words were the true expression of his feelings. "If he sometimes believed it prudent to hide his opinions, he never disguised them." His only means of deceiving the British Ministry had been to tell them the literal truth. The American Revolution would never have taken place had they believed him at the time of his examination at the House of Commons.

Advanced age did not in the least diminish his sensibilities. One day walking in the Bois de Boulogne with a friend, he spoke of his son who had died at the age of seven over forty years previously and tears came to his eyes. He said to his friend, "Do not be surprised at the grief which such a distant loss still causes. Alas! I still imagine that this son would have been the best of my children." Franklin's tenderness toward all children is reported by Pougens, who records one of his typical sayings, "Children should be treated like strangers who arrive from an unknown country and who must be politely taught the customs of ours."

An anecdote in other papers of the abbé de la Roche reveals that Franklin held a very low opinion of political oratory. [44] During his twenty years of service at the British court he observed that the ministers who shone most brilliantly by their eloquence in Parliament were the most inept in handling of great affairs and discussion of details. The verbiage of these orators so completely blocked and confused the progress of affairs that the King was forced to take them into the ministry in order to put an end to it. Franklin had heard the elder Pitt, for example, speak admirably for entire half-days on subjects concerning which Franklin wished to negotiate, but he would never have had any results without the aid of his clerks and secretary. At the beginning of the American troubles, Pitt was strongly desirous of bringing about reconciliation. Although he no longer held office of any kind, he frequently visited Franklin's apartments incognito in order to lay the foundation for negotiations. He always spoke at great length, never listened to replies, and left without concluding anything. One day Franklin visited him at his country estate, carrying with him documents incorporating a plan of reconciliation. Franklin arrived at nine in the morning, listened for six hours to Pitt's wit and eloquence, and left at three in the afternoon with his papers untouched and the subject of the conference not even broached.

Most of the anecdotes recorded by de la Roche, since they are not available elsewhere, give a novel and colorful view of Franklin's personality. Many of those presented by Cabanis, on the other hand, are based upon Franklin's *Memoirs* and consequently serve to support the conventional view of Franklin's character rather than to furnish new light upon his behavior and personality. Cabanis sees Franklin through Franklin's own eyes, that is to say, he sees essentially what Franklin had taught him to look for. The epitome of Franklin's own notions as expressed in his *Memoirs* are revealed in Cabanis' theory of the art of biography:

> The fundamental facts in the history of great men are without doubt the important events in which they have taken part or the works which they have executed. But frequently there results from a knowledge of these facts no precise idea concerning the temper of their mind and character. Those among them who most deserve to stand as models, those whose memory is accompanied by the most useful lessons, need to be studied in the details which concern their intimate day to day existence. . . . This truth . . . is especially applicable to the great men who are distinguished primarily by their character, who are not content to afford to fame merely some moments or some days of a sort of theatrical representation, who do not owe their reputation to some transitory flashes, but who have established it upon a continuous plan of conduct, or a regular system of habits of every moment. Such was Benjamin Franklin, no doubt in the eyes of his friends more extraordinary, more worthy of being observed in the intimate details of his life, than he was great in the eyes of America and Europe." [45]

This definition or estimate of a great man was tailor-made for Franklin, since Franklin himself attributed his eminence to a number of systematic, moral, and physical exercises and wrote his autobiography partly to vindicate his modes of self-examination. Cabanis, who believed that Franklin's character was even more important than his scientific discoveries or his brilliant political exploits, wrote his "Notice" on Franklin as a supplementary vindication. As a result, his work is deadly serious—with no lively anecdotes such as those of his friends Morellet and de la Roche.

Franklin, aware of the philosophical earnestness of Cabanis, probably exposed to him only the serious side of his own character. As a matter of fact, Franklin seems to have pulled his leg at least once. In one of his most serious works, *Rapports du physique et du moral de l'homme,* Cabanis says that he had several times heard Franklin tell that he had "observed in the forests of North America a sort of bird which, like the horned screamer or the horned lapwing, carries two horned tubercles at the joints of the wings. These two tubercles at the death of the bird become the sprouts of two vegetable stalks which grow at first in sucking the juice from its cadavre and which subsequently attach themselves to the earth in order to live in the manner of plants and trees." [46] Completely *au sérieux* Cabanis remarks in his next sentence, "Several other learned naturalists, among others my illustrious colleague Lacépède, to whom I have spoken of this fact, ignore it absolutely; therefore in spite of the great veracity of Franklin, I cite it with a great deal of reserve, and I draw from it no conclusion." Franklin's "great veracity" in this tale is of a piece with his stories of the grand leap of the whales up the falls of the Niagara and of the North American sheep with so much wool that each requires a four-wheeled wagon to support it.[47] Cabanis reports also that Franklin believed that he had several times received a revelation in his dreams of the outcome of his affairs, and that despite his strong mind that was otherwise completely devoid of prejudice he was unable entirely to escape a grain of superstition because of these inner voices.[48]

Cabanis prepared his recollections of Franklin when only the first part of Franklin's *Memoirs* had appeared, and he considered his own work as a temporary substitute for the complete ver-

sion. Many of his reminiscences duplicate sections of the autobiography, but some details in his recounting vary from Franklin.[49] On the subject of early intellectual influences, for example,
Franklin merely mentions Plutarch and attributes to Xenophon a
considerable influence on his early thought. Cabanis reverses the
emphasis: "It was before leaving his father's house that there fell
into his hands some volumes of Plutarch; he devoured them.
Nothing had ever made a stronger impression on him than the
great and simple manner and the philosophy at the same time
wise and generous of this writer, if it was not perhaps the exquisite good sense and the plainer virtue of Socrates . . . in the
Memorabilia of Xenophon. . . . Having read the tract on 'The
Eating of Flesh,' Franklin became convinced of the barbarousness and the pernicious effects of this custom; he resolved never
more to eat anything which had once had life." In a note Cabanis
points out that in his *Memoirs* Franklin attributes this resolution
to the reading of a book by Tryon on vegetable diet, but at Paris
he had spoken only of Plutarch. The abbé de la Roche also says
that Franklin adopted his rule against eating meat from Plutarch.

Cabanis follows the *Memoirs* in reporting that Franklin's reading of Anthony Collins gave him such a skeptical turn of mind
that he began to question all matters of dogma, the divinity of
the Scriptures, revelation, and the mysteries. According to Cabanis,
he never reached the final step of denying the reality of moral
distinctions. (Cabanis had never read his *Dissertation on Liberty
and Necessity!*) "As for morality, he constantly repeated that it
was the single rational design of individual happiness as it was
the sole guarantee of public happiness. One day when he had
already spoken at length on this point, he finished by telling
us . . . : 'If rascals knew all the advantages of virtue, they would
become honest out of rascality. ' " ("Si les coquins savaient tous les
avantages de la vertu, ils deviendraient honnêtes gens par co-
quinerie." Elsewhere in his works Cabanis repeats the same
thought in slightly different words: "Si les fripons, disait le sage
Franklin, pouvaient connaître tous les avantages attachés à l'habi-
tude des vertus, ils seraient honnêtes gens par friponnerie.") [50] It
is not surprising that Franklin should have said this—even though
he did not include a proverb to this effect in *Poor Richard*. As
a matter of fact, he printed one of the opposite view, "Poor Plain

Dealing! dead without Issue" (September, 1750). He did not even say in *Poor Richard* that "honesty is the best policy." This proverb is from Cervantes, not Franklin. Yet a major portion of *Poor Richard,* including all of *The Way to Wealth,* reflects principles of prudential morality. As we have already pointed out, the original *Poor Richard* has no comprehensive theme—especially in the early years. When Franklin first began publication he tried to make it entertaining as well as useful, and his chief emphasis was upon entertainment. Then after perceiving that it was almost universally read in Pennsylvania, he "considered it as a proper vehicle for conveying instruction among the common people." This is his own retrospective view in the *Memoirs,* but it is quite possible that he there attributes to himself a higher motive than actually prevailed at the time. He explains that he chose "proverbial sentences, chiefly such as inculcated industry and frugality, as the means of procuring wealth, and thereby securing virtue; it being more difficult for a man in want, to act always honestly, as, to use here one of those proverbs, *it is hard for an empty sack to stand upright."* [51] It is worthy of special mention that even this prudential morality is not quite the same thing as the sublime virtue that Dubourg and other French commentators attempted to read into *The Way to Wealth.*

Cabanis also reports Franklin's device for attaining moral perfection, which is described in great detail in the *Memoirs.* Franklin explains that in order to acquire perfection in the practice of what he considered to be the thirteen primary virtues, he arranged in a notebook a chart with a list of these virtues and spaces opposite them for the seven days of the week. Checking with black marks each fault committed, he attempted gradually to eradicate every offense. The importance of the recapitulation of Franklin's method by Cabanis is the evidence that Franklin took his notebook with him to France. "We have had in our hands this precious little book. One perceives in it a sort of chronological history of Franklin's mind and character. One sees him develop, fortify and mold all the actions which constitute spiritual perfection, and the art of life and virtue taught in the same manner as that of playing an instrument or manufacturing weapons."

Solely on the basis of his own observation Cabanis adds what amounts to a fourteenth virtue—politeness. This must have been one of Franklin's most admirable characteristics, and a recognition of it should do much to counterbalance aspersions on his behavior based on the apparent smugness or moral materialism of the thirteen original virtues. According to Cabanis, Franklin considered politeness to be a kind of amiable benevolence, not the artificial etiquette of social relations expressed in gestures and formalities. "That which he esteemed was the politeness of the heart, the evidence of a habitual obligingness. He made of it a virtue—he thought that one is obliged to be amiable—almost as one must pay one's debts—and that only a higher interest may excuse a good man for offending another—even in indifferent concerns. 'The most irreconcilable discords, the most violent hates, often stem,' he said, 'from minor pricks such as those which released the winds enclosed in Ulysses' leathern bag. One may easily avoid many chagrins and misfortunes by a little attention to one's self and consideration for others—and even if an open rupture comes about one is at fault if one does not make the people with whom one lives as happy as one can.' "

Cabanis reveals much about Franklin's early life that is not in the *Memoirs,* particularly about his reading habits. He read Bacon's *Essays* and was impressed by "Of Atheism." "He loved to cite two sentences of Bacon, one that it requires more credulousness to be an atheist than to believe in God; the other 'that a little philosophy inclineth man's mind to atheism; but depth in philosophy bringeth men's minds about to religion.' " Cabanis also attributes much greater influence to the Bible than Franklin admits in his own works. "In reading the Bible, which he did often, the Book of Proverbs attracted his attention in a particular manner. One notices in those books called wisdom books a great knowledge of the human heart and of society. The Proverbs contains excellent lessons applicable to common life and compressed in energetic and piquant phrases. Franklin there read: 'Length of days is in her right hand, and in her left hand riches and honor.' " The pronoun in this proverb refers to Virtue. For some reason Cabanis converts the pronoun to the second person: "La longue vie est dans ta main droite, et la fortune dans ta main gauche." In his *Memoirs,* Franklin cites this proverb as one of several in his notebook on moral perfection, but he does not give it the preeminence that Cabanis does.[52] He also clearly indicates that it is virtue and not merely personal persistence that guarantees fortune and long life. Cabanis cites Franklin's determination at the age of twenty to confirm this proverb in his own life. At the age of eighty he recalled this circumstance to his friends and added, "Judge whether I have been deceived. My health was not more firm then than today. I enjoy, not opulence, but easy circumstances far above my needs; and it is well known in the world that King George has little reason to be content with his quarrels with the journeyman printer."

When Franklin announced to his family his determination to follow a vegetarian diet, "his mother let him have his way persuaded that his eccentricity would not last. But she soon perceived that she was mistaken; and when his friends asked her what could have put such a thing in the head of her son, she replied, 'He is a mad philosopher.' She added, 'There is nothing bad in it; this will give him the habit of empire over himself; he will learn that one can do anything with a strong will.' " The abbé de la Roche tells the same story, but with a completely different emphasis. According to his account, when one of Franklin's friends asked her why he ate only fruits and vegetables, his mother replied, 'Apparently he read it in some old mad philosopher.' " De la Roche adds that "this light sarcasm touched him little." [53] Another version of this story appeared in print before Franklin's death and before the publication of any part of his *Memoirs,* indeed before the revised copy was sent to Le Veillard and La Rochefoucauld. In the *Journal de Paris,* March 27, 1786, and later in *Almanach littéraire, ou étrennes d'Apollon* (Paris, 1787) appeared an anecdote on Franklin at the age of twenty determining to pursue a diet of bread and water exclusively. It was told that he lived for six weeks on a pound of bread a day and no other beverage but water without perceiving any debilitation of mind or body. "His mother, who was asked why he lived such a strange life, replied, 'He has read some crazy philosopher, a certain Plutarch, but I leave him alone; he will soon get tired of it.' " [54]

According to Cabanis, Franklin maintained that man is complete only when he is associated with a wife worthy of providing his happiness. Until then his existence is imperfect; it is only the half of a whole, which cannot remain thus divided without great disadvantages. Nature always punishes us by the faults and particular misfortunes of a system that contradicts hers. In 1768 Franklin had written in similar terms to a young man congratulating him on marrying early in life. "An odd Volume of a Set of Books," he wrote, "is not worth its proportion of the Set, and what think you of the Usefulness of an odd Half of a Pair of Scissors. It cannot well cut any thing. It may possibly serve to scrape a Trencher." [55] Later in Passy he wrote to another friend, "Man & Woman have each of them Qualities & Tempers, in which the other is deficient, and which in Union contribute to the common Felicity. Single and separate, they are not the compleat human Being; they are like the odd Halves of Scissors; they cannot answer the End of their Formation." [56] Cabanis quotes Franklin as saying of his own wife, "I discovered that she always knew what I did not know, and if something escaped me, I was sure that it was precisely that which she had seized."

On the subject of material wealth, Cabanis reported that Franklin was pleased to have a competency, but did not wish to be wealthy. He had often said that he was rather disturbed at being as rich as he was than at not being any richer. "My heirs," he added, "will find it more difficult to deserve something than if the need of making their own way inspired their activity; and I should consider myself culpable toward them if I sought to heap advantages upon them which one ordinarily enjoys wholesomely only when one has acquired it by one's own labor."

Cabanis relates an anecdote concerning Washington that caused the American general to become a symbol of militarism during the French Revolution. At the outbreak of the War for Independence, the patriots were somewhat dubious about Washington because he seemed to vacillate between the British military service and the voice of his country. "His first incertitudes had left some doubts in the mind of ardent republicans, and, at the outset, when he ventured some remarks on political affairs, they were known to say to him, 'Mr. Washington, do not concern yourself with that—get up on your white horse.'" In the French National Assembly, July 21, 1792, M. Torné used this story in a speech directed against Lafayette. According to Torné, Franklin often remarked with complacence that Washington "appeared one day in Congress to talk on public affairs. 'Get back on your battle

horse,' said the president of the Congress, 'it is up to us to regu-
late internal affairs.' " [57]

Volney, who during his youth was a close friend of Cabanis and
actually lived for a time in the house of Mme. Helvétius, a fact
little known, reports in one of his letters a saying concerning old
age.[58]

> "My dear Franklin," Mme. Helvétius said to him, "I like to be-
> lieve that you are happy." "I become more so every day," he re-
> plied. "I have never had the misfortune of finding myself ill. First
> poor, then rich, I have always been content with what I have, with-
> out thinking about what I have not; but since I have begun to age,
> since my passions have diminished, I feel a well-being of mind and
> heart that I never knew before and which is impossible to know at
> the age of these young people," he said, in pointing at us, Cabanis
> and me. "At that age, the spirit is *exterior;* at mine, it is *interior;*
> it looks out the window at the stir of those who pass by without
> taking part in their disputes."

Franklin's swan song, according to Cabanis, was a letter he sent
to Mme. Helvétius after his return to America. In it he reported
that "nearly all his days were passed among workmen constructing
commodious houses for his grandchildren, that he sometimes re-
newed acquaintance with the sages of all the centuries and he
tried to reassemble in his home those of his own country, that he
also devoted some moments to the arrangement of his papers and
to the writing of the last part of his memoirs. I extend, he added,
my arms toward you despite the immensity of the seas which separate us, in awaiting the celestial kiss which I firmly hope to give
you one day."

Of all the French anecdotes concerning Franklin, perhaps the
most significant concerns his social and economic station. According to de la Roche, the Queen, struck with his modest and
simple demeanor, asked a courtier what his occupation had been
before being made ambassador. "Overseer of a printing-house,"
was the answer. Another, overhearing it, remarked, "In France
he could never have risen to be higher than a bookseller." Pougens tells the same story except that it is a duke who refers dis-
dainfully to Franklin's occupation in America, and a man of
letters who replies sardonically, "Too bad that he was not born
in France; he would have been able with your protection to become one of the thirty-six printers in Paris."

This anecdote reveals an aspect of Franklin's reputation apparent in more serious sources—that he became the first symbol in France of the American ideal, or the American legend, of the rise from rags to riches. This theme received its primary statement in an anonymous English work, *A View of the History of Great-Britain, during the Administration of Lord North,* 1782, from which it was taken up and circulated in France.[59] Because of its importance I shall quote it *in extenso.*

> . . . This man (who formerly for many years carried on the business of a printer at Philadelphia) may be considered as the first fruits of American genius: and perhaps no man ever owed more to the time and place of his birth: had he been a native of London instead of Boston, and born into the same rank of society [His father was a tallow-chandler], the world would probably never have heard his name either as a philosopher or politician. Pent within a populous city, his occupation would have been more laborious, and his incentives to cultivate speculative science, would have been suppressed by every consideration of interest or ambition. He might have distinguished himself as an ingenious artist, but he would neither have formed an hypothesis to account for the phenomenon of the *Aurora Borealis,* nor have traced out the principles and operations of the electrical fluid; and what is much more important, he would never have become a powerful engine to shake a great empire, and to erect a congeries of republics from its dismembered parts; nor would he have had the appropriated distinction of being the principal agent to introduce a new aera in the history of mankind, which may prove as important as any which have yet elapsed, by procuring a legislative power to the western hemisphere. In this view he may be considered as a greater enemy to England than even Philip II or Louis XIV.

This paragraph and three subsequent ones devoted to Franklin were translated literally by Hilliard d'Auberteuil in his *Histoire de l'administration de Lord North,* 1784, a work that is a paraphrase and extension of the anonymous London publication.[60] The section on Franklin from the English work was also independently translated and incorporated in *Annecdotes* (sic) *historiques sur les principaux personnages qui jouent maintenant un rôle en Angleterre,* 1784.[61]

Condorcet presumably borrowed the theme from one of these sources for his *De l'influence de la révolution d'Amérique sur l'Europe,* 1786,[62] in which he cites Franklin as evidence that de-

pendence upon the mother country would not have extinguished
the natural genius of Americans. But this dependence "would
nearly always have directed genius toward other objects. The desire of being something in England would have stifled all other
sentiments in the mind of an American born with energy and
talents, and he would have chosen the quickest and the surest
means of attaining his end. Those who would not have been
able to nourish this ambition would have fallen into indolence
and discouragement."

The English work from which this concept derives presents
perhaps the best epitome of contemporary opinion concerning
Franklin.[63]

> Trammelled in no system, he may be said to be a philosopher
> without the rules, a politician without adopting the Roman pan-
> dects, and a statesman without having sacrificed to the graces: pos-
> sessing a diversity of genius without a versatility of temper.

Even today this statement could hardly be improved upon.

13. EULOGIES

Perhaps the most remarkable evidence of the respect and affection Franklin enjoyed in France is found in the official tributes
and eulogies after his death. Most famous of all declarations made
anywhere concerning Franklin was the dramatic announcement
of his passing by Mirabeau to the National Assembly, June 11,
1790.[1] It was eventually printed by nearly every newspaper in
France, London, and the United States, and came to be considered one of the symbolic statements of the French Revolution.

Mirabeau, the outstanding orator of the Assembly, used his
sonorous voice and dramatic delivery in a brief but highly significant tribute. In asking the French nation to observe a period of
mourning, he drew a contrast between the old regime symbolized
by insincere adulation of royalty and the revolutionary regime

Notes to this chapter begin on page 254.

of enlightenment symbolized by universal love of truth and benevolence.

Franklin is dead. He has returned to the bosom of the Divinity, the genius who freed America and shed torrents of light upon Europe.

The sage whom two worlds claim, the man about whom the history of sciences and the history of empires dispute, will doubtless maintain a high place in the annals of the human race.

Long enough the cabinets of statesmen have announced the death of those whose greatness is to be found only in funeral elegies. Long enough court etiquette has proclaimed hypocritical mourning periods. Nations should wear mourning only for their benefactors. The representatives of nations should recommend only the heroes of humanity for homage.

Congress has ordered in the fourteen confederated states a mourning period of two months for the death of Franklin, and America at this moment acquits its tribute of veneration for one of the fathers of its constitution.

Would it not be worthy of you, gentlemen, to join in this truly religious act, to participate in this homage rendered before the entire world both to the rights of man and to the philosopher who has contributed most to spreading them throughout the world. Antiquity would have raised altars to this mighty genius, who for the advantage of human beings, embraced both heavens and earth in his thoughts, who was able to conquer both thunderbolts and tyrants. Free and enlightened Europe owes at least a token of remembrance and regret to one of the greatest men who have ever served philosophy and liberty.

I propose that it be decreed that the National Assembly for three days wear mourning for Benjamin Franklin.

The place in which this stirring tribute was delivered—the floor of the National Assembly—contributed to the dramatic intensity of Mirabeau's words, and his voice and oratorical skill made an unforgettable impression upon his auditors.[2] His speech immediately won international attention because of its compactness, cogency, and intellectual ingenuity. It contained a single idea—an idea to grip the imagination of the world that had not before realized the significance of the revolutions in the two hemispheres. The age of privilege had given way to the age of merit, Franklin was the symbol of the new order, and Mirabeau's speech was the agent to crystallize it in men's minds.

The Assembly applauded Mirabeau with transport, mourning

was decreed for a period of three days, and the discourse was ordered to be printed and circulated. A member of the right raised
doubts about the authenticity of the news of Franklin's death, but
was assured of its truth by La Rochefoucauld and Lafayette.[3] According to legend, the decree proved very embarrassing for Robespierre, who was then a delegate and very poor. He is supposed to
have borrowed from a much taller man a black coat, which was
so long that it trailed on the ground.[4]

It should not be overlooked that the homage paid to Franklin
was the first honor of the kind ever to be accorded by the Assembly. The full significance of the gesture was pointed out in the
Journal de la Société de 1789, 24 juillet 1790. By consecrating
the memory of Franklin, the Assembly had symbolically embraced and professed his doctrine—an action that served as a fore-
runner of the act to abolish titles and the nobility, for the greatest honor that a man could hope from his peers had been accorded to a journeyman printer. Until that moment, in deference to the custom of *deuil de cour* (court-mourning), the whole
nation had been merely an antechamber of Versailles; the entire
population had been constrained to envelop itself in black at the
decease of a crowned embryo or of a collateral despot. But by
honoring Franklin, the National Assembly had converted *deuil
de cour* to *deuil de nation* (national mourning). At this moment
the French Assembly became "the representative assembly of the
human race, the Areopagus of the universe. What the Delphic
oracle had done for Socrates, it had done for Franklin; it had
declared him the greatest, that is, the wisest of mortals." Louis
Marie Prudhomme in his *Révolutions de Paris* (June 5-12, 1790)
declared that this sublime gesture gave hope that the French
might eventually surpass the ancient Romans, that by this single
act all the insane periods of state mourning forced upon them
by their tyrants were expiated.

Brissot, writing in the same strain, asserted that the Assembly
acquired honor and glory by its action, that the homage to Franklin elevated the Assembly to a sublime height beyond that of
any other political body in Europe.[5] It must be remembered
that at this moment the French Revolution had not initiated its
most drastic reforms. Brissot complimented the Assembly on its
victory over prejudice in paying homage to a man who from the

profession of journeyman printer and colporteur rose to the rank
of legislator and helped to place his nation among the powers of
the earth.

After Mirabeau's own death, Chénier put the theme of his
discourse into verse.[6]

> Adoptez ces lugubres marques,
> Français qui chérissez les lois!
> On porte le deuil des monarques;
> Un seul grand homme vaut cent rois.
> Ce Franklin, qui dans l'Amérique
> Fit régner la raison publique,
> Au monde était plus précieux
> Que tous ces princes dont la gloire
> Expire et s'éteint dans l'histoire,
> Dès qu'on leur a fermé les yeux.

Not all was sweetness and light, however, even at the epoch
of Mirabeau's speech. Prudhomme soon moderated his initial enthusiasm. In the next number of his journal (June 12-19), he reported that the mourning that had been observed for Franklin
had overheated the heads of some Frenchmen. "They do not
realize that there is in the beautiful, in the pathetic, a point beyond which one finds only exaggeration and ridicule." A café had
been turned into a temple, for example, by being draped in black
in the fashion of a church prepared for a funeral ceremony. The
bust of Franklin "had been placed under a pall between cypress
branches. The word *vir* had been inscribed at the base of the
bust, and on the door of the 'chapel' the first words of Mirabeau's
discourse, 'Franklin est mort.' An orator pronounced a funeral
oration, and almsgiving concluded the ceremonies and undoubtedly atoned for the patriotic inconsistencies of these good citizens."

The royalist organ *l'Ami du Roi* (June 12, 1790) remarked
that no doubt America owed Franklin a debt of gratitude. Mirabeau's eulogy was merited perhaps, "but in making it the orator
had elevated his hero to such an elevation that he, so to speak,
made him unrecognizable." Another journalist, Marat, whose political views were the extreme opposite, nevertheless agreed with
this opinion—probably because he had no love for either Franklin or Mirabeau. He published an essay in his *Ami du peuple*
(June 16, 1790) that could well bear the title, "Humbug con-

cerning Franklin." Several years earlier Marat had treated Franklin's electrical discoveries in a patronizing manner, apparently an
outgrowth of his bellicose spirit.[7] He had once invited Franklin
to witness his own electrical experiments. Franklin had admired
his dexterity, but treated his knowledge as superficial. Marat immediately set out to destroy Franklin as he had previously attempted to destroy the reputation of Newton's *Optics*. To this
end, he invited Voltaire as honor guest to witness further experiments, but Voltaire also went away without giving his approbation.[8] Marat, in his essay on Mirabeau's discourse, remarked that
all that was missing on this day of exalted sentiments, noble
maxims, and edifying scenes was a little sincerity and good faith.
The whole proceedings he condemned as farcical.

> At the reading of this touching motion I was unable to fight off
> a melancholy sentiment, and I regretted bitterly that it was not
> made by some good patriot. Yes, it is time that the people stopped
> prostrating themselves before the idols of fortune and that they
> learned to respect their defenders, to cherish their benefactors, to
> feel their loss, and to demonstrate publicly their affliction. Doubt-
> less Franklin was one of the liberators of his country, one of the
> first to declare himself against the tyrannical government of Great
> Britain. He swore to it an eternal hatred; he devoted all of his
> efforts to casting off its yoke, to ruin the empire, and he never
> contradicted himself.

Marat did not object to the eulogy of Franklin—he had contributed his own faint praise—but he felt that Mirabeau had donned
the mask of patriotism to conceal his own authoritarian record.
He charged that the greatest enemy of public liberty had proposed honor to the apostle of liberty and that he had done so to
gain a false popularity. Even Mirabeau's oratorical skill, he
argued, is not what it seems. "Although he does not lack eloquence, it is, however, to his vast lungs that he owes his success,
the prodigious ascendancy he holds over our deputies, who are
contented meekly to echo the views of the priesthood." Marat
had consequently a hundred times wished Mirabeau an eternal
whooping-cough; Mirabeau's good health he considered a public
calamity.

Finally, there appeared in the *Apocalypse* a very amusing and
mordant satire from the royalist point of view on the mourning

for Franklin—a report of a ceremony purported to have taken
place at the Jacobins Club.[9] At these alleged proceedings, Mirabeau proposed mourning for six days, but the other members considered such a long period extremely inconvenient. They engaged
therewith in a debate on the appropriate colors for their observance, none of them relishing the traditional black. Each member
argued for a different color until one of them proposed to submit the question to the committee on the constitution. The
Apocalypse then ridicules an imaginary ceremony during which
La Rochefoucauld pronounces a funeral oration.

As a matter of fact, the first official eulogy of Franklin actually
to be pronounced in France was that delivered June 13 by La
Rochefoucauld before the Société de 1789, two days after Mirabeau's discourse.[10] Probably it was La Rochefoucauld himself
who acquainted Mirabeau with the news of Franklin's death, for
he had learned it himself from a letter that Benjamin Vaughan
wrote to him, June 4, 1790,[11] in which letter Vaughan asked that
La Rochefoucauld communicate the news of Franklin's death to
Lafayette, Mirabeau, and Target. He asked in addition that La
Rochefoucauld disclose the fact to the National Assembly and
that Le Roy announce it to the Academy of Science and to Franklin's friends at Passy. Apparently La Rochefoucauld deferred to
Mirabeau in the Assembly because of the latter's superior talents at oratory. Paradoxically, La Rochefoucauld's eulogy at the
Société de 1789 presents the most authentic view of Franklin's
career, but is the least effusive and emotional in style. Based directly on the manuscript of Franklin's *Memoirs* then in his possession, it consists for the most part of a chronological record of
Franklin's life. Despite La Rochefoucauld's friendship and intimate association with Franklin, he allows himself only a few personal references or digressions. Of all the eulogies, it is the closest
to Franklin's own smooth, clear, and precise style, presenting the
facts without emotion or exaggeration. Franklin would probably
have preferred this to all the other pronouncements; yet it is the
most obscure, not listed in most bibliographies of Franklin materials. In addition to details from Franklin's autobiography, and
a section on Franklin's unicameral theories, which has been discussed in a previous chapter, La Rochefoucauld gives one or two
personal anecdotes. He had made Franklin's acquaintance many

years previously on a voyage to London. It was he who had taken Turgot to visit Franklin, and he had experienced great joy in seeing these two great men embrace for the first time. On the day Franklin signed the treaty ending the American war he said to La Rochefoucauld, "Could I have hoped at my age to have experienced such happiness?" Of his literary work, La Rochefoucauld observed that he produced nothing but short pieces, "but all, even his pleasantries, carried the imprint of his genius of observation and his mild philosophy. . . . He knew how to reduce useful truths to maxims easy to retain, sometimes in proverbs and in little tales." La Rochefoucauld generously closed his remarks with a forecast of Condorcet's formal eulogy, which was to be the "precursor of history, which will place the name of Franklin among the names of the most celebrated benefactors of humanity."

Preceding Condorcet, Michaud pronounced his poetic eulogy at the Lodge of the Nine Sisters, July 14.[12] Then the abbé Fauchet delivered a Civic Eulogy in the name of the Commune of Paris, July 21, in the *Halle des bleds* of the Rotund.[13] "It was entirely draped in black. A pulpit had been erected, in front of which had been placed the bust of Franklin on a kind of altar. . . . The Commune of Paris, several members of the National Assembly, Bailly [the mayor] and Lafayette were present at the ceremonies." [14] Apparently because of all these dignitaries there arose a question of protocol, for *l'Ami du Roi* reported, July 23, that "the deputation which the assembly sent to the ceremony had not been received with the proper honors due to the representatives of the governing body of the nation, for there arose at the beginning of the proceedings a ridiculously serious discussion on the ceremony to be observed in receiving deputations."

Unlike La Rochefoucauld and later eulogists, Fauchet did not attempt to summarize Franklin's entire career, but limited himself to merely two aspects, his moral or religious opinions and his legislative career. He proposed to leave to scientific societies and learned groups the honor of eulogizing Franklin's intellectual achievements for the reason that these were the only ones capable of picturing the scientist or the scholar. Fauchet felt qualified to treat only his theories of social morality and his contributions to the liberty of nations. Indeed Fauchet's oration is as much a public plea for enlightened morality, reason, and toleration in religion and social legislation as it is a tribute to Franklin. Fauchet, along with Condorcet, Nicolas Bonneville, and later, Thomas Paine, was a leading member of Le Cercle Social, a political-philanthropic club with Masonic antecedents, which professed the same idealistic purpose as the French Revolution itself, the regeneration of the human race. Condorcet and Bonneville emphasized the Masonic aspects of the club, believing that the spirit of rationalism and free inquiry held the solution of the problems of the Revolution, whereas Fauchet emphasized the Christian elements of brotherhood and faith. Fauchet's eulogy of Franklin is a public manifesto of these ideas.

Fauchet points out that Franklin's father emigrated to America in order to resist religious persecution, for the English, who are very changeable in matters of religion, have always been persecutors. After delineating Franklin's humble origin and his earliest trade as a candle-maker, Fauchet compares him to a French bishop with the same origin, a passage that was later satirized. Jumping to Franklin's sojourn in Philadelphia, Fauchet warmly praises that city and William Penn. Philadelphia, he maintains, is worthy of being called "the capital of humanity." "It is open to all human nature without restriction, for the law which forbids atheists and idlers admission to the city of brotherly love as not being men presents, as Franklin himself nobly said, only a comminatory exception without effect, 'for if there existed an atheist in the rest of the world, he would be converted on entering a city where everything is so fine.' " This observation, which Fauchet characterizes as worthy of Franklin's nobility and wisdom, is actually not Franklin's at all, but Dubourg's. It comes straight from the preface to his edition of Franklin's *Œuvres*.[15] This tribute to Philadelphia leads to a long section in which Fauchet explains why he, a Catholic priest, is able to eulogize Quakers and Franklin, the philosopher of protestantism *par excellence*, "who without the perfection of belief had the perfection of evangelical benevolence." Obviously addressing an audience of Catholics, Fauchet vigorously defends religious tolerance, arguing that only God has the right to judge conscience. He admits the truth of the maxim that outside of Catholicism there is no salvation, but he broadens his definition of Catholicism to include all men of good conscience. "It is among the avowed principles of the catholic church that all those who faithfully observe natural law, that is, all virtuous men, belong to the true church."

As an example of Franklin's dedication to the religion of virtue, Fauchet cites and translates Franklin's "Parable Against Persecution" and Franklin's epitaph in which his life is compared to a book, which he hopes will be reissued in an improved edition.[16] Fauchet praises the evangelical faith and the religious hope of this sentiment.

This is not a place for a detailed discussion of Franklin's religious views, but it is nevertheless appropriate to contrast Fauchet's tribute to Franklin's religion of virtue with a conversation that allegedly took place between Marbois and John Adams in June, 1779, when both were crossing the Atlantic Ocean. Adams records in his diary that he hinted that Franklin had no religion.[17]

> "No," said M. Marbois, "Mr Franklin adores only great Nature, which has interested a great many people of both sexes in his favor." "Yes," said I, laughing, "all the atheists, deists, and libertines, as well as the philosophers and ladies, are in his train,—another Voltaire, and thence—" "Yes," said M. Marbois, "he is celebrated as the great philosopher and the great legislator of America." "He is," said I, "a great philosopher, but as a legislator of America he has done very little."

Adams is as wrong about Franklin's philosophic acquaintances in France as he is about his legislative accomplishments. As we have already seen, Franklin's closest friends in France were not the atheists and libertines, but priests and constitutional moderates. Apart from his feminine conquests, his closest friends seem to have been Turgot, Dubourg, Le Veillard, Le Roy, La Rochefoucauld, du Pont de Nemours, Cabanis, and the abbés de la Roche, Morellet, and Soulavie.

Fauchet hardly merits inclusion in this list, although he claimed to have dined with Franklin several times in his apartments in Passy. By means of his own observation or the suggestions of Fleury and Le Roy, he discovered Franklin's fondness for attractive women and his uniform success with the fair sex. This information Fauchet uses to praise Franklin's psychological penetration; he argues that Franklin's knowledge of human nature revealed to him that women are the arbiters of morality and

that he devoted himself to winning their graceful cooperation
in seeking the triumph of virtue. Franklin's writings, Fauchet
declares, are addressed to all conditions and ages of mankind, and
all reflect his desire to serve society and virtue. He descended "to
the most naive details; to the most ingenuous familiarities; to the
first principles of the rural, commercial, civil and patriotic life;
to the conversation of children and old men, filled with the
verdure and the maturity of wisdom. In inculcating morality, this
virtuous man gave to his modest lessons the immense weight of
his reputation as one of the foremost scientists of the universe."

Turning to the second phase of his discourse, Franklin's political career, Fauchet describes an imaginary monument erected in
the midst of the Atlantic Ocean. A pyramid bears the august
visage of Franklin, and on the two sides facing America and Europe are inscribed the words, "Men, love humanity; be free and
open the doors of the nation to all." In this section Fauchet presents some of the principal political events in Franklin's life, his
tenure as postmaster in the colonies and his appearance before
the House of Commons in London. François L. T. de Fleury,
Lieutenant-Colonel in the Continental Army, had apparently
seen some of Franklin's plans for the Pennsylvania militia in the
French and Indian War and had mistaken them for early military
planning for the Revolution. On the basis of Fleury's notes,
Fauchet reported, "The philosopher of humanity, the friend of
peace, Franklin, held in readiness for ten years, all the plans of
the insurgent army. The inventories of regiments and companies,
the accounts, the instructions, all the military details written in
his hand a decade before the insurrection and placed in the
Philadelphia archives attest to the extent and the prescience of
his thoughts."

In a passage that was later scorned for its ludicrousness, Fauchet
described Franklin's mission to France. "He left at a moment's
notice; neither he nor his country owned a piece of gold; he arrived at Paris with a cargo of tobacco—as in the past at the moment when Holland sought her liberty, her deputies came to
Brussels with a convoy of herring to pay their expenses." This unfortunate reflection was copied verbatim in a life of Franklin attributed to J. B. Say.[18] Like La Rochefoucauld, Fauchet suggests
that Franklin's constitution of Pennsylvania was the nucleus of

the national governments of the United States and France. Joining primitivist theories with the doctrine of natural rights, he
argues that "the rights of man were developed for the first time in
laws simple and fertile like those of nature; the rights of citizens are based upon the fundamental bases of society." Fauchet
concludes with the exhortation to his fellow-citizens to regard
Franklin as one of the principal founders of the French constitution, which aims to attain the full elevation of reason and justice
and the perfection of the order of nature and of society, and which
will become the beacon light of the human race.

In the printed version of his discourse, Fauchet adds a long
letter from Le Roy, giving additional biographical information,
much of which is erroneous. Le Roy's only authentic information
not available in other sources is his account of dining with Franklin on the day Lord Stormont left Paris because of the French
rupture with England. Franklin, ordinarily very calm and tranquil, appeared to him on this day transformed with joy. Of chief
value is Le Roy's interpretation of Franklin's character. As Professor Chinard remarks, it can hardly be surpassed as a thumbnail
portrait.[19]

 Tranquil, calm and circumspect, like the people of his country,
one is unable to cite during his entire sojourn here amid the delicate circumstances in which he found himself, a word, a reflection
with which one could reproach him or which could compromise
him, which is indeed rare for a man whom everybody observed
closely in view of the role he played here. He had all the courage
necessary to meet emergencies—the type of firm courage which belongs to superior minds, who, having considered everything, consider emergencies as the necessary and inevitable consequence of
the order of things. As for his mind, he had a particular characteristic which has not been sufficiently noticed, which was of always
considering in any circumstance the most simple point of view. In
his philosophical and political views, he always seized in every
question the simplest aspect. If it was an explanation in natural
philosophy, he did the same thing. In the arrangement of a machine, it was the same procedure. Whereas the generality of men
arrive at the true and the simple only after a long circuit and
multiplied efforts, his excellent mind, by a happy privilege, led
him to the simplest means to explain the arranged phenomenon,
to construct the apparatus which he needed, finally, to find the
expedients the most proper to bring to a successful conclusion the
projects or commissions with which he was charged.

Fauchet's eulogy was given a very poor reception by the press, including representatives of all shades of political opinion. A conservative royalist organ, *Les Actes des Apôtres,* devoted five pages to ridicule of his style, attacking particularly his habit of mentioning crude and mundane objects amidst sonorous and sententious phrases.[20] Considered most ludicrous were Fauchet's references to Franklin's candle-making, "the cargo of tobacco with which Franklin arrived in Paris, not having a piece of gold," and "the convoy of herring with which the deputies from Holland formerly came to Brussels." The *Mercure de France,* an eclectic review, accused Fauchet of bombast, poor taste, and empty declamation.[21] *Les Révolutions de Paris,* a radical organ, ridiculed Fauchet's affected sublimity and condemned him for addressing himself to the mayor instead of first of all to the public.[22] This seems a rather unreasonable objection since the occasion represented an official gesture of the municipality. After enumerating a number of particular objections to Fauchet's falsely sublime and ludicrous sentiments, the reviewer concluded that the discourse may have given pleasure through the magic of utterance, but the silent reading of it was hardly supportable. "One perceives throughout an immoderate ambition to please by singularity, scant justness in the accessory ideas (the principal ideas are common to all those who have written for the Revolution), a pusillanimous discretion for every special interest, and everywhere truth sacrificed for the desire of producing an effect."

The *Journal Général de France* objected to Fauchet's elaborate praise of the Pennsylvania constitution and suggested that he deliberately concealed the fact that the new constitution of the United States was closer to that of England than to the one Franklin sponsored.[23] "But he believed no doubt that it was not necessary to reason too logically in order to carry away the crowd. He is right, and a discourse more solid than his would have had less success. Piled up apostrophes, the words *patriotism, liberty,* and *universal fraternity,* rang out under the vaults of the hall. A little verve in some passages, a strong and sonorous voice, that is all that was needed, and everyone left persuaded that M. Fauchet was more eloquent than Bossuet."

Condorcet's eulogy that followed, November 13, 1790, does not develop merely one or two particular themes like Fauchet's but elaborates the ideological significance of Franklin's career.[24] Although speaking as the representative of the Academy of Sciences, Condorcet devotes practically no attention to Franklin's scientific discoveries.

We have already pointed out that there exist four manuscript drafts of Condorcet's eulogy.[25] The third draft, the most interesting, contains a number of passages that Condorcet deleted in the final version.

A mystery surrounds Condorcet's source for the following passage on Franklin's colonial currency scheme, which was not carried over to the final draft.

> A long time previously he had brought about a new creation of paper money in the state of Pennsylvania. The majority of wage-earners had no sooner put aside some savings than they hastened into business, and their number still very small in relation to that of the proprietors had pushed the value of their wages very high. It was at the same time the prices-current in England and not the American specie which controlled the prices of manufactured objects and even of a large number of commodities which had to be imported from Europe. A paper money was then necessary, and this necessity maintained its value. Interest was paid on this money as one would have paid for the silver which this paper replaced, and as the state reserved the right to withdraw it at certain periods from those who had borrowed it, it would be maintained as long as it never exceeded the demand and the amount advanced to individuals never exceeded a certain part of their wealth.

None of this economic discussion appears in Franklin's *Memoirs*, which states merely that Franklin composed a pamphlet, *The Nature and Necessity of a Paper Currency*. This pamphlet was not translated into French, and even in English it was impossible to find at the end of the century. There seems to be no explanation for Condorcet's knowledge of Franklin's currency scheme unless he received it directly from Franklin himself or indirectly from Turgot or, more probably, Thomas Paine, who also wrote on Franklin's project.

Condorcet deleted also from his final draft a long paragraph concerning Franklin's vegetarianism as well as original comments on Franklin's relations with George III.

In the history of thought Condorcet is considered as an ideologist, an advocate of idealistic reforms, and, in analyzing the career of Franklin, he emphasizes episodes favorable to his own theories of perfectibility. Even though Franklin is noted for his practical experimental method in both science and politics, he was a projector in his early youth, and throughout his life he envisaged many schemes of moral and social reform that admirers of his practical good sense might call visionary. Condorcet considered his scheme to obtain moral perfection as essentially the same that Pythagoras had conceived and executed more than 2000 years previously, but with different means. It had been commonplace to designate Franklin as the Pythagoras of the new world, but Condorcet was the first to develop an extended parallel between the two sages.

> The Greek philosopher wished by the force of habit to substitute for natural impulses or sentiments the principles with which he believed it necessary to inspire men; the American philosopher wished only to purify, fortify, and direct the movements of nature. The one proposed to subdue man and to transform him; the other aspired only to enlighten and to perfect him. The one had formed a system which could in one nation at a given period of time produce a fortunate revolution and amaze the populace by great virtues, but which soon, overwhelmed by the irresistible force of nature the laws of which it had opposed, was reduced to exist only in memory. The methods of the other, conforming to the laws of nature, suited to all countries and to all times, led to a slow but lasting perfection, and, without producing the glory of any century, could contribute to the happiness of all.

Using as a focus of discussion two treaties with the Indians in which Franklin participated, Condorcet attributes to Franklin primitivistic theories that are Condorcet's own. In his *Memoirs* Franklin says nothing whatsoever about the moral characteristics of American aborigines, and the only work in which he does treat the subject that Condorcet could have read was the *Remarks concerning the Savages of North America* and, possibly, the "Mithologie et Morale Iroquoises" in the *Ephémérides du Citoyen*. It is possible though that Condorcet acquired his notions of Franklin's primitivism from conversation rather than from printed works. That Franklin held these opinions is seen in his marginal notations in a British pamphlet, *Reflections Moral and Political on Great Britain and Her Colonies*, 1770. Here Franklin asserts, "Happiness is more generally & equally diffus'd among

Savages than in our Societies. The Care & Labour of providing for artificial and fashionable Wants, the Sight of so many Rich wallowing in superfluous Plenty, whereby so many are kept poor & distress'd by Want: The Insolence of Office, the Snares & Plagues of Law, the Restraints of Custom, all contribute to disgust them with what we call civil Society." [26] Whatever his source, Condorcet concludes that Franklin had a low opinion of the achievements of civilization for the masses. According to his interpretation, Franklin "found that we had done much for the class of enlightened men, but little for the generality of the human species, and that if the virtuous man who exercises his reason is superior to the inhabitant of the forests of Ohio, the ordinary man has often merely changed his savage ferocity for debasing vices and his ignorance for prejudices." Condorcet held that Franklin "contrasts the native good sense of the Indians with the arrogant reason of civilized men, their unalterable calm and profound indifference with the passions which arouse us by imaginary interests. He appeared to believe that the savage differed less than the greater part of us from the ideal of man perfected by reason without ceasing to be submitted to nature." Condorcet's primitivistic proclivities appear also as he contrasts the new American nation—its virtues derived from its proximity to nature—with the European world—its corruptions based upon centuries of civilization. "One must not conclude that the Americans surpass us in intelligence; but men agree easily when a mild equality has preserved them from the sophisms of interest and vanity: truth is easy to discover among a burgeoning people without prejudices, and the old nations have need of all the resources of instruction, all the strength of genius, to defend themselves against the systematic errors of corruption and habit."

In treating Franklin's unicameralism, which, as we have already seen, Condorcet himself adopted and proposed for the French constitution, Condorcet portrays Franklin's theories as evidence of optimism and perfectibility. The constitution of Pennsylvania, Condorcet maintains, distinguished itself from all the other state constitutions by the principle of equality, particularly in its unicameralism for which Franklin alone was responsible. "He considered that wisdom must naturally make rapid progress, especially in a land where the revolution was going to provide new relations; it was necessary to promote the means of perfecting legislation and not encumber it with foreign obstacles. . . . Franklin was aware that one may find in the form of the deliberations of a single assembly all that is necessary to give to its decisions that caution, that maturity, which guarantees their truth and their wisdom, whereas the establishment of two houses permits the avoidance of new faults only in perpetuating established errors." Emphasizing the moral and psychological basis of the conflict between the two systems, Condorcet scornfully describes the arguments for bicameralism as a result of "that discouraging philosophy which considers error and corruption as the habitual condition of society, the moments of virtue and reason as a sort of prodigy which one must not hope to render permanent."

As far as political theory is concerned, Condorcet does not attempt to portray Franklin as a planner or as an ideologist who sought to mold his thoughts into systems—as Condorcet himself is considered to be. Indeed, Condorcet clearly foreshadows the conclusions of one of the most recent analysts of Franklin's political ideas—that he was not a systematic political philosopher, that his political thought was pragmatic, that it was based upon observation and a strong sense of tactics.[27]

> Franklin had not formed a general system of politics; he examined questions in proportion as the order of events or his foresight presented them to his mind, and he resolved them with the principles which he drew from a pure mind and in a just and acute spirit. In general he appeared not to seek to give the greatest degree of perfection to human institutions all at once; he believed it more certain to wait the passage of time; he did not insist upon delivering a frontal attack upon abuses, but found it more prudent first to attack the errors which are their source. He had in politics as in morality this type of indulgence which demands little because it hopes much and which pardons at the present in favor of the future. . . . In a word, his politics was that of a man who believed in the power of reason and the reality of virtue and who had wished to make himself teacher of his fellow citizens before being called to be their legislator.

As an example of Franklin's tact in political negotiations, Condorcet explains why Franklin had not suggested means of attacking England to the French government. He realized that if his military strategy failed, France might blame him and lose inter-

est in the struggle. He attempted instead to keep alive in France
the concept of the constancy and resources of America. As an example of Franklin's spirit of compromise, Condorcet reports his
accepting for the sake of unanimity the American constitution
even though he was opposed to its provisions of two legislative
houses and the veto power of the president. According to Condorcet, his political sagacity enabled him to predict the French
Revolution. "It was easy for him to foresee that a people already
worthy of liberty must soon win it and that the revolution of
France like that of America was one of these events which human reason can remove from the empire of chance and passion."

Modern critics have maintained that Franklin made little use
of the theory of natural rights, especially during his period in
London as a colonial agent.[28] Condorcet, however, interprets the
high point of his agency, the appearance before the House of
Commons, as a defense of the theory. "It was doubtless a magnificent spectacle to see the deputy of the free citizens of America
defending justice and the eternal rights of nature before the men
who, considering themselves also the representatives of a free
people, could not without betraying their duty, refuse to regard
an identical liberty as a property equal and inalienable for the
entire human race—to hear him contrasting the simplicity of courage and reason with the pride of riches and power." In a sense
Franklin could be all things to all men. We have seen how the
physiocrats interpreted his appearance at the bar of the House of
Commons as a vindication of physiocratic principles. Here Condorcet sees him upholding the doctrine of natural rights.

In the final words of his address Condorcet touches upon Franklin's electrical theories and ends on the note that there is no incompatibility between his political and his scientific discoveries.
The third draft of his discourse presents a stronger statement of
the pre-eminence of science and the inevitable march of political
progress through science than appears in the final form. To illustrate his contention, he contrasts the two revolutions in seven-
teenth-century England, the earlier in a period of fanaticism—
that of the contemporaries of Penn—and the later in a period
of enlightenment—that of the contemporaries of Boyle and Newton. One violently enforced a despotism; the other mildly created
the freest constitution that had existed on the earth and that

could be surpassed only in a century when the sciences made
new progress and became more widespread. In defending the role
of science, he declares that the savants do not refuse their knowledge to political leaders, for they realize that men must not be left
subject to ignorance merely because they are subject to servitude.
The savants do not compromise the cause of liberty by imprudent
clamor because they recognize that political revolutions like the
operations of nature have a prescribed course that cannot be disturbed without delaying or endangering progress. Science needs
no apology in an enlightened nation that realizes there can be
no question of choosing between cultivating the sciences or sur-
rendering to prejudice—that in the order of nature political
knowledge depends upon scientific knowledge. Those who before
kings accuse the scientists of being republican and before the
people accuse them of being despots do so because of chicanery
and ignorance. They know that people deprived of knowledge
are easier to deceive than an enlightened people. "They hide their
desire for power under a false enthusiasm for liberty and seem
to have divined only too well that under no matter what constitution an ignorant populace is always enslaved."

These ideas are toned down somewhat in the printed version.
Condorcet contrasts the unfruitful attempts of unenlightened
centuries sullied by wars and massacres with the happy efforts of
America and France; then he compares the fanatical and blood-
thirsty revolution of the era of Prynne and Knox in England
with the peaceable, constitutional change effected in the time of
Newton and Boyle. He substitutes Prynne and Knox for Penn as
symbols of the early seventeenth century presumably because
Penn had been generally considered in France as a democratic
constitution-maker.

Contrasting the cultivation of science with submission to prejudice, Condorcet repeats from his earlier draft the assertion that in
the order of nature political enlightenment is a consequence of
scientific progress. He duplicates the warning against envious detractors who accuse the sciences of thriving under despotism, for
these detractors realize that ignorant people are the easiest to
control. These demagogues, he adds, fear the patriotism of reason
and virtue, which hypocrisy cannot imitate. "Hiding their urge to
dominate under the mask of enthusiasm for liberty, they seem

to have understood that even under the freest constitutions an ignorant people is always enslaved." Condorcet still defends science, but he is less vigorous in suggesting that knowledge is superior to political institution.

Despite the principles of revolutionary philosophy that Condorcet expresses in his eulogy, it was given an unflattering review in the *Mercure de France*,[29] the reviewer remarking that they had had declamation from Fauchet and a philosophical discourse from Condorcet, and now he was looking for an oration, both philosophical and well written.

Some critics felt that such an oration was supplied in the next year by Vicq d'Azyr, Franklin's personal friend and secretary of the Royal Society of Medicine.[30] Condorcet's eulogy and Vicq's were frequently compared—and at least one critic preferred Vicq's. This was Lemontey, who several years later became in turn Vicq's eulogist at the French Academy. Admitting that Condorcet's discourse possesses ideas, useful opinions, and a certain enthusiasm, he argues that this is all extinguished in a verbose and colorless style. He feels that Vicq's is superior because of the vigor of his talent and the diversity of his knowledge. The eulogy of Franklin, considered his *chef d'oeuvre*, was oddly enough the only one of Vicq's fifty orations that was never published in his complete works. It had originally been destined for the Memoirs of the Royal Society of Medicine, but during the Revolution the manuscript passed to the files of the School of Medicine and the archives of the Royal Academy of Medicine. Vicq's eulogy created a great sensation when delivered March 14, 1791. His first sentence especially enjoyed a great vogue and was everywhere repeated:

Un homme est mort, et deux mondes sont en deuil.

The printed version, however, reads:

Un homme est mort, et des nations ont pris le deuil

—a phrase less rhetorical, but more conformable to historical exactitude. Vicq may have written one, but said the other.

Of all the eulogists of Franklin, Vicq was the only one to imitate the theme of the pastoral elegy that we should not weep for death. He reminded his auditors that Franklin had lived almost as long as his century. "Upon the ladder of life, he always ascended, never descended." "He lived long enough to see tranquil days succeed disastrous ones, to enjoy the happiness of his countrymen and the respect of two worlds."

Most of Vicq's material came directly from Franklin's *Memoirs;* the rest from personal knowledge or reminiscences of Franklin's acquaintances. Vicq interjects few philosophical or political opinions, but occasionally he presents an individual interpretation of an event in Franklin's life. In considering, for example, Franklin's tale of some very bad poetry he had written in his youth that his brother had printed and forced Franklin to hawk on the streets of Boston, Vicq was much affected by Franklin's adolescent hardship. "When one sees Franklin submitted to such trials," he wrote, "one can hardly keep from fearing that amid so many misfortunes he may lose courage and miss the happy destiny which awaits him."

Like all other Frenchmen, Vicq knew nothing of the original *Poor Richard's Almanac,* to which he devotes special attention, but was forced to base all his observations on *The Way to Wealth.* He remarks that Franklin "always places his maxims in the mouth of an old man, and to make them even more respected he invoked proverbial language." Vicq gives extended quotations from *La Science du Bonhomme Richard* and follows Fauchet in paraphrasing "A Parable Against Persecution" and Franklin's epitaph.

Discussing the outbreak of the American Revolution, Vicq compares Franklin to Cato as the moderator of decisions and conduct, although he considers Franklin less austere and more fortunate than the Roman hero. Later in France, Franklin appeared as the symbol of liberty as well as of virtuous old age. Wherever people were found in large numbers, he showed himself as though to demonstrate that his interests and theirs were common. "Never perhaps was there so much calm and goodness in physiognomy, so much harmony in simplicity of apparel, of bearing, of character and of language; never perhaps was to be found an old age both so imposing and so amiable." When the time came for leaving his friends and habitation at Passy to return to America, his eyes filled with tears. "I had thought," he said, "that my friends of Passy would close my eyes, but destiny confides to others the care which I expected from you."

If there is any identifying characteristic of Vicq's eulogy, it is that he devotes more attention than any of his predecessors to summarizing Franklin's scientific accomplishments, chiefly electrical. Undoubtedly with the example of Condorcet in view, Vicq concludes his discourse with a parallel between Franklin and Pythagoras, but considers them from perspectives that Condorcet had not touched. Still emphasizing practical science, Vicq pointed out that they both amused themselves with combinations of numbers (Franklin's magic squares and circles).

> Born in the most obscure condition, both gained the confidence of their countrymen, to whom they gave lessons and left examples. Pythagoras absented himself from his country because it trembled under the oppression of tyrants. Franklin did better; he preserved his from the evils of slavery. They did not confine themselves to discoursing on virtue; both practiced it constantly; both taught men the art of self-improvement by a written method. Full of respect for the sovereign author of the universe, they employed their entire lives to seek the true and to do good, that is, to study the divinity in his works and to serve him in his designs; both rejected the class of nourishment which one obtains only by murder—in this decision, one obeying an opinion and the other giving way to the pure instinct of sentiment. Both knew the value of time and the price of silence. Both meditated on the phenomenon of thunder, which Pythagoras explained by ingenious systems and Franklin by a theory based upon experience. Both lived to an old age and died with a celebrity that nothing could augment and nothing could decrease.

One other eulogy characteristic of its author and audience was pronounced August 10, 1790, at a memorial observance organized by the journeymen printers of Paris.[31] Franklin's bust was elevated upon a column in the middle of the room, a civic crown upon his head. Below were compositors' cases, a press, and other symbols of the printing art. While an apprentice delivered the oration, others were composing and printing it, and it was distributed to the spectators at the conclusion. The speaker knew the essential facts of Franklin's life, which he perhaps obtained from La Rochefoucauld's eulogy. After a brief résumé of Franklin's most important political achievements, he asserted that it was not Franklin's period of glory and elevation that he wished to consider, but Franklin's career as journeyman printer and simple citizen. Franklin's example, the speaker asserted, would make them honor their own estate and make of it an instrument of happiness. "Franklin was born as poor as the poorest among us, but he had the courage not to be ashamed of poverty." The orator urged his auditors to imitate Franklin's reading habits in youth, his love of books, and faith in instruction as a defense of liberty. Developing the theme that workers must instruct themselves fully in their rights and duties, he exhorted them to follow Franklin's example of forming clubs for mutual improvement and for exchanging books. Franklin, he asserted, considered the art of printing to be the principal lever to be used in overthrowing despotism in America.

After this discourse, another speaker, a soldier of the Battalion of Veterans, addressed the same gathering,[32] paying tribute to Franklin in an oration that was less a eulogy than a patriotic effusion on the ideals of the French Revolution. Although admitting that free speech is the *sine qua non* of political liberty, he warned the printers against sullying their hands with anti-revolutionary writings and exhorted them to be their own censors in the service of reason and truth.

Le Moniteur, July 8, 1790, presented a warm tribute to Franklin, in an extract from an anonymous letter from New York. Comparison with a document in the Ministry of Foreign Affairs shows that it is a paraphrase of a report from Louis Otto, French consul in New York, to his superior, the Count de Montmorin.[33]

> A few minutes before dying, this great man repeated these words, founded on the religion that he had made for himself, "that a man is perfectly born only after his death." France has lost in him a sincere friend; America, one of its ornaments; the literary world, a man who has enriched it and has created models in several genres [fait époque en plusieurs genres]. Although the stone, with which he was tormented for eight years, and his gradual weakening should have prepared the public for the event, it has nonetheless made a great sensation. It was about 65 years ago that Franklin arrived in Philadelphia as journeyman printer. He was obliged, on arriving, to spend several nights in a church, not having the means of paying for lodging. He has since been raised to the highest dignities that his country can confer. His name is celebrated in the two hemispheres, and he died at the moment when the calm re-established in his country gave the brightest hopes for the future. Few men have

been so completely happy; few men have so well deserved to be happy.

It is apparent from these eulogies alone that in France Franklin was sincerely admired by all classes of society, the high and the low, intellectuals and workers. French men of letters accorded him a much higher tribute than did his colleagues in the United States or England. Neither country produced collections of personal reminiscences to match those of Morellet, Cabanis, or de la Roche. In England, Franklin was understandably given no official eulogy.[34] In America he was accorded only one—a half-hearted, colorless piece, not worthy to be compared with the warm and spirited tributes of La Rochefoucauld, Condorcet, Fauchet, and Vicq d'Azyr. The American Philosophical Society appointed as its official American eulogist, William Smith, who was actually Franklin's principal literary enemy. Throughout his life Smith's relations with Franklin had been colored by personal jealousy and political disagreement. Benjamin Rush, who was both a genuine admirer and a close friend of Franklin and who in addition was an experienced orator, would have been an appropriate choice, but unfortunately destiny limited his participation to supplying Smith with biographical details. The latter's eulogy is exactly what one would expect from a mind balancing between indifference and animosity—an artificial, uninspired, rhetorical exercise.[35] Strangely enough, no other American body or author sought to compensate for the deficiencies of Smith's discourse by preparing a supplementary eulogy. Yet such minor figures by comparison as James Bowdoin and Cotton Mather were each honored with at least a dozen published funeral discourses. Even the generality of Americans were less demonstrative than the common people of France. Louis Otto reported to his superiors, December 12, 1790, that "the memory of Dr. Franklin has been infinitely more honored in France than in America. People are hardly susceptible to enthusiasm in this country—they praise and they blame coldly. General Washington is the only one who has the talent of touching the heart of his compatriots and of making a durable impression." [36] From the perspective of the end of the eighteenth century, therefore, France, not the United States, would seem to be the country of Franklin.[37]

14. CONCLUSION

In the course of our survey of the influence of Franklin in France, we have seen how Franklin came to adopt his pose of primitive moralist and how this pose came to be identified with him in popular thought; we have seen Franklin portrayed in French letters as a symbol not only of primitive morality and daily thrift but also of political liberty; and, finally, we have seen the Franklin of real life—Franklin the man—exposed in his own memoirs and light pieces and in the anecdotes and serious eulogies and souvenirs of his friends.

From this mass of evidence certain conclusions are self-evident and undeniable. Others are merely conjectural.

First of all, it would seem that the actual information that was available to the French public concerning the achievements and character of Franklin would hardly justify the extreme adulation with which he was received. Today we know Franklin as a man of extremely versatile talents, but the French knew him only as scientist, man of letters, and diplomat.

In his character as scientist, few laymen at that time understood the significance of his electrical theories. The greater part were forced to accept their value on hearsay.

In his character of man of letters, nearly everyone knew the *Science du Bonhomme Richard,* but even if everyone viewed it with the eyes of Dubourg, Condorcet, or Fauchet, this work by itself would hardly elevate Franklin to a position of great eminence. His *Memoirs* and some of his bagatelles were known in France after his death, but they never even approached the enormous vogue of *Bonhomme Richard.* In a sense the French public —even Franklin's intimate friends—did not understand or correctly interpret his literary work. As we have seen, Polly Baker was accepted *au sérieux,* and Poor Richard was considered a work of sublime morality. The editors of the *Ephémérides* saw in his Indian farce concerning William Henry only "mythologie et mo-

rale Iroquoises," and other men of letters considered his bagatelles in the light of *opuscules moraux*. Only his *Memoirs* seem
to have been understood in the sense in which Franklin really
intended them.

In his character as diplomat, Franklin's achievements were truly
magnificent. But his contemporaries viewed only his successes
without considering the means by which they were attained. It is
doubtful that the French public realized the qualities of finesse
and tact necessary for the accomplishment of his mission. They
knew, of course, that largely through his efforts the French government had agreed to the treaty of alliance with America. But
even before this treaty he had been universally considered a symbol of American liberty and the spirit of independence.

The question immediately occurs: Was Franklin known to his
French contemporaries then as a symbol or as a man? We have
seen that there were some relatively faithful reports of his activities and personality. The portrayal in the *Mémoires secrets* was
somewhat caustic and that in the *Espion anglois* somewhat sentimental, but together they present a detailed and reasonably accurate view of his life in Paris. These seem to have had little effect, however, on popular opinion. From the moment of his arrival in France in 1776, Franklin became identified with Father
Abraham. He stood as the symbol of prudential wisdom and patriarchal morality, which Father Abraham also represents to a limited degree, and of political liberty and Quaker manners, which
Father Abraham has absolutely nothing to do with. By means of
Turgot's epigram Franklin's prior scientific achievement was
brought into harmony with his political renown, and by and
large the moral and political aspects of his reputation engulfed
the scientific. Turgot's epigram is in itself evidence of the symbolic force of Franklin's personality—and most of the formal literary tributes to Franklin, especially those in verse, treat him as
symbol alone and ignore the real man.

This does not mean, however, that in French thought and history Franklin's influence was that of a symbol alone. In addition
to his achievements in negotiating the alliance between France
and America, he had a direct influence upon actual events of the
French Revolution. Indeed, he may have been partly aware of
the effect his writings would have on French history. One may

ask, for example, whether he planned the publication of his letter on the Society of the Cincinnati because of the situation in America or because of the situation in France. On the surface it would seem that the letter was directed exclusively toward America—the accepted view—but analysis seems to show that the most telling blows are directed against the European system of aristocracy. Whether intended primarily for France or not, the work because of Mirabeau's translation and many subsequent reprintings had an undeniable influence on French public opinion. As we have seen, the same is true of Franklin's unicameral theories.

If we accept the conclusion that Franklin was better known in France as a symbol than as a real person, we must not stop here. We must still inquire why Franklin rather than someone else should have been considered as the symbol of American liberty. John Adams, for example, Franklin's fellow commissioner at Paris, certainly had equal literary talents, and his diplomatic skill was probably not inferior to Franklin's. Yet Adams made practically no impression upon the French public. Today hardly anyone would recognize either his name or his physiognomy. Even in America, where Adams later became president, few but professional historians could now recognize his portrait. Yet Franklin's features are even today well known in France, and during the eighteenth century they were almost as familiar as Voltaire's. The only explanation seems to be that Franklin's personality—his human qualities—endeared him to the French people, whereas Adams lacked this personal appeal. In any case Adams could hardly have posed as the symbol of American liberty, for in many ways his ideas were extremely conservative. Franklin was, of course, the ideal symbol, for he really believed in political and individual liberty.

Naturally enough, the French were by no means unanimous in revering the name of Franklin. For contrast let us put side by side two views. First a sardonic one:

This gentleman became very skilled in electricity. He forced the thunder to fall where he ordered it; he commanded it to withdraw and it withdrew. He did surprising things. He electrified a dog on the opposite bank of a river, making him howl like a martyr without having the least suspicion of the author of his sufferings.

Next, a panegyrical view of the same achievement:

> Jupiter who disposed of the thunder at his pleasure was a fable
> in Greece, and in our day it has become a reality in America.
> Franklin said to the thunder, "fall," and the thunder fell. But
> whereas the god of Greece governed the thunder like a man to
> seek revenge and to destroy, the man of America governed it like
> a god; he ended its destruction and annulled it by diverting it from
> human beings.

Contrary opinions such as these existed, but, as we have seen, the
favorable—even the adulatory—were far in the majority.

This undeniable fact leads to another interesting point of speculation. Why did Franklin appear as a greater hero in France
than he did in his own country? Again evidence from belles lettres may provide the explanation. As Chamfort remarked in comparing Turgot's epigram with the verse of Odell, perhaps the
contrast betokens a difference in the spirit of the two peoples.
Perhaps the personality of Franklin—symbolic or real—was more
congenial to the somewhat effusive and emotional French than to
the more austere and conventional Americans of the epoch. It
may not have been a completely absurd gesture for the French
to attempt by tracing his genealogy to claim him as a true Gaul.

Against this hypothesis, however, it must be remembered that
very little evidence concerning the human side of Franklin—his
character as a man—was available to the masses until after his
death. At this time appeared the formal eulogies and shortly afterwards the narratives and anecdotes of Morellet and Cabanis.
Although some of Franklin's bagatelles appeared concurrently in
the periodical press, it does not seem that they had a wide circulation. In other words, the average man had no way of knowing
Franklin as we know him today or as Mesdames Brillon and Helvétius knew him then. But as the great historian Michelet recognized the influence of the masses upon the French Revolution and
attributed that great social movement to the people themselves
rather than to the leaders, perhaps we can likewise attribute the
enormous vogue of Franklin at least partly to the intuition of the
people. Even if the evidence were incomplete and imperfect, it
may be that they sensed that here was a man who represented
true democracy and warm humanity, and that without knowing
why they did so, they responded intuitively to Franklin's grandeur
of spirit with almost universal praise and admiration.

NOTES

CHAPTER 1

1. *Œuvres de Voltaire,* ed. Beuchot (72 vols.; Paris: J. Didot, 1827-1829), I, 289. All translations of French texts in this book are my own with the exception of the passages from Soulavie's *Mémoires historiques,* which are from the London edition of 1802.
2. Letter to the abbé Gaultier, 21 février 1778. *Œuvres de Voltaire,* LXX, 450. Voltaire became acquainted with Franklin as early as 1767. He wrote to A. M. Mariott, 26 février 1767: ". . . Si vous voyez M. Franklin, je vous supplie, monsieur, de vouloir bien l'assurer de mon estime et de ma reconnaissance." *Œuvres complètes* (52 vols.; Paris: Garnier frères, 1877-1885), XLV, 137.
3. "Extrait d'une Lettre de Charles Villette sur Voltaire," *La Bouche de Fer.* No. X. Octobre, 1790, p. 149.
4. *Vie de Voltaire,* in *Œuvres de Voltaire,* I, 290.
5. Lettre LXXXIII, *Correspondance Littéraire* (6 vols.; Paris: Migneret imprimeur, 1801-1807), II, 210-211.
6. *Vie de Voltaire, loc. cit.*
7. La Harpe, *loc. cit.*
8. 22 février 1778.
9. *Souvenirs de la marquise de Créquy,* ed. Maurice Cousin, Cte de Courchamps (10 vols.; Paris: Garnier frères, 1903), VI, 8.
10. François Astori to Franklin, March 13, 1779. *Calendar of the Papers of Benjamin Franklin in the Library of the American Philosophical Society,* ed. I. Minis Hays (5 vols.; Philadelphia: Printed for the American Philosophical Society, 1908), II, 42.
11. Letter of Etienne Catherine Baillot, May 1, 1778. Ernest Choullier, *Voltaire et Franklin à l'Académie des Sciences* (Troyes: imp. de P. Nouel, 1898), p. 4.
12. *Vie de Voltaire, loc. cit.,* p. 290.
13. "Autobiography," *Works of John Adams* (10 vols.; Boston: Little, Brown, 1850-1856), III, 147.
14. Hays, ed., *Calendar,* IV, 241. Voltaire to Mme. Duboccage. November 2, 1777.
15. Francis Hervé, ed., *Madame Tussaud's Memoirs and Reminiscences of France* (London: Saunders & Otley, 1838), p. 56.
16. George de Cadoudal, *Les serviteurs des hommes* (Paris: C. Dillet, 1864), p. 24.

CHAPTER 2

1. The following discussion of the reception of Franklin's scientific works in France is based on I. Bernard Cohen, ed., *Benjamin Franklin's Experiments* (Cambridge, Mass.: Harvard University Press, 1941), pp. 100-118.
2. Franklin cites this paragraph in a letter to Jared Eliot, April 12, 1753. Albert Henry Smyth, ed.,

The Writings of Benjamin Franklin (10 vols.; New York: Macmillan Co., 1905-1907), III, 124.

3. *Op. cit.* (Paris: chez Rollin, 1752), p. 185.

4. Hays, *Calendar,* I, 11.

5. Manuscript letter, March 10, 1755. New York Historical Society.

6. Smyth, ed., *Writings,* I, 419.

7. Cohen, *op. cit.,* pp. 113-116.

8. *Memoirs of the Life of Sir Samuel Romilly* (Third edition, 2 vols.; London: J. Murray, 1841), II, 447-458.

9. *Ephémérides,* 1769, I (i), 68.

10. *Œuvres de Turgot,* ed. Gustave Schelle (5 vols.; Paris: F. Alcan, 1913-1923), III, 13.

11. Smyth, ed., *Writings,* V, 409.

12. *Ephémérides,* 1767, I (ii), 5-18. The abbé M. was probably Morellet.

13. *Ephémérides,* 1768, IV (i), 28-91; (ii), 159-192.

14. *Ephémérides,* 1769, V (ii), 5-14.

15. Janvier 1780, *Correspondance Littéraire,* ed. Maurice Tourneux (16 vols.; Paris: Garnier frères, 1877-1882), XII, 356-358. Although I here and elsewhere speak of Grimm as author of all the letters in this collection, it is understood that he had several collaborators.

16. *Ephémérides,* 1769, II (i), 68-78. My reason for believing that Dubourg is the author of these letters is that a contrast between agricultural and military establishments in America (only agricultural communities increase in population) is found both in these letters and in the preface to Dubourg's translation of John Dickinson's *Letters from a Farmer in Pennsylvania* (*Lettres d'un fermier de Pensylvanie, aux habitans de l'Amérique septentrionale,* Amsterdam [i.e. Paris]: Aux

dépens de la compagnie, 1769, p. xiii). The two letters were reprinted from the *Ephémérides* by G. G. de Beaurieu as an appendix to his novel *L'élève de la nature* (Amsterdam & Lille: J. B. Henry, 1771). Because of this Emile Légouis has assumed that Beaurieu is the author of the letters (*Beaurieu et son élève de la nature,* Oxford: Clarendon Press, 1925, p. 7), but Beaurieu nowhere even suggests that he is.

17. *Ephémérides,* 1769, IV (ii), 39-52.

18. "Achenwall's Observations on North America, 1767," *Pennsylvania Magazine,* XXVII (1903) 4-5, 15. Gottfried Achenwall, *Herrn Hofrath Achenwalls in Göttingen Anmerkungen über Nordamerika und über Dasige Grosbritannische Colonien aus Mündlichen Nachrichten des Herrn Dr. Franklins* (Frankfurt und Leipzig: 1769).

19. *Œuvres de Turgot,* ed. Schelle, III, 70.

20. *Ephémérides,* 1772, I (i), 213-227.

21. Hays, ed., *Calendar,* I, 140. Baron F. de Westerholt to Franklin. November 12, 1772.

22. *Ephémérides,* 1769, VI (i), 56-78.

23. For a fuller discussion and evidence that the work is Franklin's see: A. O. Aldridge, "Franklin's Deistical Indians," *Proceedings of the American Philosophical Society,* XCIV (1950), 398-410. James R. Masterson ["A Foolish Oneida Tale," *American Literature,* X (1938) 53-65] discusses several versions of the tobacco story, including that of William Henry, but does not attribute it to Franklin.

24. *Indian Treaties Printed by Benjamin Franklin 1736-1762.* With an Introduction by Carl Van Doren and Historical and Bibliographical Notes by Julian P.

Boyd (Philadelphia: Hist. Soc.
Pa., 1938), pp. 72 ff.

25. Masterson, *loc. cit.*, points out
that this version was translated
into French in *Précis de l'état
actuel des colonies angloises dans
l'Amérique septentrionale par*

M. *Dominique de Blackford*
(Milan, 1771).

26. For more details concerning this
work see Chapter 11.

27. Manuscript letter. Bache Collection, Library of the American
Philosophical Society.

28. Smyth, ed., *Writings*, X, 98-99.

CHAPTER 3

1. *Œuvres* (2 vols.; Paris: Quillau
l'aîné, 1773), II, 171-181.

2. *La science du bonhomme Richard, ou moyen facile de payer les
impôts* . . . (Philadelphie, et se
trouve à Paris, chez Ruault,
1777). There were two editions
in 1777, two others in 1778.

3. A. O. Aldridge, "Jacques Barbeu-Dubourg, A French Disciple
of Benjamin Franklin," *Proceedings of the American Philosophical Society*, XCV (1951), 342-
343.

4. Manuscript in Archives Nationales. Paris. M1773. No. 2.

5. Tome IV, 219-236.

6. *Port Royal*, 1. II, chap. XVIII
(Edition commentaire . . . 9 vols.;
Paris: la Connaissance, 1926-
1929), II, 457-458.

7. Smyth, ed., *Writings*, VII, 347.

8. Jeanne Louise Henriette Cam-
pan (Genet), *Mémoires sur la vie
de Marie-Antoinette* (Paris: Fir-
min-Didot, s.d.), p. 177.

9. *Essais historiques et politiques
sur les Anglo-Américains* (2 vols.;
Bruxelles, et se trouve à Paris
chez l'auteur), II, 44-47.

10. A Lausanne: chez Hignon, 1795.

11. J. Castéra, ed., *Vie de Benjamin
Franklin* (2 vols.; Paris: Buisson,
An VI).

12. Paris: chez Delaunay, Librairie,
1817.

13. 10 octobre 1791. J. L. Tallien reprinted this essay in his *Ami des
citoyens, journal fraternel*, 19
octobre 1791.

14. P. J. B. Buchez & P. C. Roux,
*Histoire parlementaire de la
Révolution Française* (40 vols.;
Paris: Paulin, 1834-1838), XIV,
139.

15. *Eloge civique de Benjamin
Franklin* (Paris: J. R. Lottin,
1790), p. 13.

16. Novembre 1777. Tourneaux, ed.,
Correspondance, XII, 29.

17. *Œuvres diverses* (Paris: Guillaumin, 1848), p. 614.

18. *La science du bonhomme Richard de Benjamin Franklin,
précédée d'un abrégé de la vie
de Franklin, et suivie de son inter-
rogatoire devant la Chambre des
Communes* (Paris: Imprimerie
des Sciences et Arts, An II). Say
was a director of this press. This
edition has nothing remarkable
except a footnote, not found in
other editions, concerning Father Abraham's statement that a
creditor has the right to keep his
debtor in prison for life or to
sell him as a servant. The footnote merely states: "Example of
the barbarousness of the English
law."

19. 30 thermidor An II.

20. 16 pluviôse An III. Manuscript
letter. Archives Nationales. Paris.
F^{17} 1331^B dossier 6. No. 167.

21. *Sur l'éducation nationale dans
les États-Unis d'Amérique*. Seconde édition (Paris: Le Nor-
mant, 1812), p. 34.

22. Smyth, ed., *Writings*, IX, 477.

23. See introduction to: *La science*

du bonhomme Richard par Franklin, imprimeur, suivi . . . du Testament de Fortuné Ricard (Paris: Klefer, 1831).

24. *Œuvres complètes de Frédéric Bastiat* (6 vols.; Paris: Guillaumin, 1854-1855), I, 19.

25. P. Ronce, *Frédéric Bastiat, sa vie et son oeuvre* (Paris: Guillaumin, 1905), p. 145.

26. *Œuvres du Marquis de Condorcet,* publiées par A. Condorcet O'Connor et M. F. Arago (12 vols.; Paris: Firmin Didot Frères, 1847-1849), III, 378-379.

27. 23 juin 1791.

28. 29 septembre 1791.

29. See especially II, 252, 291; III, 31, 37, 395. 1 messidor An III— 17 floréal An IV.

30. *Journal des théâtres, ou le nouveau spectateur,* Tome Troisième, 1 mars 1778. A similar allusion exists in [L. S. Mercier] *Tableau de Paris* (12 vols.; Amsterdam: no printer's name, 1783-1789), XII, 8.

31. An VI. Tome IV, 81-92.

32. For further comments on the moral significance of *Poor Richard:* see the end of Chapter 12 of the present work.

33. There exists at the Bibliothèque Nationale and at the New York Public Library another edition of the almanac without the conversation between Sancho Pança and Bonhomme Richard: *Calendrier de Philadelphie pour l'année* MDCCLXXVII, Londres [i.e. Paris] 1777. This is unquestionably the original work of Dubourg, but he seems to have had nothing to do with any subsequent edition.

34. Vol. III, 358.

35. John Keats, October 14-31, 1818. Lionel Trilling, ed., *The Selected Letters of John Keats* (New York: Farrar, Straus, 1951), p. 160.

36. Leigh Hunt, *Autobiography* (2 vols.; New York: Harper & Bros., 1850), I, 130.

CHAPTER 4

1. *L'espion anglois* (10 vols.; Londres: John Adamson, 1777-1786), V, 2 ff. Volumes 1-4 were written by Mathieu François Pidauzat de Mairobert, 1777-1778. The volumes that concern Franklin (5-10) were written anonymously after Mairobert's death. They may have been published in Amsterdam, the London reference being perhaps a blind.

2. Simeon Prosper Hardy, "Mes loisirs ou Journal d'événemens tels qu'ils proviennent à ma connoissance." Bibliothèque Nationale, MSS Français 6682, folio 308.

3. Verner W. Crane, *Benjamin Franklin and a Rising People* (Boston: Little, Brown, 1954), pp. 166, 171. For the most thorough analysis of Franklin's political opinions see: Gerald Stourzh, *Benjamin Franklin and American Foreign Policy* (Chicago: University of Chicago Press, 1954).

4. *Œuvres de Bernard Palissy, revues sur les exemplaires de la bibliothèque du roi, avec des notes; par M. Faujas de Saint Ford, et des Additions par M. Gobet* (Paris, Ruault, 1777).

5. *L'espion anglois,* VII, 242-243.

6. *États-Unis de l'Amérique septentrionale, comparés avec les ligues achéenne, suisse et hollandoise* (2 vols.; Genève: Cuchet, 1787), II, 100-101.

7. Reprinted in *Pennsylvania Packet,* June 3, 1780; quoted from Frank Moore, *Diary of the*

American Revolution (2 vols.; New York: Scribners, 1860), II, 434.

8. For a discussion of Franklin's part in *Affaires de l'Angleterre et de l'Amérique* see: Gilbert Chinard, "Adventures in a Library," *Newberry Library Bulletin*, Second Series No. 8 (March, 1952), pp. 225-236.

9. La Rochefoucauld, ed., *Constitutions des Treize États-Unis de l'Amérique* . . . (Paris: Ph D. Pierres, 1783).

10. Ministère des Affaires Étrangères. Correspondance Politique. États-Unis, 23, f. 372

11. John Lewis Soulavie, *Historical and Political Memoirs of the Reign of Lewis XVI* . . . (6 vols.; London: G. & J. Robinson, 1802), V, 160-179.

12. 26 juin 1782.

13. William Smith, *Eulogium on Benjamin Franklin* . . . (Philadelphia: B. F. Bache, 1792), Appendix No. 1.

14. Smyth, ed., *Writings*, VIII, 597.

15. März 1797.

16. *Vie de Benjamin Franklin* (2 vols.; Paris: Buisson, An VI), II, 336-337.

17. Jared Sparks, ed., *Works of Benjamin Franklin* (10 vols.; Boston: Hilliard, Gray & Co., 1836-1840), II, 434-447.

CHAPTER 5

1. Smyth, ed., *Writings*, III, 124.

2. *Ibid.*, V, 47.

3. *Ibid.*, V, 53-54.

4. *Ibid.*, VII, 103.

5. *Ibid.*, VII, 289-290.

6. *Ibid.*, VII, 393-394.

7. *Ibid.*, IX, 667-669.

8. *Ibid.*, IX, 665.

9. *Ibid.*, X, 50.

10. *Pennsylvania Evening Herald.* February 26, 1785.

11. 21 août 1791.

12. *Les Jardins de Betz, Poème, Accompagné de notes instructives . . . fait en 1785 par M. Cerutti, et publié en 1792* (Paris: Desenne, 1792), pp. 40-41. The note on American independence appeared first in *La Feuille Villageoise,* 9 février 1792.

13. Helen Maria Williams, *Souvenirs de la Révolution française* (Paris: 1827), pp. 12-13.

14. 16 août 1792.

15. Bernard Faÿ, "Franklin et Mirabeau collaborateurs," *Revue de littérature comparée*, VIII (1928), 5-28.

16. Smyth, ed., *Writings*, IX, 162.

17. Morellet's letter is printed by Faÿ, *loc. cit.*

18. Smyth, ed., *Writings*, X, 354.

19. *Ibid.*, IX, 270.

20. René des Genettes, *Souvenirs de la fin du XVIIIe siècle et du commencement du XIXe* (2 vols.; Paris: Didot frères, 1835-1836), I, 117.

21. *Lettres de Mirabeau à Chamfort* . . . (Paris: chez le directeur de la *Décade philosophique*, An V), p. 29.

22. *Ibid.*, p. 43.

23. *Ibid.*, p. 56.

24. *Ibid.*, p. 87.

25. *Œuvres complètes de Chamfort recueillies . . . par P. R. Auguis* (5 vols.; Paris: Chaumerot jeune, 1824-1825), V, 1825.

26. *Œuvres de Chamfort* (4 vols.; Paris: Imprimerie des Sciences et Arts, An III), I, xii.

27. *Vie de Benjamin Franklin* (Paris: Buisson, An VI), II, 376.

28. *Journal de la Société de 1789,* 24 juillet 1790. After writing this chapter, I discovered that Durand Eccheverria published Morellet's text in *Bulletin de*

l'Institut Français de Washington, n.s. III, 119-126.

29. *La Feuille Villageoise,* 26 janvier 1792.

30. No. XVII, p. lix.

31. Paris: Ruault, Libraire, 1777, pp. 82-145.

32. Regnier trad., *Recueil des loix constitutives des colonies angloises* (Philadelphie, et se vend à Paris: . . . chez Cellot & Jombert, 1778).

33. La Rochefoucauld, ed., *Constitutions des Treize États-Unis de l'Amérique* . . . (Paris: Ph D. Pierres, 1783). The French editions of the constitution of Pennsylvania pose a number of problems, including that of the identity of the translator. The *Recueil des loix constitutives* is generally attributed to Regnier—yet the translations of the Pennsylvania constitution in the three volumes mentioned above are identical. Regnier wrote to Franklin (October 12, 1782) on the subject of a collection of laws of the United States he was making. He pointed out that he had presented his first volume to La Rochefoucauld, who had approved the plan of publishing a second volume. He asked Franklin for permission to copy documents that he lacked and asked whether he might later submit the work for Franklin's criticism and advice. [Hays, *Calendar,* II, 502.] The first volume, 1778, had been dedicated to Franklin in an address signed by Regnier. For the influence of these editions see: J. Paul Selsam and Joseph G. Rayback, "French Comment on the Pennsylvania Constitution of 1776," *Pennsylvania Magazine of History and Biography,* LXXVI (1952), pp. 311-325. Gilbert Chinard gives a full discussion of the texts of Regnier and La Rochefoucauld

in American Philosophical Society, *Year Book* 1943 (Philadelphia, 1944), pp. 88-106.

34. *Journal de la Société de 1789,* 19 juin 1790.

35. Séance du vendredi 7 octobre 1791. *Correspondance patriotique,* I (1791), 67.

36. John Adams, *Works* (10 vols.; Boston: Little, Brown & Co., 1850-1856), IX, 622-623. To Samuel Perley, June 19, 1809.

37. *The Life of Thomas Paine* (London: John Maxwell, 1817), p. 165.

38. Philip S. Foner, ed., *The Complete Writings of Thomas Paine* (2 vols.; New York: Citadel Press, 1945), II, 270.

39. *Ibid.,* II, 1006.

40. Smyth, ed., *Writings,* X, 58.

41. M. R. Eiselen, *Franklin's Political Theories* (Garden City, N. Y.: Doubleday, Doran & Co., 1928), pp. 57-58; J. Paul Selsam, *The Pennsylvania Constitution of 1776* (Philadelphia: University of Pennsylvania Press, 1926), *passim;* Charles M. Anderson, *The Colonial Period of American History* (4 vols.; New Haven: Yale University Press, 1934-1938), III, 320.

42. *Qu'est-ce que la constitution de 93? Constitution de Massachusett* (sic) (Paris: chez Migneret, An III), pp. 27-33.

43. Smyth, ed., *Writings,* X, 35.

44. *Ibid.,* X, 68-69.

45. *Private Correspondence* (London: H. Colburn, 1817), I, 68-69.

46. 2 janvier 1790.

47. Smyth, ed., *Writings,* X, 72.

48. *Gazetteer and New Daily Advertiser* (London), July 5, 1790.

49. *Les contemporains de 1789 et 1790, ou les opinions débattues pendant la première législature . . . rédigé par M. de Luchet* (3 vols.; Paris: chez Lejay fils, 1790), II, 34-35.

CHAPTER 6

1. *Illusions perdues,* II Partie, *Un grand homme de province à Paris.*
2. *Histoire philosophique et politique des établissemens et du commerce des européens dans les deux Indes* (6 vols.; Amsterdam: no printer's name, 1770), VI, 257-262. Three excellent scholarly works treat Raynal's use of the Polly Baker story: Anatole Feugère, *L'Abbé Raynal* (Angoulême: Imprimerie ouvrière, 1922); Johan Viktor Johansson, *Études sur Denis Diderot* (Goteborg, Paris; Champion, 1927); Gilbert Chinard, ed., Diderot. *Supplément au Voyage de Bougainville* (Paris: E. Droz, 1935). Johansson's work is the most thorough study of the textual history of Polly Baker and the influence of Raynal's version.
3. *Writings* (20 vols.; Washington: Jefferson Memorial Association, 1903-1904), XVIII, 170.
4. *Op. cit.* (4 vols.; Paris: chez Froullé, 1788), III, 23-24.
5. See in particular Feugère, *L'Abbé Raynal,* p. 219.
6. *Œuvres complètes de Voltaire* (70 vols.; Imprimerie de la société littéraire typographique, 1784-1789), XXXVII, 277-278.
7. Smyth, ed., *Writings,* II, 465.
8. Brissot de Warville, *Mémoires* (4 vols.; Paris: Ladvocat, 1830-1832), III, 83.
9. Lettre II, Mai 1774. *Correspondance Littéraire* (6 vols.; Paris: Migneret imprimeur, 1801-1807), I, 18.
10. Chinard, ed., *Supplément au Voyage de Bougainville,* pp. 155-159. The digression concerning Polly Baker does not appear in any of the editions of the *Voyage* published during Diderot's lifetime, but in a manuscript of the work discovered in the Leningrad public library.
11. Johansson, *Études,* p. 189.
12. 17 juin, II, 40. The heroine is termed Mary Baker in a note concerning credulity by the translator [Joel Barlow?] of Brissot's *Travels:* "Accounts like this put one in mind of Dr. Franklin's romance of *Mary Baker,* so religiously believed and copied by the Abbé Raynal, in his History of the Two Indies." J. P. Brissot de Warville, *New Travels in the United States of America* (Dublin: W. Corbet, 1792), p. 330.
13. *Op. cit.,* VIII, 363-368.
14. *Op. cit.,* p. 158.
15. Egide Louis Edmé Joseph de Lespinasse, Chevalier de Langeac, *Anecdotes anglaises et américaines* . . . (2 vols.; Paris: Delaunay, 1813), II, 130-139.
16. Johansson, *op. cit.,* p. 181.
17. *Recherches historiques* . . . *sur les États-Unis,* III, 25.

CHAPTER 7

1. This and other details of Dubourg's early life are documented in A. O. Aldridge, "Jacques Barbeu-Dubourg," *loc. cit.*
2. The edition of the Bibliothèque Nationale [T⁷.15.8⁰] has neither date nor place, but can be dated 1779 because of an account of it in *Mémoires secrets,* 13 février 1779.
3. *Vicomte de Barjac, ou Mémoires pour servir à l'histoire de ce siècle* (London: no printer's name, 1784), pp. 78, 120.

4. Maurice Cousin, Cte de Cour-champs, ed., *Souvenirs de la marquise de Créquy* (10 vols.; Paris: Garnier frères, 1903). According to Sainte-Beuve, ". . . on arriverait, rien qu'avec les Lettres qu'on publie et dont j'ai les originaux sous les yeux, à être assuré que les prétendus Mémoires ne sont, *à aucun degré*, de la Marquise de Créqui elle-même." *Lettres inédites de la marquise de Créqui* (Paris: L. Potier, 1856), p. xiv.

5. *Op. cit.,* V, 179.

6. Emmanuel Duc de Croÿ, "Mémoires du Duc de Croÿ sur les Cours de Louis XV et de Louis XVI (1727-1784)," *Nouvelle Revue Rétrospective,* V (1896), 339. See also an expanded but less colorful account in Groucy & Cottin, eds., *Journal inédit du duc de Croÿ, 1718-1784* (4 vols.; Paris: E. Flammarion, 1907), III, 301-302.

7. Winslow C. Watson, ed., *Men and Times of the Revolution: or Memoirs of Elkanah Watson* (2d ed.; New York: Dana & Co., 1857), p. 103.

8. Carl Van Doren, ed., *The Letters of Benjamin Franklin and Jane Mecom* (Princeton: Princeton University Press, 1950), pp. 336-337.

9. All of the following details concerning Crèvecoeur are taken from the excellent study by Percy G. Adams, "Crèvecoeur and Franklin," *Pennsylvania History,* XIV (1947), 2-8.

10. Manuscrit 596. Bibliothèque Municipale de Verdun.

11. Versions of this anecdote appeared in a number of newspapers after Franklin's death and in John F. Watson's *Annals of Philadelphia,* 1844, but its apparent source appeared only recently: "An Article Found Among the Papers of Roberts Vaux," *Pennsylvania Magazine,* XLVIII (1924), 383.

12. *Portrait du Comte de Vergennes* (n.p., 1778), p. 58.

13. *Histoire d'un pou françois* (Paris: Imprimerie royale, 1779), p. 26.

14. *Journal inédit,* III, 295.

15. Quoted in Jules Bellendy, *J.-S. Duplessis, peintre du roi. 1725-1802* (Chartres: Imprimerie Durand, 1913), p. 86.

16. *Op. cit.,* pp. 61-62.

17. *Mercure de France.* Supplément au No. 1 (janvier 1793).

18. Jones's *Fragment of Polybius* is printed in full in Sparks, ed., *Works of Benjamin Franklin,* VIII, 543-547.

19. (Paris: Ph D. Pierres, 1783), pp. 28-29.

CHAPTER 8

1. Schelle, ed., *Œuvres de Turgot,* V, 647.

2. Georges Giacometti, *Le statuaire Jean-Antoine Houdon et son époque* (3 vols.; Paris: Joune & Cie., 1918-1919), III, 239, 336.

3. Charles Henry Hart, "An Unpublished Life Portrait of Franklin," *McClure's Magazine,* VIII (March, 1897), 453.

4. Baron Roger Portalis, *Honoré Fragonard, sa vie et son oeuvre* (Paris: J. Rothschild, 1889), pp. 141-142. The engraving is described and praised in *Journal de Paris,* 15 novembre 1778.

5. P. 197.

6. *Œuvres choisies de Servan* (5 vols.; Paris: chez les éditeurs, 1825), III, 116.

7. At his revolutionary trial, 7 thermidor An II. George Hilt.

"Des Freiherrn von Trenck letzte Stunden," *Die Gartenlaube,* 1863 (no volume number), pp. 8-11.

8. Schelle, ed., *Œuvres,* V, 494.
9. Adams, *Works,* IX, 625.
10. *Ibid.,* I, 662.
11. O'Connor et Arago, eds., *Œuvres,* V, 162.
12. Smyth, ed., *Writings,* VIII, 93.
13. *Ibid.,* VIII, 215.
14. Ernest Choullier, *Voltaire et Franklin à l'Académie des Sciences* (Troyes, 1898), p. 6.
15. *Mémoires de Condorcet sur le règne de Louis XVI et la révolution. Extraits de sa correspondance et de celles de ses amis. Tomes VII et VIII des Œuvres choisies de M. le Marquis de la Rochefoucauld-Liancourt* (2 vols.; Paris: imprimerie de Morris, 1862), I, 155-157.
16. Vol. II, p. 365.
17. Vol. IV, p. 20.
18. Tourneux, ed., XII, 85.
19. Charles Sumner, "Monograph from an Old Note-Book," *Atlantic Monthly,* XII (1863), 648-662. Reprinted in *Works of Charles Sumner* (15 vols.; Boston: Lee & Shepard, 1873-1883), VIII, 1-38.
20. Pp. 134-136. This review can be identified as Chamfort's because it is reprinted in his *Œuvres complètes,* III, 316-324.
21. Horace W. Smith, *Life and Correspondence of the Rev. William Smith, D.D.* (2 vols.; Philadelphia: Ferguson Bros., 1880), II, 346.
22. Winthrop Sargent, ed., *The Loyal Verses of Joseph Stansbury and Doctor Jonathan Odell* (Albany: no printer's name, 1860), p. 112: "The Inscription on Franklin's Stove was undoubtedly written by Dr. Odell. Independently of the assertion of his family, and the fact of a manuscript version in his handwriting, dated 1776, being now before me, abundant evidence of his authorship will be found in contemporaneous authorities. It is so stated in the Gentleman's Magazine for April, 1777; in Towne's Evening Post; Philadelphia, Nov. 29th, 1777; in Boucher's View of the American Revolution (London, 1797), p. 449; and in Rev. W. Smith's Works (Philadelphia, 1803)."
23. Masson to Franklin, June 22, 1778. Hays, ed., *Calendar,* I, 444.
24. Du Pont de Nemours, ed., *Œuvres de Mr. Turgot* (9 vols.; Paris: Impr. de A. Belin, 1808-1811), IX, 140.
25. Smyth, ed., *Writings,* VIII, 215-216. Nogaret's translation was immediately printed below a portrait of Franklin engraved after a painting by L. C. Carmontelle. It is described in *Journal de Paris,* 31 mars 1781.
26. Morellet, *Mémoires,* I, 288.
27. *Voyage d'Amérique* (à Londres et se trouve à Paris, chez Pichard, 1786), p. 22.
28. (A Paris: Impr. L. Potier de Lille, 1790.)
29. *Public Advertiser,* February 16, 1774. Verner W. Crane, *Benjamin Franklin's Letters to the Press* (Chapel Hill: University of North Carolina Press, 1950), p. xxix.
30. Coder to Franklin, June 16, 1777. Hays, ed., *Calendar,* I, 257.
31. Tourneux, ed., *op. cit.,* XII, 3.
32. (5 vols.; Paris: Migneret, 1801-1807), II, 70. It is to be noted that the first line in this quatrain and in Turgot's French verses are identical. Madame du Deffand sent a copy of Target's quatrain (unaware of its authorship) to Horace Walpole, March 1, 1777. W. S. Lewis and W. H.

Smith, eds., *Horace Walpole's Correspondence with Madame Du Deffand* (6 vols.; New Haven: Yale University Press, 1939), IV, 413. Madame Du Deffand cited the epigram in a letter to the Duchesse de Choiseul, April 22, 1778, and quoted d'Alembert's verses, May 2, 1778. Saint-Aulaire, ed., *Correspondance complète de Mme. du Deffand* (3 vols.; Paris: Michel Levy frères, 1866-1877), III, 313-314.

33. Nicholas Hans, "Franklin, Jefferson, and the English Radicals at the End of the Eighteenth Century," *Proceedings of the American Philosophical Society*, XCVIII (1954), 423.

34. L. S. Livingston, *Franklin and His Press at Passy* (New York, 1914), p. 196.

35. *Nouveaux opuscules de M. Feutry* (Dijon, et se trouve à Paris, 1779), p. 59. There are other verses on Franklin on pp. 18-20 and 94.

36. *Portrait du Comte de Vergennes* (n.p., 1788), pp. 60-61.

37. Livingston, *op. cit.*, p. 190.

38. Cubières-Palmézeaux (Michel de Cubières), ed., *Poésies philosophiques et descriptives des auteurs qui se sont distingués dans le dix-huitième siècle* (3 vols.; Paris: no printer's name, 1792), III, 79-87.

39. *Le tribut de la société nationale des neuf soeurs, ou recueil de mémoires sur les sciences, belles lettres et arts, et d'autres pièces lues dans les séances de cette société* (Paris: 1791), pp. 51-57 [Z6 1748]. The separate printing has no title page [Ye 27763].

40. *Recueil d'apologues et de faits historiques, mis en vers, et relatifs aux révolutions française, américaine, etc.* (Paris: Laran, An V), pp. 22-24. For information on this author see: Gilbert Chinard, ed., *Vashington ou la liberté du nouveau monde* (Princeton: Princeton University Press, 1941).

41. *Ibid.*, pp. 57-60.

42. Caen: L. J. Poisson, 1787.

CHAPTER 9

1. See Chapter 7.

2. My treatment of this play and the two following is based on K. N. McKee, "The Popularity of the 'American' on the French Stage During the Revolution," *Proceedings of the American Philosophical Society*, LXXXIII (1940), 479-491.

3. Bernard Faÿ also treats this work: *L'esprit révolutionnaire en France et aux Etats Unis à la fin du XVIIIᵉ siècle* (Paris: Edouard Champion, 1925), pp. 196-197.

4. I. Bernard Cohen, "A note concerning Diderot and Franklin," *Isis*, XLVI (1955), 269-270.

5. Roland Mortier, *Diderot en Allemagne* (Paris: Presses Universitaires, 1954), p. 217.

6. *La mort de Robespierre, Tragédie en trois actes et en vers* (Paris: chez Monoroy, Libraire, An IX), pp. 215-221.

CHAPTER 10

1. There have been countless studies of Franklin's *Memoirs*. The most complete printing of texts is Max Farrand, ed., *Memoirs*. Parallel text edition (Berkeley: University of California Press, 1949). Best discussion is Jack C. Barnes, *Franklin and His Memoirs*, unpublished doctoral dissertation, University of Maryland, 1954.

2. "Anecdotes sur Franklin," 15 juillet 1790.

3. Pierre Jean Georges Cabanis, "Notice sur Benjamin Franklin," *Œuvres complètes* (5 vols.; Paris: Bossange frères, 1823-1825), V, 219-274.

4. Bibliothèque Municipale. Mantes.

5. *Mémoires de la vie privée de Benjamin Franklin, écrits par lui-même et adressés à son fils* (Paris: Buisson, 1791).

6. This letter was subsequently printed in *Mercure de France*, 12 mars 1791 (where it is dated 23 février) and in *Journal de Paris*, 24 mars.

7. Manuscript letter. Morgan Library. New York City. Photostat in Library of Congress.

8. Manuscript Division. Library of Congress.

9. O'Connor and Arago, eds., *Œuvres . . . de Condorcet*, III, 411.

10. Papers of abbé de la Roche. Bibliothèque de l'Institut de France.

11. This translation is apparently not entirely the work of Le Veillard since W. T. Franklin in a letter to Le Veillard (February 28, 1792) refers to the latter's remark that the translation is being done by a M. Feuillet, who, however, could not complete it. [Manuscript letter. Morgan Library. New York City. Photostat in Library of Congress.] Somewhat later Benjamin Vaughan knew of the existence of Le Veillard's translation. When interrogated by French officials on landing in France, June 2, 1794, he reported: ". . . Le Docteur Franklin m'a envoyé une Copie en manuscrit de sa vie pour y ajouter mes réflexions avec le Docteur Price, avant que d'être imprimée; et dans sa vie qu'a traduit le M. Le Veillard on trouvera une Longue Lettre de ma part, pour lui décider d'écrire sa vie." Ministère des Affaires Étrangères. Angleterre, 588, ff. 171-176.

12. 30 pluviôse, An VI (18 février 1798), pp. 348-358.

13. J. Castéra, trad., *Vie de Benjamin Franklin* (Paris: Buisson, An VI), I, i-ii.

14. Gilbert Chinard, "Les amitiés américaines de Mme. d'Houdetot d'après sa correspondance inédite avec Benjamin Franklin et Thomas Jefferson," *Bibliothèque de la Revue de littérature comparée*, VIII (1924), 5-10.

15. Bibliothèque de l'Institut de France.

16. *Mercure de France*, 25 juin 1791; Chamfort, *Œuvres complètes*, III, 316-324.

17. 5 août 1791.

18. 21 août 1791.

19. "Hommage rendu par le voeu unanime de la société de 1789 à Benjamin Franklin, objet de l'admiration et des regrets des amis de la liberté," *Journal de la Société de 1789*, 19 juin 1790.

CHAPTER 11

1. Richard E. Amacher, ed., *Franklin's Wit and Folly. The Bagatelles* (New Brunswick: Rutgers University Press, 1953), p. 19. See also L. S. Livingston, *Franklin and His Press at Passy* (New York: Grolier Club, 1914), p. 17.

2. *Memoirs of the Life and Writings of Benjamin Franklin* (3 vols.; London: H. Colburn, 1817-1818), III, 307.

3. W. C. Bruce, *Benjamin Franklin, Self-Revealed* (2d ed.; 2 vols.; New York: G. P. Putnam, 1923), I, 476.

4. Pierre Jean Georges Cabanis, *Œuvres complètes* (5 vols.; Paris: Bossange frères, 1823-1825), V, 256.

5. *Mémoires inédits de l'abbé Morellet* (2ième ed.; 2 vols.; Paris: Ladvocat, 1822), I, 379-380.

6. Gilbert Chinard, "Abbé Lefebvre de la Roche's Recollections of Benjamin Franklin," *Proceedings of the American Philosophical Society*, XCIV (1950), 215-216.

7. Smyth, ed., *Writings*, X, 442. Sparks quite properly printed this letter as a bagatelle, *Works of Benjamin Franklin* (10 vols.; Boston: Hilliard, Gray & Co., 1836-1840), II, 202-203.

8. Poupon was a lap dog. September 19, 1779. Paul McPharlin, ed., *Satires and Bagatelles* (Detroit: Fine Book Circle, 1937), p. 106.

9. June 24 [1780?], Schelle, ed., *Œuvres de Turgot*, V, 628.

10. Smyth, ed., *Writings*, VII, 204-206.

11. Maurice Tourneux, ed., *op. cit.*, XII, 385-386.

12. *Op. cit.*, I, 300-302.

13. L. S. Livingston, *Benjamin Franklin's Letters to Madame Helvétius and Madame La Freté*

14. C. F. Adams, ed., *Letters of Mrs. Adams* (2d ed.; 2 vols.; Boston: C. C. Little & J. Brown, 1840), II, 55-56.

(Cambridge: Harvard Univ. Press, 1924); McPharlin, *op. cit.*, p. 109; Amacher, *op. cit.*, p. 148.

15. This letter and others by Mme. Brillon, although written in French, are printed by Smyth in English translation: *Writings*, X, 409. Bernard Faÿ discovered an interesting anecdote about Franklin and Mme. Brillon in the *American Museum*, August, 1791. One day she was "sitting on his knee and combing his grey locks. 'Why,' asked he, 'have you that have so often invited me to dine and sup with you never requested me to stay and sleep?' She smiled, perhaps she blushed, and answered that she would be happy to be favored with his company that very night. Fortunately it was summer time. 'Hum, hum,' said the old gentleman a little embarrassed, not expecting so warm a reply, but taking out a memorandum book. 'I'll make a minute of the invitation, and, when the nights are longer, will have the pleasure of waiting on you.' " "His Excellency Mr. Franklin. The Last Loves of the First American," *The Forum*, LXXIX (1928), 330.

16. To William Carmichael, June 17, 1780. *Writings*, VIII, 100.

17. November 18, 1780. *Ibid.*, X, 416.

18. Papers of abbé de la Roche. Bibliothèque de l'Institut de France.

19. Smyth, ed., *Writings*, X, 436.

20. *Ibid.*, X, 208.

21. *Ibid.*, X, 100.

22. "The Vanity and Ambition of

the Human Mind." This essay appeared originally in *The Freethinker*, April 24, 1719.

23. Papers of abbé de la Roche. Bibliothèque de l'Institut de France.
24. Smyth, ed., *Writings*, X, 436.
25. Amacher, *op. cit.*, pp. 158-159.
26. Smyth, ed., *Writings*, VIII, 154-162.
27. *Ibid.*, X, 427.
28. *Ibid.*, VII, 414-416.
29. *Œuvres complètes*, V, 222-223.
30. Chinard, "Recollections," *Proceedings of the American Philosophical Society*, XCIV (1950), 219.
31. Smyth, ed., *Writings*, VIII, 162-164.
32. A. A. Barbier, ed., *Correspondance inédite de l'abbé Ferdinand Galiani, Conseilleur du roi de Naples . . .* (2 vols.; Paris: Treuttel et Würtz, 1818), II, 512.
33. *Ibid.*, I, liv.
34. Amacher, *op. cit.*, pp. 66-69.
35. A. O. Aldridge, "Franklin's Letter on Indians and Germans," *Proceedings of the American Philosophical Society*, XCIV (1950), 391-395.
36. Smyth, ed., *Writings*, IX, 176-177.
37. Hays, ed., *Calendar of the Papers of Benjamin Franklin*, I, 496.
38. Chinard, "Recollections," *loc. cit.*, p. 221. All critics of Franklin's bagatelles agree that the *Information* and the *Remarks* should not be included in the group, but persist in including them because of the mechanical circumstance that Franklin printed them himself and sent copies to Mme. Brillon. In his accompanying letter to Mme. Brillon, however, he clearly indicated that he considered the two propaganda tracts to belong to a different category.

39. Papers of abbé de la Roche. Bibliothèque de l'Institut de France.
40. 17 février.
41. Amacher, *op. cit.*, p. 153.
42. *Ibid.*, p. 155.
43. 23 juin 1791. Even before Cerutti's article, the abbé Fauchet had paraphrased the parable in his eulogy of Franklin, July 21, 1790. See Chapter 11.
44. Ministère des Affaires Étrangères. Correspondance Politique. États-Unis, Vol. 23, f. 386.
45. Bibliothèque Municipale Nantes.
46. Smyth, ed., *Writings*, V, 553-555. On another occasion Franklin attended a dinner at which bread made with potatoes—the discovery of Parmentier—was a feature. C. Hippeau, *Le Gouvernement de Normandie au XVIIe et XVIIIe Siècle . . .* Deuxième Partie (9 vols.; Caen: G. de Laporte, 1863-1870), I, 127.
47. Smyth, ed., *Writings*, IX, 183-189.
48. *Benjamin Franklin* (New York: Viking Press, 1938), p. 710.
49. J. Castéra, ed., *Vie de Benjamin Franklin* (2 vols.; Paris: Buisson, An VI).
50. C. Couderc, "Economies proposées par B. Franklin et Mercier de Saint-Léger," *Bulletin de la Société de l'histoire de Paris*, 43e année 1916, pp. 93-101.
51. There exists in the Boston Public Library a newspaper clipping of "La main gauche, pétition adressée à tous ceux qui ont des enfants à élever." This clipping has neither name nor date, but it states that the petition is extracted from a "petit almanach de 1787 (Etrennes à l'humanité)." Unfortunately this edition does not exist at the Bibliothèque Nationale. It is not even mentioned by J. Grand Carteret in *Les almanacs français*.
52. 10 pluviôse An VI.

53. Letter of M. Grouvelle, *Journal de la Société de 1789*, 24 juillet 1790.
54. Sparks, ed., *Works*, X, 314.
55. Smyth, ed., *Writings*, VIII, 162.
56. A full account of this work is available in A. O. Aldridge, "Jacques Barbeu Dubourg, A French Disciple of Benjamin Franklin," *Proceedings of the American Philosophical Society*, XCV (1951), 331-392.
57. The great historian of the French Revolution, A. Aulard, has presented nearly everything that is known about Gargaz. "Le forçat Gargaz, Franklin et la Société des Nations," *La Revue de Paris*. Trentième Année. Tome Cinquième (septembre, 1923), pp. 44-55. There is a second edition of the *Contrat social* printed in reformed spelling. Paris. Archives Nationales. AD XVII 49.

CHAPTER 12

1. Gilbert Chinard, "La Roche's Recollections," *Proceedings of the American Philosophical Society*, XCIV (1950), 218.
2. *Ibid.*, 219.
3. Jefferson, *Writings*, XVIII, 171-172. The history of the doctrine is told by Gilbert Chinard in "Eighteenth Century Theories on America as a Human Habitat," *Proceedings of the American Philosophical Society*, XCI (1947), 27-57.
4. Tourneux, ed., XII, 133. Franklin's taciturnity was frequently observed. The abbé Morellet remarked, for example, that he spoke in few words and at long intervals—that no one practiced more faithfully the maxim of La Fontaine, "Le sage est ménager du temps et des paroles." *Mémoires*, I, 204.
5. August, 1783. *Ibid.*, XIII, 349. Another version is given in *Mémoires secrets*, 24 septembre 1783.
6. Ducarne de Blaugy to Franklin, October 3, 1783. Hays, ed., *Calendar*, IV, 468.
7. *Mémoires secrets*, 5 décembre 1783.
8. "Anecdotes sur Franklin," 15 juillet 1790.
9. "Notice sur Benjamin Franklin," *Œuvres complètes*, V, 219-274.
10. *Mélanges de littérature* (4 vols.; Paris: Vᵛᵉ Lepetit, 1818), IV, 95.
11. *Vie de M. Turgot*, in O'Connor & Arago, eds., *Œuvres de Condorcet*, V, 70.
12. *Moniteur*, 15 juillet 1790.
13. Smyth, ed., *Writings*, I, 386.
14. *Œuvres*, V, 267.
15. *Œuvres complètes de Chamfort*, III, 218.
16. Cabanis, *Œuvres*, V, 249.
17. *Moniteur*, 15 juillet 1790.
18. *Lettres philosophiques . . . sur divers sujets de morale et de littérature* (Paris: F. Louis, 1826), pp. 132-136.
19. Carl Van Doren, ed., *The Letters of Benjamin Franklin and Jane Mecom* (Princeton: Princeton University Press, 1950), p. 315. See also pp. 317, 319. The story appeared also in William Cook, *Memoirs of Samuel Foote* (3 vols.; London: R. Philips, 1805), III, 370.
20. *Works*, III, 158-159.
21. 4 février 1777.
22. 25 février 1778.
23. 17 juillet 1778.
24. 26 mai 1779. The most complete record of Franklin's Masonic activities in France is found in Louis Amiable, *Une loge maçonnique d'avant 1789* [Les Neuf Soeurs] (Paris: F. Alcan, 1897).

The most important contemporary document in print is *Mémoire pour la loge des neuf-soeurs.* This work of 55 pages—without date or place—was apparently the joint work of "Court de Gebelin, Secrétaire de la Loge des Neuf-Soeurs" and "La Dixmerie, Orateur, Député & Redacteur de ce Mémoire." Amiable cites it from the Bibliothèque Nationale: H 5589.4°. It is to be found also in the Archives Nationales: AD XVII 26. Franklin is depicted as filling the void created by the death of Voltaire: "Un jour de tempête est, pour l'ordinaire, suivi d'un jour serein. Des noms fameux sont venus se joindre au grand nom de Voltaire, & enricher le Catalogue des Neuf-Soeurs. Nous vîmes bientôt accourir au milieu de nous cet homme célèbre [Franklin] ami du grand Homme que nous regrettons, ce Philosophe que le Monde ancien envia long-tems au Monde nouveau; qui scut déconcerter à la fois les effroyans mystères de la Nature & de la politique: utile à l'Univers entier par ses travaux, Protecteur & Législateur de sa Patrie par son courage & ses lumières," p. 6. We are told also that the Feast of Saint John was celebrated by the lodge in 1778 at Franklin's home in Passy. The *Mémoires secrets,* 17 juillet 1778, reports that he was present, but does not indicate that the festivities were held at his home. See also: David J. Hill, "A Missing Chapter of Franco-American History," *American Historical Review,* XXI (1916), 709-719. This is a valuable treatment of the influence of the Lodge of the Nine Sisters on the French Revolution—although the influence is greatly exaggerated. The most complete record of Franklin's Masonic activities in both France and America appears as a communication "Benjamin Franklin" by H. T. C. De Lafontaine, with addenda, in *Ars Quatuor Coronatorum,* XLI (1929), 3-40. A discussion based on manuscripts in the American Philosophical Society is given by Nicholas Hans in "Unesco of the Eighteenth Century, La Loge des Neuf Soeurs and Its Venerable Master, Benjamin Franklin," *Proceedings of the American Philosophical Society,* XCVII (1953), 513-524.

25. 10 janvier 1778.

26. 11 mars 1783.

27. 29 juin 1783.

28. 29 septembre 1782.

29. Smyth, ed., *Writings,* VIII, 595-596.

30. 17 avril 1780.

31. Hays, ed., *Calendar,* II, 363. Franquelin to Franklin. March 22, 1781.

32. 3 mai 1781.

33. July 17, 1781. M. de Lescure, *Correspondance secrète . . . sur Louis XVI, Marie Antoinette* (2 vols.; Paris: H. Plon, 1866), I, 415.

34. Cited in Frank Moore, *Diary of the American Revolution* (2 vols.; New York: Scribner, 1860), II, 82.

35. *New York Journal,* September 8, 1777. Quoted in Frank Moore, *op. cit.,* I, 389.

36. Vincent Le Ray de Chaumont, "Souvenirs des Etats-Unis," *La Semaine des Familles,* I (1859), 385-387.

37. Jefferson, *Writings,* XVIII, 168-170.

38. John Bowring, ed., *Works of Jeremy Bentham* (11 vols.; Edinburgh: Wm. Tait, 1843), X, 527.

39. *Loc. cit.*

40. New York *Public Advertiser,*

May 11, 1810. Reprinted from the *Connecticut Gazette*.

41. *Op. cit.*, p. 218.

42. Foner, ed., *Writings*, I, 285.

43. Pierre Jean Baptiste Nougaret, *Anecdotes du règne de Louis XVI* (6 vols.; no printer's name, 1791), IV, 438.

44. Papers of the abbé de la Roche. Bibliothèque de l'Institut de France.

45. *Œuvres*, V, 219.

46. *Ibid.*, IV, 253-254.

47. Verner W. Crane, *Franklin's Letters to the Press* (Chapel Hill: University of North Carolina Press, 1950), p. 34. Sainte-Beuve is much too generous toward Cabanis. Comparing him to Volney, he remarks, "Volney had none of the character of Cabanis, who corrected the dryness (sécheresse) of his doctrines by the charm (onction) of his nature; Volney was rather one to exaggerate them. If he took from Franklin his morality based on utility, he did so without a smile." *Causeries du lundi* (15 vols.; Paris: Garnier frères, 1857-1872), VII, 415. There is not even the trace of a smile in the entire essay on Franklin by Cabanis.

48. *Œuvres*, IV, 391.

49. Subsequent references to Cabanis concern his "Notice sur Benjamin Franklin."

50. *Rapports du physique et du moral de l'homme*, in *Œuvres*, III, 24.

51. Smyth, ed., *Writings*, I, 342-343.

52. *Ibid.*, I, 352.

53. Chinard, "Recollections," *Proceedings of the American Philosophical Society*, XCIV, 218.

54. J. Bennett Nolan, "A Franklin Anecdote," *Pennsylvania Magazine of History*, LXXV (1951), 192.

55. Smyth, ed., *Writings*, V, 158.

56. *Ibid.*, IX, 14.

57. *Le Moniteur*, 23 juillet 1792.

58. Jean François Bodin, *Recherches historiques sur l'Anjou* (seconde édition, 2 vols.; Angers: Cosmier et Lachèse, 1847), II, 568.

59. *A View* (Dublin: P. Byrne, 1782), p. 269.

60. *Histoire* (2 vols.; Paris: chez l'auteur, 1784), I, 220-224.

61. No place of publication. Pp. 183-186.

62. This essay was inserted in 1788 in Mazzei's *Recherches historiques*. O'Connor & Arago, eds., *Œuvres de Condorcet*, VIII, 29.

63. P. 270.

CHAPTER 13

1. *Discours du comte de Mirabeau dans la séance de 11 juin* (Paris: Baudoin, 1790). The political implications of the eulogies of Franklin are discussed by Gilbert Chinard in "The Apotheosis of Benjamin Franklin," *Proceedings of the American Philosophical Society*, XCIX (1955), 440-473.

2. Cabanis, *Œuvres*, V, 262. *Mémoires biographiques, littéraires et politiques de Mirabeau*, VIII, 7.

3. *Patriote françois*. 12 juin 1790.

4. Michelet, *Histoire de la Révolution Française*, ed. Gérard Walter (2 vols.; Angers: Bibliothèque de la Pléiade, 1952), I, 482.

5. *Patriote françois*. 12 juin 1790.

6. *Œuvres de M. J. Chénier* (8 vols.; Paris: Guillaume, 1823-1827), III, 321.

7. *Recherches physiques sur l'électricité* (Paris: Nyon, 1782), pp. 404 ff.

8. Michelet, *op. cit.*, I, 526.

9. No. XIV (1790), pp. 6-16.

10. *Journal de la Société de 1789*, 19 juin 1790.

11. Manuscrits. Bibliothèque de Mantes.

12. *Le tribut de la société nationale des neuf-soeurs* (Paris, 1791), pp. 51-57.

13. *Eloge civique de Benjamin Franklin* (Paris: J. R. Lottin, 1790).

14. *Journal général de France*, 23 juillet 1790.

15. *Œuvres de M. Franklin*, I, i.

16. The bibliographical history of this epitaph is treated by L. H. Butterfield ["B. Franklin's Epitaph," *New Colophon*, 1950, pp. 9-39], who states that the "text believed to be the first French translation of the Epitaph, was appended to the *Mémoires de la Vie Privée de Benjamin Franklin* issued over the imprint of Buisson, Libraire, Paris, in 1791." In my research I have found several other translations, including one as early as 1777.

17. John Adams, "Diary," *Works*, III, 220.

18. *La science du bonhomme Richard . . . précédée d'un abrégé de la vie de Franklin* (Paris: Imprimerie des Sciences et Arts, An II), p. x.

19. "De La Roche's Recollections," *Proceedings of the American Philosophical Society*, XCIV, 217-218.

20. No. 157 (1790), pp. 1-8.

21. 8 octobre 1790.

22. 24-31 juillet 1790.

23. 23 juillet 1790.

24. O'Connor & Arago, eds., *Œuvres de Condorcet*, III, 372-423.

25. Manuscripts Division. Library of Congress.

26. Quoted by Lewis J. Carey, *Franklin's Economic Views* (Garden City: Doubleday, Doran, 1928), p. 163.

27. Crane, *Franklin's Letters to the Press*, p. xxxvii.

28. *Ibid.*, p. xxxviii.

29. 24 décembre 1791.

30. "Eloge de Franklin," *Revue Rétrospective*, VII (1835), 375-404.

31. *Discours prononcé le 10 août 1790, à la fête célébrée en l'honneur de Benjamin Franklin par la société des Ouvriers Imprimeurs de Paris, par M. L. . . . apprenti imprimeur.* For a description of the celebration see *Le Journal Général de France*, 14 août 1790. It inspired a dramatic performance, *L'imprimeur, ou la fête de Franklin*, April 8, 1791.

32. Appendix to the *Discours prononcé le 10 août*. The provinces also paid honor to Franklin. In Meurthe, for example, it was proposed and adopted that all members of the national guard wear a brand of crêpe on their arms for three days. *Extrait du Registre du conseil général d'administration de la garde national de Nancy, département de la Meurthe. Séance du 17 juin 1790.*

33. Ministère des Affaires Etrangères. Correspondance Politique. Etats-Unis, 35, ff. 88-89.

34. The best account of Franklin's character by an English contemporary is a sketch by Joseph Priestley in *Monthly Magazine*, February, 1803. Reprinted in Franklin, *Complete Works* (3 vols.; London: J. Johnson, 1806), III, 547-552. The most entertaining account by an American is that of John Adams in his Diary, but it is fragmentary and prejudiced against Franklin.

35. *Eulogium on Benjamin Franklin, LL.D. . . . delivered March 1, 1791, in the German Lutheran Church of the City of Philadelphia before the American Philosophical Society, and agreeably to their appointment, by William Smith, D.D. . . . The memory of the deceased was honored also, at the delivery of this eulogium,*

with the presence of the president, senate and house of representatives of the United States of America. . . . Printed by Benjamin Franklin Bache. Philadelphia, 1792.

36. Ministère des Affaires Etrangères. Correspondance Politique. Etats-Unis, 35, f. 232.

37. It is not my province to discuss Franklin's reputation in Germany. I might point out for incidental interest, however, a disparaging summary of his whole career, containing adverse comments on his begetting an illegitimate son and his complicity in the affair of the Hutchinson letters. He is called the embodiment of the materialistic spirit of the age. "Auf jeden Fall wird man sich jedoch hüten müssen, ihn dem, in antiker Grösse dahstehenden, spiegelreinen Charakter Washingtons, des einzigen grossen Mannes, den Amerika bis jetzt hervorgebracht hat, auch nur von Ferne an die Seite zu stellen." N. H. Julius, *Nordamerikas sittliche Zustände* (Leipzig: Brockhaus, 1839), I, 98-99.

INDEX

DATE DUE

DEC 2 8 '62			
MR 1 1 '63			
MR 2 5 '63			
AP 23 '63			
DE 1 '63			
OC 1 8 '67			
MAR 21 '68			
APR 4 '68			
OCT 5 '69			
APR 6 '70			
FEB 1 8 '74			
NOV 1 0 '75			
GAYLORD			PRINTED IN U.S.A.